Kinship Across the Black Atlantic

Postcolonialism across the Disciplines 23

Postcolonialism across the Disciplines

Series Editors
Graham Huggan, University of Leeds
Andrew Thompson, University of Exeter

Postcolonialism across the Disciplines showcases alternative directions for postcolonial studies. It is in part an attempt to counteract the dominance in colonial and postcolonial studies of one particular discipline – English literary/cultural studies – and to make the case for a combination of disciplinary knowledges as the basis for contemporary postcolonial critique. Edited by leading scholars, the series aims to be a seminal contribution to the field, spanning the traditional range of disciplines represented in postcolonial studies but also those less acknowledged. It will also embrace new critical paradigms and examine the relationship between the transnational/cultural, the global and the postcolonial.

Kinship
Across the Black Atlantic
Writing Diasporic Relations
Gigi Adair

Liverpool University Press

First published 2019 by
Liverpool University Press
4 Cambridge Street
Liverpool L69 7ZU

Copyright © 2019 Gigi Adair

The right of Gigi Adair to be identified as the author of this book has been asserted by her in accordance with the Copyright, Design and Patents Act 1988. All rights reserved. No part of this book may be reproduced, stored in a retrieval system, or transmitted, in any form or by any means, electronic, mechanical, photocopying, recording, or otherwise, without the prior written permission of the publisher.

British Library Cataloguing-in-Publication data
A British Library CIP record is available

ISBN 978-1-78962-037-5 cased

Typeset in Amerigo by Carnegie Book Production, Lancaster
Printed and bound in Poland by BooksFactory.co.uk

Contents

Acknowledgements													vii

Introduction: Diasporic kinship across the black Atlantic					1

Part I: Rewriting anthropology

1 Postcolonial sabotage and ethnographic recovery in
   Jamaica Kincaid's *The Autobiography of My Mother*					35

2 Destabilizing structuralism in Pauline Melville's
   The Ventriloquist's Tale										59

Part II: Historiography and the afterlife of slavery

3 'As constricting as the corset they bind me in to keep me a lady':
   colonial historiography in Andrea Levy's *The Long Song*				85

4 Shattering the flow of history: Dionne Brand's *At the Full and
   Change of the Moon*										105

Part III: Queer diasporic relationality

5 Queer creolization in Patrick Chamoiseau's *Texaco*					131

6 Writing self and kin: diasporic mourning in Jackie Kay's *Trumpet*			151

Conclusion: Diasporic futures? 175

Bibliography 183

Index 195

Acknowledgements

I wish to thank Cordula Lemke, who understood what this project was about before I did, and who believed in it in the moments when I did not. Andrew James Johnston's incisive comments prevented some wrong turns, Jennifer Wawrzinek suggested new directions, and Russell West-Pavlov's advice was always spot on. A seminar with Jane Bennett and Katrin Pahl was enormously inspiring and influential. During the (lengthy) finishing stages of the book the support of Martin Lüthe and his invitation to collaborate with Robert Reid-Pharr, Hermann Bennett, Tavia Nyong'o, Gary Wilder and others on new African Atlantic diasporas helped to refine my existing analysis and generate new readings. I am grateful for the early and formative encouragement of Linnell Secomb, and for the later support and advice of Anja Schwarz, Lars Eckstein and Dirk Wiemann. In its early stages, this project was developed and written at the Friedrich Schlegel Graduate School of Literary Studies at the Freie Universität Berlin, supported by a fellowship from the German Research Foundation, and in recent years I have had the pleasure of working at the Department of English and American Studies at the University of Potsdam.

I am very grateful to Joscelyn Gardner for her permission to use an image of her artwork on the cover. Her series of lithographs entitled *Creole Portraits III: "bringing down the flowers…"*, which can be seen at www.joscelyngardner.org, depicts African braided hairstyles combined with instruments of the colonial abuse of reproduction and kinship—slave collars used to punish enslaved women accused of aborting pregnancies—and one means of their resistance: Caribbean plants used or identified as abortifacients in the eighteenth century. It thereby resonates deeply with the themes of kinship, postcolonialism and (post)slavery in the black Atlantic in this book.

My love and thanks go to my chosen family in Berlin, who were there for me when I needed them, and let me ignore them for lengthy stretches when I was writing. P. saw it through from beginning to end, and kept me on an even keel.

In memory of Roozi Araghi and Nick Salzberg,
two diasporic queers gone too soon.

Introduction: Diasporic kinship across the black Atlantic

This book is about kinship in contemporary fiction from around the black Atlantic, and about the means these literary texts find to write diasporic kinship. The six novels considered here all explicitly engage with the meanings, experiences and practices of kinship in the context of multiple black Atlantic diasporas and in the wake of slavery and colonialism. Their interrogation and rewriting of discourses of intimate bonds imagines diasporic belonging, cultural production, and ethical relationality anew. The interest in interrogating and rethinking kinship in these novels, although not necessarily new in black Atlantic fiction, broadly coincides with a surge in queer writing from the Caribbean in the 1990s.[1] Such fiction thus prefigures the 'conjunctural moment' of black/queer/diaspora proclaimed by some US-American scholars in the early twenty-first century.[2] In my readings of these texts, I seek to generate a dialogue between the literary narrations of kinship and their reshaping of diaspora, on the one hand, and recent work by cultural theorists in diaspora studies and kinship studies on the other hand, and thus to suggest some ways in which scholars in the various fields that I draw on in this book might benefit from an engagement with each other's work, and with the literary texts in which both diverse cultural concepts and practices of kinship and the consequences of attempts to naturalize and valorize particular forms of kinship are explored. I focus on three key ways in which the novels wrestle

---

1 An uptick in queer writing from the early 1990s can be clearly observed across the anglophone Caribbean; Yolanda Martínez-San Miguel similarly identifies a focus on 'alternative intimacies' in Spanish Caribbean texts from the 1990s onwards; see her 'Más allá de la homonormatividad: intimidades alternativas en el Caribe hispano', *Revista Iberoamericana* 74.225 (2008), pp. 1039–57.
2 Jafari S. Allen, 'Black/Queer/Diaspora at the Current Conjuncture', *GLQ: A Journal of Lesbian and Gay Studies* 18.2–3 (2012), pp. 211–48.

with contemporary black Atlantic diasporic kinship: interrogating colonial–anthropological texts and discourses, exploring the limits of postcolonial historiography, and experimenting with literary–textual representations of queer diasporic relationality.

The understanding of diaspora which emerges from these texts suggests that black Atlantic diasporas, and the cultures and forms of subjectivity which they generate, cannot be fully understood without a critical analysis of kinship like the one I pursue here. These novels show that diaspora is fundamentally about a displacement from national norms of kinship and relationality, and thus a displacement from national—and colonial—norms of the 'human', and that diaspora therefore necessitates a rewriting of the presumed connections between kinship and culture. This is particularly acute in black Atlantic diasporas, which are strongly marked not only by this diasporic displacement from national kinship, but also by the violent destruction of kinship and culture which resulted from the Middle Passage and colonial slavery, and by ongoing racism linked to kinship in the afterlife of slavery. Diaspora studies, therefore, remains deficient not only when it fails to consider gender and sexuality—a long-standing accusation, now often remedied in more recent work—but also when it ignores kinship. The field of queer diaspora studies that has emerged in response to this lack since the 1990s has often focused on examples other than New World black diasporas, thereby neglecting the field which may best illustrate its insights. This book therefore follows and amplifies the call for queer studies to be part of and contribute to—because it is uniquely capable of—a critique of race, nationalism and colonialism.[3] Similarly, while scholars in critical kinship studies offer crucial new ways for thinking about kinship as a technology of both colonialism and anticolonial resistance, and for analysing the relationship between discourses and kinship and claims of humanity, culture and civilization, these ideas have not yet been linked to studies of diaspora in general and the black Atlantic in particular, where they offer rich resources for thinking about culture and subjectivity.

In this introduction, I first offer a detailed overview of the developments of recent decades in the two key interdisciplinary fields—first diaspora studies, followed by critical kinship studies—that most contribute to this book. The work from these fields that I take and adapt for this study of diasporic kinship combines impulses, theories and concerns from postcolonial studies and queer studies in particular; for scholars in both fields, I suggest, there are rich possibilities to be found in interweaving their insights, concepts and methods. I then use these resources to pursue a double-pronged analysis of black diasporic kinship, in which kinship may function both and simultaneously as a technology of colonial or neocolonial rule and exploitation and a practice of collective resistance and subjective transformation. This analysis seeks to

---

3 David L. Eng with Judith Halberstam and José Esteban Muñoz, 'Introduction: What's Queer about Queer Studies Now?' *Social Text* 23.3–4 (2005), pp. 1–17.

understand the meaning and experience of black Atlantic kinship, which is also revealed as doubled: normative Euro-American kinship is understood both as an unattainable ideal which promises recognition and full personhood *and* as an oppressive and undesirable, constraining institution, while various forms of queered and diasporic kinship hold out the utopian possibility of becoming and living otherwise, but also threaten illegitimacy and illegibility.

It is worth recalling that, as diaspora studies emerged in the early 1990s, some prominent scholars doubted whether New World black communities qualified as diasporas at all. In his influential definition of the term in 1991, William Safran remains undecided as to whether black populations in the New World constitute a diaspora or not.[4] Their imagining of the homeland 'can no longer be precisely focused', he suggests; that is, black diasporas are not clearly national.[5] Perhaps more damning in his eyes is his assessment of New World black cultures, which are either 'low prestige and impede social mobility' or involve 'artificial grafts lacking a convincing connection with black experience'.[6] For Safran, 'artificial grafts' devalue black cultures and dilute their status as properly diasporic; the botanic metaphor suggests a lack of normative bodily integrity and hints at non-normative—because asexual—reproduction rather than a 'natural' diaspora guaranteed by naturalized and compulsory heterosexual kinship and patriarchy.

Yet if diasporic kinship is always denaturalized by its dislocation from national norms, then the 'artificial grafts' of black diasporic cultures, or of black diasporic families, ways of being, and forms of personhood, do not disqualify them as true diasporas but rather emphasize the centrality of black Atlantic diasporas to modernity, including and especially western modernity. Following C. L. R. James's claim that black studies 'is the history of Western Civilization', I suggest that an analysis of black diasporic kinship can tell us something about what it means to be a recognizable human subject, to have a place in a personal and shared history, to be a member of a political society, and a subject in relations with the world and other others, and can suggest ways of rethinking such relations and categories in less exclusive ways.[7]

---

4 William Safran, 'Diasporas in Modern Societies: Myths of Homeland and Return', *Diaspora* 1.1 (1991), pp. 83–99.
5 Safran, 'Diasporas in Modern Societies', p. 90.
6 Safran, 'Diasporas in Modern Societies', p. 90.
7 C. L. R. James, 'Black Studies and the Contemporary Student' [1969], in Anna Grimshaw (ed.), *The C. L. R. James Reader* (Cambridge: Blackwell, 1992), p. 397. In the same vein but more recently, Tiffany Patterson and Robin Kelley have argued that the same processes which shaped African diaspora also transformed western culture, and Paul Gilroy insists that the study of black Atlantic diasporas can, among other things, enable 'a new perspective on British culture *as a whole*'. See Tiffany Ruby Patterson and Robin D. G. Kelley, 'Unfinished Migrations: Reflections on the African Diaspora and the Making of the Modern World', *African Studies*

Of course, Safran's definition of diaspora has been challenged by numerous scholars, and not only for his discounting of black diasporas. James Clifford's focus on lateral connections rather than the homeland–hostland binary, and his suggestion that a 'shared, ongoing history of displacement, suffering, adaptation, or resistance may be as important as the projection of a specific origin' are particularly relevant to black diasporas.[8] Most influential of all has been the work of Paul Gilroy, who insists that black diaspora should be understood as a tool of contemporary and historical cultural critique, and the black Atlantic as a unit of analysis which enables an understanding of the transnational consciousness of anti-slavery movements, for example, or the way in which the black cosmopolitan writers' understandings of race, self and sociality were formed by experiences of exile and displacement, just as it enables an understanding of the exchanges between Caribbean, African-American and black British cultures in the contemporary moment.[9] Furthermore, Gilroy suggests that diasporas are characterized by their reconstruction and reworking of tradition and memory and an affective mode of ambivalence rather than nostalgia or unambiguous loss.[10] This work shifts diaspora studies away from accounts which solely consider diasporic subjects' attachment to their 'homeland' to consider the subjective transformation and complex cultural interactions which take place in the wake of mass migrations. Gilroy's desire to move 'beyond the binary opposition between national and diasporic perspectives'[11] is also taken up by Avtar Brah's concept of 'diaspora space', which she defines as

> a conceptual category [...] 'inhabited' not only by those who have migrated and their descendants but equally by those who are constructed and represented as indigenous. In other words, the concept of diaspora space (as opposed to that of diaspora) includes the entanglement of genealogies of dispersion with those of 'staying put'.[12]

This makes clear that the effects of diaspora do not only affect those subjects with a history of migration, but rather all subjects in diasporic spaces—that left behind when some people migrate, and that created by

---

Review 43.1 (2000), pp 11–45; Paul Gilroy, *There Ain't No Black in the Union Jack: The Cultural Politics of Race and Nation* (London: Routledge, 1987), p. 156, emphasis in original.

8 James Clifford, *Routes: Travel and Translation in the Late Twentieth Century* (Cambridge, MA: Harvard University Press, 1997), p. 250.
9 Paul Gilroy, *The Black Atlantic: Modernity and Double Consciousness* (Cambridge, MA: Harvard University Press, 1993).
10 Gilroy, *There Ain't No Black*; Paul Gilroy, *Against Race: Imagining Political Culture beyond the Color Line* (Cambridge, MA: Belknap Press of Harvard University Press, 2000).
11 Gilroy, *The Black Atlantic*, p. 29.
12 Avtar Brah, *Cartographies of Diaspora: Contesting Identities* (London: Routledge, 1996), p. 181.

both new arrivals *and* existing residents in the new homeland. This spatialized approach makes a focus on diasporic purity or ethnic absolutism less likely, and Brah's suggestion that diaspora should be understood as a process, characterized more by a 'homing desire' than a 'desire for a "homeland"' enables an analysis of how the attachment to or memory of a 'homeland' and distinctive diasporic subjectivities are created by social and cultural practices, and are subject to renegotiation and constant redefinition.[13]

Gilroy's work in particular has proved immensely productive over the past twenty-five years, which is not to say that it has not also been criticized for its shortcomings and omissions, in particular its centring of the US and African-American culture and its neglect of Africa.[14] Of more relevance to this study, however, are the critiques of Gilroy (and of Clifford) which point to a persistent neglect of gender and sexuality in their work.[15] While Clifford acknowledges this problem, suggesting that more must be done to account for the different experiences of differently gendered people within diaspora, rather than continuing to privilege masculine-identified diasporic experience, this work is left for others to do. This neglect of how gender and sexuality are implicated in various kinds of non-national belonging is rendered even more problematic in light of the fact that women's bodies have often been understood as the bearers and reproducers of national culture.[16] Michelle Wright castigates Gilroy and others for paying lip-service to the need for greater attention to gendered dynamics and women's experiences in diaspora studies while continuing to ignore female figures.[17] This is typical, Wright suggests, of a dominant discourse operating in African diaspora studies catalysed by 'the idea of authenticity': 'essential blackness', or the status of the most authentic, is only accorded to heterosexual male black subjects.[18] In *Becoming Black*, Wright again takes aim at Gilroy's neglect of gender and

---

13 Brah, *Cartographies of Diaspora*, p. 193. See also Brian Keith Axel, 'The Diasporic Imaginary', *Public Culture* 14.2 (2002), pp. 411–28; Brian Keith Axel, 'The Context of Diaspora', *Cultural Anthropology* 19.1 (2004), pp. 26–60.
14 An overview of key responses to and criticisms of Gilroy's *The Black Atlantic* is offered in Lucy Evans, 'The Black Atlantic: Exploring Gilroy's Legacy', *Atlantic Studies* 6.2 (2009), pp. 255–68.
15 An early critique of Gilroy in this vein is Robert F. Reid-Pharr, 'Engendering the Black Atlantic', *Found Object* 4 (1994), pp. 11–16.
16 Deniz Kandiyoti, 'Identity and its Discontents: Women and the Nation', in Patrick Williams and Laura Chrisman (eds.), *Colonial Discourse and Post-Colonial Theory* (New York: Columbia University Press, 1994), pp. 376–91. A start on such a theorization of women's writing in diaspora is offered by Sneja Gunew, 'Resident Aliens: Diasporic Women's Writing', *Contemporary Women's Writing* 3.1 (2009), pp. 28–46.
17 Michelle W. Wright, 'Can I Call You Black? The Limits of Authentic Heteronormativity in African Diasporic Discourse', *African and Black Diaspora: An International Journal* 6:1 (2013), pp. 3–16; see also T. Denean Sharpley-Whiting, 'Erasures and the Practice of Diaspora Feminism', *Small Axe* 17 (2005), pp. 129–33.
18 Wright, 'Can I Call You Black?' p. 5.

sexuality and instead offers an alternative means of defining black diasporic subjectivity, pointing to 'a twentieth-century intellectual tradition of African diasporic counterdiscourses of Black subjectivity that [...] understands Black subjectivity as that which must be negotiated between the abstract and the real, or, in theoretical terms, between the ideal and the material'.[19] From this, she develops a dialogic rather than dialectic theory of diasporic subjectivity that offers an alternative narrative of black New World cultures, with three key insights:

> that the Black male subject cannot be the sole possessor of agency because he alone cannot create other subjects; that all subjectivities are therefore 'intersubjective' in that they come into being through other subjects, not apart from them; that because all subjects are intersubjective, subjectivity cannot be produced dialectically, as thetical and antithetical relations do not exist'.[20]

According to Fatima El-Tayeb, it is such 'intersubjective' or 'dialogic' forms of diasporic identity that have been adopted by black Europeans.[21] The concept of diaspora, for El-Tayeb—as elaborated particularly in African diasporic discourses—brings together 'the experience of a population that is born into one nation, but never is fully part of it' with the 'transnational ties of that same population'.[22] She suggests that the 'disidentificatory potential' of diaspora is particularly to be found in black diasporic cultural forms which explore 'the limits of blackness'.[23] El-Tayeb's insistence on the relational aspect of diaspora is shared with Jacqueline Nassy Brown, who suggests that 'diaspora should be understood not as an existential condition of displacement and dislocation but as a kind of relation, one between and among counter/parts'.[24]

The effects of the lack of an adequate gender theory in Gilroy's work are also to be found in his theorization of the relationship between diaspora, family and kinship. He argues that, while national discourses traditionally understand the heterosexual family as the building block of the nation, and consider the primary purpose of family and women to be the production of male citizen-soldiers, diaspora challenges these radically gendered notions of citizenship and national belonging by 'valorizing sub- and supranational

---

19 Michelle M. Wright, *Becoming Black: Creating Identity in the African Diaspora* (Durham, NC: Duke University Press, 2004), p. 3.
20 Wright, *Becoming Black*, p. 22.
21 Fatima El-Tayeb, *European Others: Queering Ethnicity in Postnational Europe* (Minneapolis: University of Minnesota Press, 2011).
22 El-Tayeb, *European Others*, p. 54.
23 El-Tayeb, *European Others*, p. 60.
24 Jacqueline Nassy Brown, 'Black Europe and the African Diaspora: A Discourse on Location', in Darlene Clark Hine, Tricia Danielle Keaton and Stephen Small (eds.), *Black Europe and the African Diaspora* (Urbana: University of Illinois Press, 2009), p. 202.

Introduction

kinship', enabling 'anti-essentialist accounts of identity-formation', and generating a shift away from 'primordial identities' towards those based on 'contingency, indeterminacy, and conflict', creating a 'chaotic' rather than linear model of generation and reproduction.[25] Yet Gilroy's attempt to attend to the 'changing same' of diaspora—its iteration without reification, continuity without essence—and to imagine a non-patrilineal concept of diaspora and identify non-heteronormative identity and cultural formations within existing diasporas is hampered by the ongoing biological and patrilineal notion of diaspora which persists, despite his disavowals, in his work.[26] On this basis, Stefan Helmreich argues that Gilroy's early work on diaspora attempts yet fails to undo the patriarchal logics of kinship.[27] For Helmreich, the problem begins with etymology: 'diaspora', derived from the Greek διασπορα, 'dispersion', suggests 'scattered seeds'—or sperm—and thus diaspora 'refers us to a system of kinship reckoned through men and suggests the questions of legitimacy in paternity that patriarchy generates'.[28] The etymological baggage of the term need not render it useless, of course; however, Helmreich suggests that the heteropatriarchal traces of the word render Gilroy's focus on largely male experiences and male African-American subjects especially problematic. As a result, Gilroy's black Atlantic is a unit of study which 'relies implicitly on an appeal to historical ties of kinship', ruled by an 'arborescent image of the "family tree"' in which the roots of the family tree and the roots of diaspora both suggest 'ancestral seeds from which genealogies sprout in particular soils', creating—despite Gilroy's efforts to the contrary—a 'kinship-based model of diaspora'.[29]

Gilroy responds to Helmreich and other similar critics in *Against Race*, but I suggest that he again fails to solve this problem. First, he argues that the etymological roots of diaspora need not lead to patrilineal connotations. Instead, the 'seeds' of diaspora could just as easily be thought of as 'spores', as vectors of asexual reproduction, and that this might liberate diaspora from the 'quagmire of androcentrism'.[30] Next, Gilroy writes that the contamination of the term 'diaspora' by the 'toxins of male domination' is no *greater* than that of any other current or emergent critical or heuristic concept, and it is a matter for contemporary theorizations to define diaspora in terms of 'descent via the rhizomorphic principal' rather than the male line.[31] Gilroy's use of Deleuzian terminology in these passages nonetheless fails to annul the 'arborescent image of the family tree' identified by Helmreich, not least

---

25 Gilroy, *Against Race*, p. 128.
26 Gilroy, *Against Race*, p. 129.
27 Stefan Helmreich, 'Kinship, Nation and Paul Gilroy's Concept of Diaspora', *Diaspora* 2.2 (1992), pp. 243–49.
28 Helmreich, 'Kinship, Nation and Paul Gilroy's Concept of Diaspora', p. 245.
29 Helmreich, 'Kinship, Nation and Paul Gilroy's Concept of Diaspora', pp. 246–47.
30 Gilroy, *Against Race*, pp. 126–27.
31 Gilroy, *Against Race*, p. 127.

because Gilroy himself is unable to think diaspora without invoking metaphors of sown seeds and various modes of biological sexual reproduction: several pages earlier, for example, he writes that the concept of diaspora 'might offer seeds capable of bearing fruit'.[32] It is not sufficient for Gilroy to claim that diaspora *could* be understood in rhizomorphic terms: his own work, from its metaphors of seeds and fruits, to its almost exclusively male 'lineage' of black Atlantic cosmopolitans, demonstrates that the genealogical 'roots' of diaspora run deep and its androcentric bias is difficult to displace. By justifying the heteropatriarchal associations of diaspora on the relativizing basis that the concept is '[no] more deeply contaminated' than other critical terms, Gilroy foregoes the chance to fully investigate the ways in which diaspora, including his own use of the concept, is gendered and (hetero)sexualized, without which the routes of diaspora remain too entangled in the roots of the diasporic family tree.[33]

The development of theories of queer diaspora in response to the ongoing failure of prominent scholars to sufficiently challenge the heteronormative and genealogical logic of diaspora in their work has been one of the great gains of the field in recent years. (A similar dynamic can be observed in migration studies, which has long ignored how sexuality influences migration, in turn motivating some new work which seeks to understand how movement affects sexuality and how ideas about sexuality, including sexual propriety and sexual alterity, affect concepts of migration.)[34] The field of queer diaspora studies, most associated with the work of Gayatri Gopinath and David Eng, provides conceptual tools for such analysis and emphasizes the centrality of sexuality to liberal modernity. Since approximately the late 1990s, this has been a project which has challenged both the whiteness of queer studies and the heteronormativity of diaspora studies, seeking to make 'questions of sexuality, racialisation, colonialism, migration, and globalisation central to both a queer and a diaspora studies project'.[35] It is also a utopian project: queer diasporas imagine other ways of being in the world; they imagine— and demand—alternative futures.[36] In order to counter the 'heteronormative reproductive logic' of concepts of diaspora and enable a more effective reconceptualization of home and challenge to myths of purity and origins,[37]

32 Gilroy, *Against Race*, p. 122.
33 Gilroy, *Against Race*, p. 127.
34 Cindy Patton and Benigno Sánchez-Eppler (eds.), *Queer Diasporas* (Durham, NC: Duke University Press, 2000); Eithne Luibhéid and Lionel Cantú Jr. (eds.), *Queer Migrations: Sexuality, U.S. Citizenship, and Border Crossings* (Minneapolis: University of Minnesota Press, 2005); Eithne Luibhéid, 'Queer/Migration: An Unruly Body of Scholarship', *GLQ: A Journal of Lesbian and Gay Studies* 14.2–3 (2008), pp. 169–90.
35 Gayatri Gopinath, 'Foreword: Queer Diasporic Interventions', *Textual Practice* 25.4 (2011), pp. 635–36.
36 Gopinath, 'Foreword: Queer Diasporic Interventions'.
37 Gayatri Gopinath, *Impossible Desires: Queer Diasporas and South Asian Public Cultures* (Durham, NC: Duke University Press, 2005), p. 10, see also pp. 5–6.

Gopinath advocates a turn to 'queer diaspora', which means *not* the identification of queer diasporic subjects or subcultures, but rather the application of a 'queer diasporic frame of analysis' to diasporas in general in order to focus on the ways in which diasporic displacement generates non-heteronormative and, crucially, *non-national* subjectivities and sexualities.[38] Queering the concept of diaspora provides a way to recover not only queer sexual desires, but all 'those desires, practices, and subjectivities that are rendered impossible and unimaginable within conventional diasporic and nationalist imaginaries'.[39] Similarly, Eng argues that a reconceptualization of diaspora as queer diaspora would enable political and cultural interventions to contest traditional family and kinship structures and to reorganize communities—both national and transnational—'based not on origin, filiation, and genetics but on destination, affiliation, and the assumption of a common set of social practices or political commitments'.[40] Thus, queer diaspora not only demands a place for queer subjects as part of national and diasporic memory and 'refuses to position queer subjects as alien, inauthentic, and perennially outside the confines of these entities',[41] it also considers how diasporic experiences and formations interrupt national heteronormativity regardless of sexuality. An analysis of queer diasporas also serves to illustrate the role of sexuality in liberalism, including its role in discourses of development, Enlightenment, civilization and primitiveness, and self-determination.[42] It thus has an important role to play in the project, delineated by Lisa Lowe, of understanding how 'modern liberalism defined the "human" and universalized its attributes to European man, [as] it simultaneously differentiated populations in the colonies as less than human' and how 'the social inequalities of our time are a legacy of these processes.[43] This approach provides a more effective counterweight to national and diasporic discourses of both pure origins and pure cultural and genealogical reproduction guaranteed by normative heterosexuality than approaches, like Gilroy's, which shy away from questions of gender and sexuality.

My readings of the black Atlantic novels in this book suggest that the heteronormativity enshrined in many theories of diaspora is particularly misplaced because diaspora *necessarily* queers configurations of family and

---

38 Gayatri Gopinath, 'Bollywood Spectacles: Queer Diasporic Critique in the Aftermath of 9/11', *Social Text* 23.3–4 (2005), p. 158.
39 Gopinath, *Impossible Desires*, p. 11.
40 David L. Eng, 'Transnational Adoption and Queer Diasporas', *Social Text* 21.3 (2003), p. 4.
41 Gopinath, *Impossible Desires*, p. 15.
42 David L. Eng, *The Feeling of Kinship: Queer Liberalism and the Racialization of Intimacy* (Durham, NC: Duke University Press, 2010); David L. Eng, 'Queering the Black Atlantic, Queering the Brown Atlantic', *GLQ: A Journal of Lesbian and Gay Studies* 17.1 (2011), p. 195.
43 Lisa Lowe, *The Intimacies of Four Continents* (Durham, NC: Duke University Press, 2015), pp. 6, 3.

kinship.[44] That this has long been a feature of black Atlantic writing and other cultural forms is confirmed by Nadia Ellis's study of mid-twentieth-century works, which identifies a 'structural queerness of black global modes of belonging over particular sexual or erotic practices'.[45] That structural queerness is both a displacement of the national and a particular orientation to temporality and futurity: both in the works studied by Ellis, and in those which I analyse in this book, black diaspora is characterized by a desire to be and relate otherwise, which Ellis calls a 'queer elsewhere'.[46] I too identify a 'desire to belong and a desire to flee from community'[47] in black Atlantic novels from the late twentieth and early twenty-first centuries, where it manifests in a struggle with the double-bind of kinship discourse: an awareness of the privileges accorded to normative kinship forms, and nonetheless a diasporic longing to find alternative ways of being in the world.

The inherent displacement of diasporic subjectivities from normative national lives which this project explores in detail highlights the potential connections and affinities between such an understanding of diasporic and black Atlantic studies and other fields of study, including queer of colour critique in the USA and some Latino/a studies. In the US, the field of queer of colour critique continues to build on Roderick Ferguson's insight that estrangements from 'respectability, domesticity, heterosexuality, normativity, nationality, universality, and progress' are 'the general estrangements of African American culture' (which in turn recalls Cathy Cohen's similar insistence on the commonalities of some racialized and queer subjects).[48] Ricardo Ortíz equates the position of Cuban exiles with that of queer subjects in relation to both Cuba and the USA, both gendered and heteronormative states, and he suggests that some diasporic cultural forms offer 'an alternative (perhaps even a queer) form of continuation and contiguation toward any (future) community', despite the 'ferociously heterosexual presumption[s]' about acceptable, or even possible modes of cultural reproduction that also dominate in exilic Cuban cultures.[49] Alicia Arrizón argues that the concept of *mestizaje*, as it has been redefined by Latina feminist thinkers over the past

---

44 For a similar reading of two other black Atlantic novels, see Meg Wesling, 'Neocolonialism, Queer Kinship, and Diaspora: Contesting the Romance of the Family in Shani Mootoo's *Cereus Blooms at Night* and Edwidge Danticat's *Breath, Eyes, Memory*', *Textual Practice* 25.4 (2011), pp. 649–70.
45 Nadia Ellis, *Territories of the Soul: Queered Belonging in the Black Diaspora* (Durham, NC: Duke University Press, 2015), p. 5.
46 Ellis, *Territories of the Soul*.
47 Ellis, *Territories of the Soul*, p. 6.
48 Roderick Ferguson, *Aberrations in Black: Toward a Queer of Color Critique* (Minneapolis: University of Minnesota Press, 2004), p. 2; Cathy J. Cohen, 'Punks, Bulldaggers, and Welfare Queens: The Radical Potential of Queer Politics', *GLQ: A Journal of Lesbian and Gay Studies* 3 (1997), pp. 437–65.
49 Ricardo L. Ortíz, *Cultural Erotics in Cuban America* (Minneapolis: University of Minnesota Press, 2007), p. 13.

several decades, 'suggests diasporic interventions, hybrid epistemologies, and the borderization of space and time'.[50] These similarities suggest ample common grounds between scholars in these fields and thus potential for fruitful comparisons between regions and languages; although these fields are also sometimes criticized by scholars of black diasporas for denying and depoliticizing blackness, or for devaluing blackness as uninteresting and not cosmopolitan enough.[51] The work of scholars of the black Atlantic, however, is crucial to current work on queer globalization, migration and diaspora.[52] In bringing together and keeping balanced the terms black/queer/diaspora, as Allen suggests, it is therefore valuable to keep in sight the black/queer/diasporic *Atlantic*—not because black diasporic connections and cultural exchange are limited to the Atlantic region, but because the black Atlantic as a unit of study is still a valuable and vital framework thanks to its decentring of the nation in understanding modernity, and—if properly adapted—it still has much to add to understandings of the queerness of all diasporas.

Gopinath and Eng's work on 'queer diaspora', like Ellis's definition of black diaspora as a queer 'failed affinity', make clear that the queering of diaspora they propose has to do not only with sexuality, but at least as much with questions of intimate relationality and reproduction: matters of kinship. It is not a question of conceptualizing diaspora *without* kinship, as Helmreich suggests, but rather a demand to reconceptualize diaspora and kinship both, and thus I argue that the field of diaspora studies must enter into dialogue with the growing field of critical kinship studies.[53] When Gopinath writes of the 'genealogical, implicitly heteronormative reproductive logic' of diaspora, and of reclaiming the 'the impure, inauthentic, nonreproductive potential of the notion of diaspora', she points to the presumed relationship between sexual and cultural reproduction, on the one hand, and between kinship and subjectivity, on the other, that are key to an investigation of the relationship between kinship and diaspora.[54] Similarly, Eng's call for a diaspora based on affiliation rather than filiation points first to the ongoing importance of genealogy (filiation) to diasporic subjectivity and community; secondly, it is also a call for alternative modes of relationality and kinship, or as he writes,

---

50 Alicia Arrizón, *Queering Mestizaje: Transculturation and Performance* (Ann Arbor: University of Michigan Press, 2006), p. 48.
51 Tavia Nyong'o, *The Amalgamation Waltz: Race, Performance and the Ruses of Memory* (Minneapolis: University of Minnesota Press, 2009), p. 6; Allen, 'Black/Queer/Diaspora'.
52 Allen, 'Black/Queer/Diaspora'.
53 An overview of recent developments in the field is provided by Damien W. Riggs and Elizabeth Peel, *Critical Kinship Studies: An Introduction to the Field* (London: Palgrave Macmillan, 2016).
54 Gopinath, *Impossible Desires*, pp. 10–11.

for a rethinking of 'the parameters, not just of family and kinship, but of identity and history' in the light of non-national intimate bonds.[55]

Eng places his conceptualization of queer diaspora in clear contrast to structuralism when he writes that 'the incest taboo demands displacement from kin, or, more accurately put, establishes kinship relations precisely on the basis of that displacement', and that queer forms of kinship, and their textual representation, thus challenge 'particular mobilizations of the incest taboo and its principles of displacement that sanction and establish the Oedipal as the only livable, knowable, or inevitable form of family and kinship'.[56] Eng therefore suggests that a focus on queer diasporas might offer a key tool for developing a much needed, but as yet lacking, 'retheorization of family and kinship relationships after poststructuralism'.[57] This engagement with kinship puts the work of Eng and Gopinath, and in turn this book, into dialogue and contestation with the field and history of kinship studies in anthropology. Conceptualizations of queer diaspora, alongside recent work on kinship in queer and indigenous studies, both engage with and reject elements of these anthropological traditions, such as Claude Lévi-Strauss's assertion that human culture and human kinship structures came into being simultaneously through the establishment of the incest taboo, which mandates exogamous reproduction—and thus that certain kinship rules are essential to culture—or the earlier claim of A. R. Radcliffe-Brown, who argues that the 'elementary family' ('a man and his wife and their child or children') is the basic unit of all kinship systems, and that a society's kinship system is the most fundamental structuring principle of its social system.[58]

These claims, however, and indeed the anthropological field of kinship studies as a whole, have also been comprehensively challenged from within the discipline, most significantly by David Schneider's *A Critique of the Study of Kinship*, and it is this critical tradition within anthropology on which much of the more recent work in critical kinship studies is based. Schneider argues that the study of kinship within anthropology, including the theory of what constitutes kinship, is entirely untenable and unsupported by anthropological evidence; yet these claims have long appeared 'a very compelling set of ideas', indeed, 'self-evident', because they are 'essentially our own cultural conceptions'.[59] Western anthropologists have imposed Eurocentric notions of

---

55 Eng, 'Transnational Adoption and Queer Diasporas'; Eng, *The Feeling of Kinship*, p. 22.
56 Eng, *The Feeling of Kinship*, p. 19.
57 Eng, *The Feeling of Kinship*, p. 16.
58 Claude Lévi-Strauss, *The Elementary Structures of Kinship*, trans. James Harle Bell (Boston, MA: Beacon Press, 1969); A. R. Radcliffe-Brown, 'The Study of Kinship Systems', *The Journal of the Royal Anthropological Institute of Great Britain and Ireland* 71.1–2 (1941), p. 2.
59 David M. Schneider, *A Critique of the Study of Kinship* (Ann Arbor: University of Michigan Press, 1984), p. 3.

kinship—primarily the importance of consanguinity or its legal fiction and the assumption of a basic nuclear-family unit—upon the social arrangements of the societies they study, through both the process of translation (of terms of address and relationship as well as ideas) and the filtering of information deemed relevant and important. He concludes that all theories of kinship and all forms of kinship studies serve more to obfuscate than to explain the structures and cultural practices of the societies being studied, and that kinship studies as taught and practised in the field of anthropology should be abandoned.

Most critically for this book, Schneider insists that kinship studies relies upon and reifies the 'fundamental assumption' that 'Blood Is Thicker Than Water'.[60] The assumption of a 'biological' basis for kinship renders kinship bonds, on the one hand, as *states of being*, not of *doing* or performance', and renders them 'unquestioned and unquestionable'.[61] Even Lévi-Strauss's insistence on exchange rather than descent as the primary mechanism of kinship and sociality rests on the assumption of 'natural links of kinship', that is, 'blood', onto which the 'artificial links' of a social order are laid.[62] Yet this premise, Schneider argues, is not only *not* universal, it is specifically European, a 'fundamental axiom of European culture', but not of others.[63] Kinship studies, as practised by anthropologists, forcibly imposes European categories onto other cultures, thereby distorting them. In fact, the relationship of biology to kinship is less simple than is commonly assumed even in Euro-American cultures. Schneider writes in his analysis of US-American kinship, first published in 1968, that so-called natural or blood relatives are defined by their 'biogenetic' relationship, so that 'if science discovers new facts about biogenetic relationship, then that is what kinship is and was all along, although it may not have been known at the time'.[64] More recent anthropological work, however, argues for a more complex interweaving of biological and cultural explanations in European and American understandings of kinship.[65] In addition, as Myra Hird points out, newly discovered biological phenomena, such as chimerism and mosaicism, 'demonstrate [...] that *nature* can contradict the *cultural* assumption that children are biologically related to their (non-adoptive) parents, at the same time that this cultural assumption is supposed to be grounded in biological explanation'.[66] As a result, she suggests that 'just as anthropologists found that "primitive" cultures use classificatory

---

60 Schneider, *A Critique of the Study of Kinship*, p. 165.
61 Schneider, *A Critique of the Study of Kinship*, p. 165.
62 Claude Lévi-Strauss qtd in Schneider, *A Critique of the Study of Kinship*, p. 173.
63 Schneider, *A Critique of the Study of Kinship*, p. 199.
64 David M. Schneider, *American Kinship: A Cultural Account* (Chicago: University of Chicago Press, 1980), pp. 27, 23.
65 Janet Carsten, *After Kinship* (Cambridge: Cambridge University Press, 2004).
66 Myra J. Hird, 'Chimerism, Mosaicism and the Cultural Construction of Kinship', *Sexualities* 7.2 (2004), p. 224, emphasis in original.

systems, we could well argue that western cultures use classificatory systems, even whilst they depend upon strong notions of "biology"'.[67] Rather than a biological guarantee of identity and belonging, genealogy is primarily a story we tell ourselves—or that we tell about others.

Schneider's arguments are compelling, but his conclusions are not intended to apply beyond the anthropological traditions within which his work is situated and which constitute the target of his criticism. Within cultural criticism and literary studies, scholars interested in kinship have drawn different conclusions from Schneider's work than Schneider himself. Among them, Judith Butler's work on kinship emphasizes the possibility and necessity of reconceptualizing kinship as a kind of 'doing' rather than 'being', whilst also focusing on the imbrication of kinship and the state. In *Antigone's Claim*, she argues against Hegel and Lacan's positioning of kinship outside of the political or social order.[68] For them, kinship occupies a subordinate and supporting position in which its function is, respectively, to produce male citizens for the modern universal state or to make signification within the symbolic possible. Butler questions this separation of kinship and the state through her reading of Sophocles' play; she argues that the play reveals that kinship and the state are deeply imbricated and mutually dependent. In Hegel and Lacan, the incest taboo functions to preserve and ensure the stability and intelligibility of the social and political order, and the forms of kinship it mandates are therefore deemed essential to that order. Butler's reading therefore focuses critical attention on 'the relation between kinship and reigning epistemes of cultural intelligibility, and both of these to the possibility of social transformation'.[69] In following work she analyses the presumed connection between culture and certain models of normative sexual relations to consider, first, how compulsory heterosexuality may be mandated by Lévi-Straussian arguments about the reproduction of culture, and secondly how normative and non-normative forms of sexuality, desire and kinship are connected to questions of life and the 'human'.[70] Thus her analysis in *Antigone's Claim* of which forms of normative kinship are understood to be structurally mandated by the incest taboo leads on to other questions: 'who counts as human? Whose lives count as lives?'[71] She suggests that in order to challenge the tradition which installs heteropatriarchy as the necessary foundation of political order, citizenship, culture and civilization, and to work against a political order which defines those with non-normative kinship or intimate lives as liminal or subhuman, kinship

---

67 Hird, 'Chimerism, Mosaicism', p. 222.
68 Judith Butler, *Antigone's Claim. Kinship Between Life and Death* (New York: Columbia University Press, 2000).
69 Butler, *Antigone's Claim*, p. 24.
70 Judith Butler, 'Is Kinship Always Already Heterosexual?', *differences: A Journal of Feminist Cultural Studies* 13.1 (2002), pp. 14–44.
71 Butler, *Antigone's Claim*, p. 30; Judith Butler, *Precarious Life: The Powers of Mourning and Violence* (London: Verso, 2004), p. 20, emphasis in original.

must be reconceptualized. (Butler thus adopts a different approach than Gayle Rubin, who accepts Lévi-Strauss's analysis and concludes that 'the feminist program must include a task even more onerous than the extermination of men; it must attempt to get rid of culture and substitute some entirely new phenomena on the face of the earth'.)[72] Drawing on the distinction made by Schneider (albeit in a way not entirely endorsed by Schneider himself), Butler argues that kinship should be defined as durable, intimate relationships not necessarily linked to sexuality, and should be understood as an enacted practice rather than a given structure.[73]

This analysis of kinship as 'doing' or performative is not the same as Erving Goffman's much earlier 'dramaturgical' approach to family, although Goffman's work continues to inspire analyses of 'doing family', sometimes in combination with Schneider's analysis.[74] Goffman does not question what kinship is—he quotes Radcliffe-Brown's definition of kinship without quarrel—but rather seeks to denaturalize the behaviour which adheres to kinship roles and positions in the (classed) family. While for Goffman, a performance might fail—that is, not be accepted as convincing by others—he does not account for the possibility of certain people being structurally excluded from certain roles, or their performances deemed culturally unintelligible due to factors such as race, although his observation that 'we may not find a perfect fit between the specific character of a performance and the general socialized guise in which it appears to us' would appear to invite precisely such an analysis of the potential social vectors that might cause such disjunctures.[75]

The relationship between kinship and the state is also taken up by Elizabeth Povinelli, who likewise rejects the Hegelian claim of separation to argue that kinship remains a central, albeit often denied, technology of the

---

72 Gayle S. Rubin, 'The Traffic in Women: Notes on the "Political Economy" of Sex', *Deviations: A Gayle Rubin Reader* (Durham, NC: Duke University Press, 2011), p. 46. An interview between Gayle Rubin and Judith Butler further clarifies some of the differences in their thinking on kinship: see Gayle S. Rubin and Judith Butler, 'Sexual Traffic', *differences: A Journal of Feminist Cultural Studies* 6.2–3 (1994), pp. 62–99; rpt. in *Deviations: A Gayle Rubin Reader*, p. 276–309.

73 Butler, 'Is Kinship Always Already Heterosexual?' Butler differs from Schneider in that she claims that we can (and should) understand kinship as a kind of 'doing', whereas Schneider argues that although such enacted practices offer better ways to account for different forms of relationality, they cannot reasonably be described as 'kinship' as the term has traditionally been understood (at least within the discipline of anthropology). See Schneider, *A Critique of the Study of Kinship*, pp. 72–75.

74 Erving Goffman, *The Presentation of Self in Everyday Life* (Edinburgh: University of Edinburgh Social Sciences Research Centre, 1956); Jessica L. Collett and Ellen Childs, 'Meaningful Performances: Considering the Contributions of the Dramaturgical Approach to Studying Family', *Sociology Compass* 3–4 (2009), pp. 689–706.

75 Goffman, *The Presentation of Self*, p. 19.

modern biopolitical state, that it continues to organize state institutions, and that this is a status inherited from kinship's central role in imperialism and settler colonialism.[76] Povinelli identifies a binary model of kinship and intimacy as one of the key products and technologies of imperialism, and she names the two discursive positions thus created the 'autological subject' and the 'genealogical society', governed respectively by 'individual freedom and social constraint'.[77] This discursive binary is not limited to the age of imperialism; rather, 'the social imaginaries of the autological subject, the genealogical society, their modes of intimacy, and their material anchors emerged from European Empire as a mode and maneuver of domination and exploitation *and continue to operate as such*'.[78] Povinelli situates the traditions of anthropology, as described and criticized by Schneider, within their imperial and colonial-historical context whilst also highlighting the ongoing efficacy of those discursive constructs. The anthropological claim of 'kin-based' societies is thus contextualized by Povinelli as part of a process in western colonial and postcolonial discourses which constructs non-western, colonized and postcolonial forms of kinship as the binary opposite to western, liberal forms of love and intimacy. Meanwhile, an often racialized discourse of 'love' has become the 'intimate event' that defines western subjectivity: the 'free' declaration of love for an other is understood as a key marker of autonomy, making love an event of self-sovereignty and the 'intimate couple' the central figure through which biopolitical power is exercised. Thus 'freely-chosen' intimacy, love and individual freedom become the markers of western kinship and subjectivity, while socially determined genealogical ties define non-western societies and kinship structures; furthermore, these are understood to be mutually exclusive and absolute; a choice of one or the other is the only possible 'foundation for governing love, sociality, and the body'.[79] Povinelli suggests that a postcolonial critique should aim to separate intimacy and genealogy, to open up new ways of seeing and experiencing sociality, to 'cut across' across colonial and liberal discourses of love, freedom and social constraint—and to question both naturalized kinship structures in Europe *and* those that have been ascribed to Europe's colonized and abjected others.[80]

In turn, Mark Rifkin draws on the work of both Schneider and Povinelli to consider how kinship discourse might be studied in the context of colonialism

---

76 Elizabeth A. Povinelli, 'Notes on Gridlock: Genealogy, Intimacy, Sexuality', *Public Culture* 14.1 (2002), pp. 215–38.
77 Elizabeth A. Povinelli, *The Empire of Love: Toward a Theory of Intimacy, Genealogy, and Carnality* (Durham, NC: Duke University Press, 2006), p. 2.
78 Povinelli, *The Empire of Love*, pp. 16–17, emphasis added.
79 Povinelli, *The Empire of Love*, pp. 3, 9.
80 Povinelli, *The Empire of Love*. See also Elizabeth A. Povinelli and Kim Turcot DiFruscia, 'A Conversation with Elizabeth A. Povinelli', *Trans-Scripts* 2 (2012), pp. 76–90.

and indigenous studies; he simultaneously makes clear that the field of contemporary kinship studies holds both contradictions and dangers for any anti or postcolonial project.[81] Rifkin rewrites Schneider's claim that biological reproduction is the 'underlying reference' of all kinship relationships to show how anthropological kinship studies thereby imposes both heteronormativity and nuclear-family norms upon the community being studied.[82] In the case of Native American cultures, he argues that studying kinship in this way risks obscuring the specific modes of peoplehood and political autonomy of indigenous societies and making them visible only as 'a "special"/ "savage" aberration from the nuclear household'.[83] A focus on kinship risks reifying cultural difference: either because, as Povinelli points out, non-white and non-western others are simply inserted into the category already provided in western, liberal discourses of sociality and affiliation, or because, as Rifkin argues, forms of governance and political organization are reduced and privatized to become questions of sexuality and family. Nonetheless, Rifkin also comes to different conclusions than Schneider about the utility and value of kinship studies. Rather than advocating an end to kinship studies, he suggests that kinship should be studied 'as a vector of imperial governance' and a 'key technology of settler imperialism'.[84]

Povinelli, Butler and Rifkin all insist that questions of race and empire must be central to contemporary reconsiderations of kinship discourses, and that modes of relationality or kinship should be understood as processes, that is, as enacted 'doings' informed by discourses of kinship and intimacy rather than fixed and immutable structures. It is important to note, however, a longer history of such demands, made particularly by indigenous, primarily Native American and Amerindian, scholars and activists, and by black scholars, particularly women of colour in the US. I therefore echo calls by other scholars to recognized the ongoing relevance and influence of women of colour feminism to recent fields such as queer of colour critique and to situate such new work, including this project on diasporic kinship, as emerging more from women of colour feminism than from predominantly white Euro-American queer theory, even as I maintain the importance and value of queer theory's interventions.[85] In Grace Hong's assessment of the continuing potential of an analysis built on women of colour feminism, she recognizes that kinship is a key element of this, although she does not identify it as an independent field

---

81 Mark Rifkin, *When did Indians Become Straight? Kinship, the History of Sexuality, and Native Sovereignty* (Oxford: Oxford University Press, 2011).
82 Schneider, *A Critique of the Study of Kinship*, p. 99.
83 Rifkin, *When did Indians Become Straight?*, p. 10.
84 Rifkin, *When did Indians Become Straight?*, pp. 13, 15.
85 Grace Kyungwon Hong and Roderick A. Ferguson, 'Introduction', in Grace Kyungwon Hong and Roderick A. Ferguson (eds.), *Strange Affinities: The Gender and Sexual Politics of Comparative Racialization* (Durham, NC: Duke University Press, 2011), pp. 1–22.

of study.[86] Daniel Heath Justice, a Native American scholar, makes an argument which resonates with elements of Schneider's and Butler's work, and which is drawn on extensively by Rifkin: 'kinship is best thought of as a verb, rather than a noun, because kinship, in most indigenous contexts, is something that's *done* more than something that simply *is*'.[87] Chela Sandoval's call for a new politics of love is also a call for a new model of kinship, understood as enduring connection and collectivity; she begins with a quotation from the Native American scholar and activist Bea Medicine which makes this explicit: 'All my kinspersons, with a good heart, and strong hands, I welcome you'.[88] This greeting, Sandoval suggests, works to 'interpellate connection-by-affinity'; that is, it is a way of making kin.[89] Sandoval's call for a politics of love is just one recent iteration of a long tradition of black women's love politics, which has long been interested in new ways of thinking about intimacy, relationality, and their political potential and meaning.[90] This critique of relationality, in turn, must be understood not as limited to intimate bonds or political organizing structures, but as a broader critique of 'the epistemological foundation of the white supremacist moment of global capital organized around colonial capitalism'.[91]

Kinship has also been extensively discussed—and sometimes mourned—in postslavery contexts. In the colonies of the New World, slave owners and traders destroyed both kinship bonds and traditional kinship structures by separating, often deliberately, members of kinship and cultural groups; at the same time, various slave codes created and instituted different forms of legally recognized kinship for African slaves and free residents.[92] This bears

---

86 Grace Kyungwon Hong, 'Existentially Surplus: Women of Color Feminism and the New Crises of Capitalism', *GLQ: A Journal of Lesbian and Gay Studies* 18.1 (2012), pp. 87–106.
87 Daniel Heath Justice, '"Go Away, Water!": Kinship Criticism and the Decolonization Imperative', in Craig S. Womack, Daniel Heath Justice and Christopher B. Teuton (eds.), *Reasoning Together: The Native Critics Collective* (Norman: University of Oklahoma Press, 2008), p. 150.
88 Bea Medicine qtd in Chela Sandoval, 'Dissident Globalizations, Emancipatory Methods, Social-Erotics', in Arnaldo Cruz-Malavé and Martin F. Manalansan IV (eds.), *Queer Globalizations: Citizenship and the Afterlife of Colonialism* (New York: New York University Press, 2002), pp. 20–32 (p. 20). See also Chela Sandoval, *Methodology of the Oppressed* (Minneapolis: University of Minnesota Press, 2000).
89 Sandoval, 'Dissident Globalizations', p. 20.
90 A summary and historical overview is provided in Jennifer C. Nash, 'Practicing Love: Black Feminism, Love-Politics, and Post-Intersectionality', *Meridians: feminism, race, transnationalism* 11.2 (2013), pp. 1–24.
91 Grace Kyungwon Hong, 'The Future of our Worlds: Black Feminism and the Politics of Knowledge in the University under Globalization', *Meridians: feminism, race, transnationalism* 8.2 (2008), p. 101.
92 Orlando Patterson, *Rituals of Blood: Consequences of Slavery in Two American Centuries* (Washington: Civitas Counterpoint, 1998); Orlando Patterson, *Slavery and Social Death: A Comparative Study* (Cambridge, MA: Harvard University Press, 1982);

repeating because, as Hortense Spillers emphasizes, 'the destruction of the African name, of kin, of linguistic, and ritual connections is so obvious [...] that we tend to overlook it'.[93] As a result of this destruction and denial, many have drawn on the trope of 'wounded kinship' to describe kinship in the wake of slavery.[94] Saidiya Hartman suggests that 'wounded kinship' 'defines the diaspora', which continues to be haunted by this loss; she writes: 'Slavery denied the captive all claims of kin and community; this loss of natal affiliation and the enduring pain of ancestors who remain anonymous still haunt the descendants of the enslaved'.[95] Shifting to the realm of literary studies, Valérie Loichot suggests that the narrative transmission of stories became a means of creating or repairing the ties destroyed by slavery, and that this is perhaps one reason why postslavery and postcolonial fiction has so often told family stories.[96] Moreover, when those family stories focus on shared history and mixed racial heritage, they *may* (but do not necessarily) challenge or twist racist and chauvinist nationalist claims to dominance based on racial purity and ancestry.[97] There are risks involved, however, in the narration of genealogy as a means of reconstructing destroyed or damaged kinship. Hartman is critical of such narratives and claims of kinship in the context of contemporary slavery tourism, suggesting that these 'redemptive narratives' offer 'the promise of restored affiliations', but that such a promise is 'a placebo, a pretend cure for an irreparable injury'.[98] Another problem, not addressed by Hartman, is that narrating genealogy as a means of *re*creating kinship implies that kinship is or should be properly based on genealogy or consanguinity. Orlando Patterson invokes the term 'fictive kinship' to describe the ties of, for example, those who survived the Middle Passage together; this term is taken up by Loichot in her

---

Hortense J. Spillers, 'Mama's Baby, Papa's Maybe: An American Grammar Book', in *Black, White and in Color: Essays on American Literature and Culture* (Chicago: University of Chicago Press, 2003), pp. 203–29.

93 Spillers, 'Mama's Baby, Papa's Maybe', p. 216.
94 The term 'wounded kinship' is generally taken from the work of Nathaniel Mackey. See Nathaniel Mackey, 'Sound and Sentiment, Sound and Symbol', *Callaloo* 30 (1987), pp. 29–54; Nathaniel Mackey, *Bedouin Hornbook* (Charlottesville: University Press of Virginia, 1986). Mackey's phrase is taken up by Fred Moten, *In the Break: The Aesthetics of the Black Radical Tradition* (Minneapolis: University of Minnesota Press, 2003), and by Saidiya V. Hartman, 'The Time of Slavery', *The South Atlantic Quarterly* 101.4 (2002), pp. 757–77. Hartman's work is in turn referenced in Butler, 'Is Kinship Always Already Heterosexual?'
95 Hartman, 'The Time of Slavery', pp. 762, 764.
96 Valérie Loichot, *Orphan Narratives* (Charlottesville: University Press of Virginia, 2007).
97 Loichot, *Orphan Narratives*; George B. Handley, *Postslavery Literatures in the Americas: Family Portraits in Black and White* (Charlottesville: University Press of Virginia, 2000); Chris Weedon, 'Migration, Identity, and Belonging in British Black and South Asian Women's Writing', *Contemporary Women's Writing* 2.1 (2008), pp. 17–35.
98 Hartman, 'The Time of Slavery', pp. 759, 762.

study of 'postplantation' literature.[99] Schneider, however, argues that the very concept of 'fictive kinship' reinstates the primacy and indispensable position of biological or 'blood' ties, devaluing all others.[100] This is particularly obvious in Patterson's work, in which he understands the practice of enslaved people to 'use kinship as the idiom for the expression of all important relationships and rankings' as, nonetheless, inferior to 'real' kinship, by which he means legal (heterosexual) marriage and genealogical lineage, and particularly legal paternity.[101] (Judith Butler suggests that Patterson's work therefore seems to mourn primarily the erosion of enslaved black men's 'natural' patriarchal authority.)[102] As Alexander Weheliye writes, Patterson's concept of social death 'neglect[s] and/or actively dispute[s] the existence of alternative modes of life alongside the violence, subjection, exploitation, and racialization that define the modern human'.[103] If kinship is reduced to questions of conjugality, blood and paternity, this risks, first, the inaccurate, limited description of relationality as detailed by Schneider; secondly, an accession to the colonial imposition of certain kinship norms upon colonized, enslaved and oppressed populations as a method of control, as discussed by Povinelli and Rifkin, and finally the elision or marginalization of the history of resistance, cultural creation and forms of alternative, sometimes subversive relationality that those enslaved and oppressed peoples developed and practised—and still do today.

In an immensely important and influential essay, Spillers argues that the destruction of kinship, lineage and legitimacy in slavery was one important means (but not the only means) by which slaves were degendered, and she analyses this abolition of legal kinship as a means of investigating the workings of gender under enslavement and for African-Americans since slavery. Spillers argues that 'kinlessness' was a requirement of property, that is, of making enslaved people into the property of others.[104] This is not to say that enslaved Africans did not have 'powerful ties of sympathy', but rather that under enslavement kinship has no legal efficacy; it 'loses meaning, *since it can be invaded at any given and arbitrary moment by the property relations*'.[105] Spillers's primary interest is in gender, rather than in kinship, and this is made clear when she writes that 'trying to understand how the confusions of consanguinity

---

99 Patterson, *Rituals of Blood*, p. 27; Loichot, *Orphan Narratives*.
100 Schneider, *A Critique of the Study of Kinship*, pp. 97–112. Note that in *Slavery and Social Death*, Patterson instead uses 'fictive kinship' to refer to either the adoption of slaves into the owner's family in various societies (but not in colonial Atlantic slavery) or the discourse of slave owner paternalism prominent in the Americas and Caribbean.
101 Patterson, *Rituals of Blood*, pp. 25–28.
102 Butler, *Antigone's Claim*, pp. 73–74.
103 Alexander G. Weheliye, *Habeas Viscus: Racializing Assemblages, Biopolitics, and Black Feminist Theories of the Human* (Durham, NC: Duke University Press, 2014), pp. 1–2.
104 Spillers, 'Mama's Baby, Papa's Maybe', p. 217.
105 Spillers, 'Mama's Baby, Papa's Maybe', p. 218, emphasis in original.

[caused by slavery] worked [...] goes far to explain the rule of gender and its application to African females in captivity'.[106] As a result, she accepts that kinship means only blood ties of descent or legally recognized heterosexual unions, or rather she accepts this definition because she is interested only in legally efficacious kinship.

Spillers's approach, focused on legal questions and the destruction of gender and legal kinship by both the Middle Passage and New World slave codes, might be compared with that of Omise'eke Natasha Tinsley, who argues for an analysis of the forms of kinship—not legally recognized, but nonetheless powerful—that were created during and after the Middle Passage.[107] Tinsley's investigation of the Creole world *mati*, used by women for their female lovers, and which 'literally [...] means mate, as in shipmate—she who survived the Middle Passage with me', leads to her claim that the queer bonds formed on the slave ships and plantations were means by which captive Africans 'resisted the commodification of their bought and sold bodies by *feeling* and *feeling for* their co-occupants on these ships'.[108] Spillers's and Tinsley's respective approaches map out the ends of a double-pronged approach to studying kinship as suggested by Rifkin: one which understands kinship as potentially *both* a technology of control, a means of granting or restricting legal rights, a delimitation of the human and thereby a means of dehumanization, *and* a means and record of resistance to enslavement and oppression, of imagining other ways of being and relating than those prescribed by liberal modernity and the racism and denial of race that have long defined it.

The possibility and ethical desirability of alternative models of intimacy has been extensively explored by queer theory and politics in recent decades; the question of kinship, on the other hand, has been a vexed one for queer scholars. Rifkin argues that kinship within queer studies has either been figured as the constituting horizon of queerness, as that which, by definition, queers are excluded from (and which, by extension, they should reject), or scholars and activists have sought to transform and queer kinship, undercutting in particular the importance of procreation to the concept.[109] Many of these queer(ed) conceptualizations of kinship are not limited to queer contexts, especially in light of the argument that kinship should be understood as enacted, rather than pregiven, bonds. Elizabeth Freeman argues that the focus on reproduction in traditional notions of kinship can be effectively replaced by a notion of renewal: 'kinship can [...] be viewed as the process by which bodies and the potential for physical and emotional attachment are

---

106 Spillers, 'Mama's Baby, Papa's Maybe', p. 217.
107 Omise'eke Natasha Tinsley, 'Black Atlantic, Queer Atlantic: Queer Imaginings of the Middle Passage', *GLQ: A Journal of Lesbian and Gay Studies* 14.2–3 (2008), pp. 191–215; Omise'eke Natasha Tinsley, *Thiefing Sugar: Eroticism Between Women in Caribbean Literature* (Durham, NC: Duke University Press, 2010).
108 Tinsley, 'Black Atlantic, Queer Atlantic', 192.
109 Rifkin, *When did Indians Become Straight?*

created, transformed, and sustained over time'.[110] This leads her to a consideration of kinship's relationship to temporality. She offers a self-consciously false etymology of (queer) belonging as 'the longing to "be *long*"', that is, a longing for a temporal dimension which extends over a long period, or a way to conceive of timescales longer than one's own lifetime.[111] While David Eng's call for queer diaspora suggests that abandoning structuralist understandings of kinship to instead pay attention to 'collective, communal and consensual affiliations as well as [...] psychic, affective, and visceral bonds' would create an account of kinship less committed to futurity and less connected to linear time, I suggest that this should not be understood in the sense of the anti-futurity strain of queer thinking most associated with the work of Lee Edelman.[112] Rather, the black diasporic kinship imagined in the novels analysed in this book suggests that a lessened attachment to personal genealogical futurity might be accompanied by a strong drive to imagine alternative futures for black Atlantic subjects to come.

Kinship has often had an ambivalent relationship to friendship, which has sometimes conceptualized as a form of 'fictive kinship', but more often placed in a marginal or devalued position in relationship to 'real' kinship.[113] In contrast, Kath Weston's work insists on a place for friendship as, potentially, a means of making and keeping kin; her gay and lesbian fieldwork subjects 'pictured kinship as an extension of friendship, rather than viewing the two as competitors or assimilating friendships to biogenetic relationships regarded as somehow more fundamental'.[114] More recently, Ramón Rivera-Severa blurs these categories in his theorization of 'queer latinidad' as 'an affective tie among friends, family members, and even strangers' which creates a 'community in pleasure'.[115] In contrast to the devaluation of friendship as a mode of kinship in normative western discourses, Rifkin notes that some Native American texts

---

110 Elizabeth Freeman, 'Queer Belongings: Kinship Theory and Queer Theory', in George E. Haggerty and Molly McGarry (eds.), *A Companion to Lesbian, Gay, Bisexual, Transgender, and Queer Studies* (Oxford: Blackwell, 2007), p. 298.
111 Freeman, 'Queer Belongings', p. 299.
112 Eng, *The Feeling of Kinship*, pp. 2, 14; Lee Edelman, *No Future: Queer Theory and the Death Drive* (Durham, NC: Duke University Press, 2004); for critiques of Edelman's work particularly related to race, see Chandan Reddy, *Freedom with Violence: Race, Sexuality, and the US State* (Durham, NC: Duke University Press, 2011); José Esteban Muñoz, *Cruising Utopia: The Then and There of Queer Futurity* (New York: New York University Press, 2009); Deborah Cohler, 'Queer Kinship, Queer Eugenics: Edith Lees Ellis, Reproductive Futury, and Sexual Citizenship', *Feminist Formations* 26.3 (2014), pp. 122–46.
113 Kath Weston, 'Forever Is a Long Time: Romancing the Real in Gay Kinship Ideologies', in Sylvia Yanagisako and Carol Delaney (eds.), *Naturalizing Power: Essays in Feminist Cultural Analysis* (New York: Routledge, 1995), pp. 87–110.
114 Kath Weston, *Families We Choose: Lesbians, Gays, Kinship* (New York: Columbia University Press, 1991), p. 118.
115 Ramón H. Rivera-Servera, *Performing Queer Latinidad: Dance, Sexuality, Politics* (Ann Arbor: University of Michigan Press, 2012), p. 3.

not only do not distinguish between enduring friendship and kinship, but even define kinship *as* enduring friendship, suggesting that we might read texts of and on friendship as ways of imagining kinship.[116]

In Freeman's account, the 'doing' of kinship creates not only a bond between subjects, it also creates those subjects and their bodies.[117] In this account, the enaction and imagination of kinship is a key force in shaping embodied subjectivity—just as normative accounts of kinship may create 'impossible subjects'.[118] These impossible subjects, however, interrupt in turn those normative categories, 'demarcating alternative material structures and psychic formations that demand a new language for family and kinship'.[119] An insistence on alternative forms of kinship *as* kinship is a means to '[focus] attention on the epistemological and ontological limits of the liberal humanist tradition, [to] bring into relief disparate ways of knowing and being in the world that evade the purview of capitalist modernity'.[120]

In this project, I combine this work on queer kinship and racialized kinship to understand diasporic kinship. Very similar concerns are also to be found, however, in recent work in adoption studies, particular literary studies of adoption narratives, suggesting again that the study of diasporic kinship might reverberate outside the circle of those commonly identified as diasporic subjects. While John McLeod acknowledges that the administration of adoption 'has frequently sought to confirm normative models of filial relations exemplified by the heterosexual, patrician and nuclear family', nonetheless he argues that 'transcultural adoption has also made possible firm grounds for the critique of such filial norms and opened up alternative ways of imagining families in transcultural, non-biocentric, post-racial and queer terms, amongst others'.[121] Adoption studies, too, reveals the constructedness of race via particular logics of family and kinship, and the political nature of all family structures.[122] Dominant discourses of adoption normalize particular modes of personhood focused on individuation, claiming that both racial boundaries and knowledge of biological origins are necessary conditions for 'self-possession, singularity, and continuity of self', for a historical identity and socially legible and legitimate subjectivity.[123] These scholars emphasize

---

116 Mark Rifkin, 'Remapping the Family of Nations: The Geopolitics of Kinship in Hendrick Aupaumut's "A Short Narration"', *Studies in American Indian Literatures* 22.4 (2010), pp. 1–31.
117 Freeman, 'Queer Belongings'.
118 Gopinath, *Impossible Desires*. The term 'impossible subject' is also adapted to apply to queer migrants in Luibhéid, 'Queer/Migration'.
119 Eng, *The Feeling of Kinship*, p. 16.
120 Eng, *The Feeling of Kinship*, p. 15.
121 John McLeod, *Life Lines: Writing Transcultural Adoption* (London: Bloomsbury, 2015), p. 5.
122 Mark C. Jerng, *Claiming Others: Transracial Adoption and National Belonging* (Minneapolis: University of Minnesota Press, 2010).
123 Jerng, *Claiming Others*, pp. 210–11.

the importance of literature as an archive of responses to adoption or because of the role of stories in shaping and constituting forms of personhood, and they adopt a double reading strategy, similar to that which I elaborate below, which aims to understand both the transformative potential of non-normative kinship forms and the pressures on subjectivity and personhood which kinship norms continue to exert.[124] Adoption studies like these also expand the insights gained from adoption narratives to ask what it means to be a relational subject: 'in writing transcultural adoption', McLeod asks, 'what emergent ways of thinking and being might be struck for all?'[125]

In this book, I adopt a double-pronged approach to my analysis of kinship inspired both by the preceding theorizations and by the representation of kinship in the novels themselves.[126] In accordance with Rifkin, my study of kinship is an analysis of kinship *discourses*, rather than one which seeks or claims to identify kinship as a social (let alone biological) fact. My analysis aims to navigate between a desire to explore what other forms of kinship exist, and how people might—and do—alternatively organize their intimate affiliations, on the one hand, and an awareness of how kinship has been and still is used as a tool of colonial biopolitical control, on the other. This doubled approach is also to be found in the novels. All are explicitly concerned with the meaning of kinship and its relationship to the history of colonialism and to contemporary subjectivity and cultural identity. Many of the novels display a strong ambivalence towards intimate relationality generated by the two aspects of kinship identified here: on the one hand, an awareness of the recognition, rights and privileges attendant on normative kinship, and therefore the material and social pressure to conform or attain a normative intimate and social life, on the other, an awareness that for racialized, diasporic and postcolonial subjects, such kinship is either impossible to achieve, or demands considerable political, social, and personal sacrifice. The novels make clear both the colonial and oppressive history of normative kinship demands and the strangulating normative pressures of contemporary kinship discourses, *and* they display a strong desire, a diasporic longing, for other ways of being and connecting to others. They suggest that finding other ways of being and relating is a crucial component of modern diasporic survival and flourishing. Yet at the same time, as long as material survival, citizenship rights and transnational migration options continue to be based

---

124 McLeod, *Life Lines*, p. 4; Jerng, *Claiming Others*, pp. xxiv–xv. See also Margaret Homans, *The Imprint of Another Life: Adoption Narratives and Human Possibility* (Ann Arbor: University of Michigan Press, 2013).
125 McLeod, *Life Lines*, p. 6.
126 A similarly doubled approach may be used for an analysis of love and empire, see Linnell Secomb, "Empire and the Ambiguities of Love", *Cultural Studies Review* 19.2 (2013), pp. 193–215.

upon normative, patriarchal kinship forms, black diasporic subjects must continue to subject themselves to the violence which that normativity entails as a part of their survival strategies.

While Yogita Goyal's recent work claims that Africa is central to and constitutive of black diasporic modernity, and Michelle Wright argues much African diasporic discourse endorses 'a signifying chain of authenticity that first and foremost locates itself in Africa', in these novels any connection to Africa is tenuous at best; it does not form an important point of subjective identification or attachment.[127] Even in Jackie Kay's *Trumpet*, in which the family connection to Africa is arguably strongest—Joss's father emigrated from West Africa to Scotland in the early twentieth century, we are told—this connection to Africa connection remains vague, even reluctant, and the novel explicitly counsels against investing too much meaning in it. This is not quite the same as Gilroy's identification of black modernity almost exclusively with African-Americans, prompting responses highlighting African influence and agency in the Atlantic world.[128] Rather, the impulse in these novels to reorient kinship from questions of origins to questions of lived bonds leads these novels to seek *other* ways of understanding the black diasporic present than the recourse to a shared African past. Michelle Wright's readings of the trope of the black mother resonates in some ways with these texts, but the strong focus she identifies on mothers and mother/daughter texts is not found in most of these novels, in which motherhood is not devalued, but not elevated either—sometimes it is even in doubt. Instead, these novels might be seen as developing another line of thinking in Audre Lord's poetry:

> for now we are more than kin
> who come to share
> not only blood
> but the bloodlines of our failures.[129]

In the novels considered here, becoming kin via shared experience is not only a supplement to 'blood' or 'biological' kinship, but may replace it entirely—and this, in turn, brings about a resignification of the trope of blood. By reimagining kinship these novels have the *potential* to destabilize the normative matrices and hierarchies of gender and sexuality in colonial, Euro-American and black diasporic discourses at once. However, I argue that this occurs in only some of the texts, while in others those hierarchies are instead recuperated.

---

127 Yogita Goyal, *Romance, Diaspora and Black Atlantic Literature* (Cambridge: Cambridge University Press, 2010); Wright, "Can I Call You Black?" p. 9.
128 For a summary of some of this work, see Laura Chrisman, 'Whose Black World Is This Anyway?', in Bénédicte Ledent and Pilar Cuder-Domínguez (eds.), *New Perspectives on the Black Atlantic: Definitions, Readings, Practices, Dialogues* (Bern: Peter Lang, 2012), pp. 23–57.
129 Audre Lord, 'Generations', qtd in Wright, *Becoming Black*, p. 170.

An explicit and extensive engagement with kinship after colonialism is shared among all the novels, but their differences also allow various facets of the meaning of kinship to be explored, and for the vectors of contemporary Atlantic diaspora space to become visible. This thesis considers three primary axes which intersect kinship and diaspora: anthropology, historiography, and diasporic relationality. The centrality of anthropology to kinship discourses, and of notions of indigeneity to anthropology, necessitates the inclusion of two novels which investigate and partially rewrite this relationship. While Jamaica Kincaid's *The Autobiography of My Mother* fits more easily into the category of black Atlantic literature, Pauline Melville's *The Ventriloquist's Tale*, set mostly in Amerindian communities in Guyana, initially seems little concerned with diaspora or black experiences in the Americas. Yet the novel itself addresses precisely this question and rejects such a separation of indigeneity and black diaspora in postcolonial context; instead, contemporary indigeneity is represented as part of the 'diaspora space' of Guyana, and as informed by long and multiple histories of migration and cultural contact. While other scholarship suggests that challenges to 'anthropological notions about gender, sexuality, marriage, kinship, and family', may be found among Afro-Caribbean populations in the region, Melville's novel makes clear that a querying and rewriting of the category of 'the human' and its link to kinship cannot exclude the favourite objects of anthropology's investigations—indigenous peoples and cultures.[130] The central importance of slavery and the afterlife of slavery to the black Atlantic is investigated in chapters three and four, with two novels—*The Long Song* by Andrea Levy and Dionne Brand's *At the Full and Change of the Moon*—that, despite their similarities in setting and as family stories, offer very different reflections on the relationship between history and kinship in the long wake of the slave ships and the potential for a historiographic rewriting of this relationship. Finally, forms of diasporic sociality and subjectivity and their relationship to kinship are explored in two novels which also offer reflections on the relationship of diasporic subjects to the modern nation-state and to liberalism. Patrick Chamoiseau's *Texaco* portrays the gradual and ambivalent process of formulating a distinctive diasporic culture via diasporic forms of relationality on Martinique against the idealization of mother-France, while in Jackie Kay's *Trumpet* the boundaries of diaspora space are shown to encompass a wider group than only racialized subjects, or only those with a traceable history of migration, just as the reach of diasporic queerness extends beyond queer subjects.

All the novels were published around the turn of the twenty-first century, between 1992 and 2010, but many offer longer time scales, from the early nineteenth century to the last years of the twentieth century. Several return

---

130 Gloria Wekker, *The Politics of Passion: Women's Sexual Culture in the Afro-Surinamese Diaspora* (New York: Columbia University Press, 2006), p. 1.

to the last years of slavery in the Caribbean and the immediate aftermath of emancipation; others are set entirely or in part during colonial rule in the early twentieth century. Those novels, or parts, which take place after the end of official colonial rule document both the ongoing effects of past colonial rule and the continuities between colonialism and the inequality and neocolonial exploitation of late twentieth-century postcolonial 'independence'—or, in the case of Martinique, departmentalization and assimilation to France. A postcolonial framework remains key to this analysis, given the engagement these texts display with the history of slavery and colonialism, the history of resistance to slavery and colonialism, and with the cultures which developed out of those experiences of oppression and resistance, and in order to acknowledge and address the specific 'coloniality' of black Atlantic diasporas.[131] This postcolonial framework is not one, however, which reinstates the colonial binary of metropole and colony, centre and margin; many of the novels offer no such clear colonial axis of connection. Instead, the texts engage with the meanings and experiences of centuries of transnational migration and the multiple diaspora spaces thus created, whether on the inland savannahs or in Georgetown, Guyana, on Jamaica, Trinidad, Curaçao, Dominica or Martinique, in Toronto, New York, London, Glasgow or Amsterdam. A transnational, postcolonial framework accounts both for the ongoing effects of colonialism—and its ongoing vitality in neocolonial structures and institutions—and its alteration by cultural exchanges and migratory movements between multiple diasporic locations, which act to decentre the former colonial metropoles and to demonstrate the percolation and proliferation of colonial, anticolonial and postcolonial forces and discourses around and across the Atlantic region. The texts therefore share both an interest in and often explicit engagement with kinship in the wake of colonialism, slavery, and diaspora, a desire to represent contemporary modes of diasporic subjectivity, and an exploration of the relationship between kinship, diaspora, and the possibilities of writing itself.

In chapters one and two I consider the interrelation of kinship and anthropology, diaspora and indigeneity. Any study of kinship discourses must engage with the privileged position that kinship studies has held within the discipline of anthropology, where kinship was long studied as the key to or the fundamental structure of a culture. Critiques such as Schneider's have impacted on kinship studies within anthropology, but anthropological claims about kinship and culture—particularly the work of Lévi-Strauss—continue to have a significant impact outside the discipline. The claim that cultural reproduction depends upon certain, normative kinship forms is also to be

---

131 Shalini Puri, *The Caribbean Postcolonial: Social Equality, Post/Nationalism, and Cultural Hybridity* (New York: Palgrave Macmillan, 2004); Yolanda Martínez-San Miguel, *Coloniality of Diasporas: Rethinking Intra-Colonial Migrations in a Pan-Caribbean Context* (New York: Palgrave Macmillan, 2014).

found in the traditional focus in diaspora studies on a paternal line of cultural transmission. I consider two novels that engage with this anthropological—particularly and specifically Lévi-Straussian—legacy, and which take up the intersection of kinship and anthropology in different ways.

Pauline Melville's *The Ventriloquist's Tale* directly addresses the relationship between indigenous peoples and western knowledge production, and between knowledge, narration and colonial violence; it also offers an interrogation of two of Lévi-Strauss's key themes: writing, language and cultural change, and incest, sexuality and kinship. Jamaica Kincaid's *The Autobiography of My Mother* addresses similar issues and materials through its rewriting of nineteenth-century colonial travel narratives and anthropological travel accounts, including *Tristes Tropiques*. The two texts, however, offer very different approaches to two key themes: the meaning and definition of kinship and the representation of indigeneity. I argue that the quite different reflections on past and present Caribbean indigeneity offered in Kincaid's and Melville's novels correlate with the texts' writing of kinship and their rewriting of colonial–anthropological texts and discourses, thus conditioning the effectiveness of their interventions. The potential of Kincaid's novel to imagine anticolonial alternatives for identity and subjectivity is hampered by its failure to question a genealogical norm of kinship closely allied to colonial racism, as well as by its adoption of colonial discourses of purity and extinction about indigenous peoples in the Caribbean; its rewriting strategy—although innovative and at times subversive—is thereby restricted. In contrast, although Melville's novel opens with a contemporary indigenous man contemplating perceived cultural and material threats to his indigenous identity, including from diasporic 'aliens', it goes on to suggest that discourses of indigenous cultural stasis and racial purity pose more threat to indigenous survival than cultural interaction and admixture.

Chapters three and four analyse the relationship between kinship and history in two neoslave narratives and long family stories: *The Long Song*, by Andrea Levy, and *At the Full and Change of the Moon*, by Dionne Brand. The possibility or desirability of black diasporic (linear) 'History' is of concern to historians and literary scholars alike.[132] These two novels both intervene in current historiographical debates about rewriting colonial history, the nature of temporality and the relationship of the past of the present, but they offer different approaches to archives, to colonial and national historiography, and different reflections on the uses of literature. Both retell the tale of the emergence of western capitalist and colonial modernity from the slave quarters of a Caribbean plantation, of 'the global *intimacies* out of which emerged not only modern humanism but a modern racialized division of labour', but they maintain a different relationship to that tradition of

---

132 Herman L. Bennett, 'The Subject in the Plot: National Boundaries and the "History" of the Black Atlantic', *African Studies Review* 43.1 (2000), pp. 101–24.

political liberalism or modern humanism.[133] I argue that Levy's novel primarily makes visible the editorial—or narrative—process involved in historiography, including both colonial historiography and the rewriting of colonial and slave history offered by the novel's narrator, July. As July writes her life story, she makes explicit the process of forgetting and remembering involved in any historiography. In addition, the history crafted by July is closely linked to the family story she wishes to tell; history and kinship are shown to be closely intertwined. Thus the novel explores the inclusions and omissions from history required in order to incorporate enslaved peoples and their descendants into it, and the types of bonds (and cuts)—namely the adoption and rigorous maintenance of a heteronormative, patriarchal, nuclear-family model of kinship, or what Lee Edelman terms 'the promise of sequence as the royal road to *con*sequence'[134]—required for black diasporic subjects to insert themselves into normative kinship and thereby into cultural intelligibility and history.

In contrast, Brand's novel considers both the costs and the potential of black diasporic illegitimacy and unintelligibility. The experiences of slavery and the afterlife of slavery and the forms of subjectivity arising from those experiences take precedence in Brand's novel, which suggests that colonial and/or national kinship norms can never be achieved by black Atlantic subjects, and that alternative modes of relating to others and relating to history must be found. Diasporic peoples, displaced in various ways from all nations and nation-states, are always also displaced from national heteronormativity; the experience of diaspora is therefore an experience of queering. As Tinsley argues, diasporic Africans emerge from the Atlantic '"whole and broken": brutalized and feeling, connected to the past and separate from it, divided from other diasporic migrants and linked to them'.[135] In this way, the temporal questions raised in chapter one, particularly the challenge posed to colonial–anthropological concepts of time—that is, a time that is both linear and evolutionary—are pursued. The past, it becomes clear, is neither fixed nor over; rather, both history and present subjectivities are generated in interaction with one another; they are contemporaries.[136]

In chapter five and six I pursue queer diaspora further by considering two novels which depict the role that kinship and relationality play in diasporic community and subjectivity. I read *Texaco* by Patrick Chamoiseau as a fictional reworking of and reflection on Édouard Glissant's work on Caribbean culture,

---

133 Lisa Lowe, 'The Intimacies of Four Continents', in Ann Laura Stoler (ed.), *Haunted By Empire: Geographies of Intimacy in North American History* (Durham, NC: Duke University Press, 2006), p. 192, emphasis in original.
134 Lee Edelman in Carolyn Dinshaw et al., 'Theorizing Queer Temporalities', *GLQ: A Journal of Lesbian and Gay Studies* 13.2–3 (2007), p. 181, emphasis in original.
135 Tinsley, 'Black Atlantic, Queer Atlantic', p. 203.
136 Michel-Rolph Trouillot, *Silencing the Past: Power and the Production of History* (Boston, MA: Beacon Press, 1995).

identity and community, particularly in his *Poetics of Relation*.[137] The novel is less concerned with the destruction of kinship under slavery, as in Levy and Brand, nor with the way in which colonial norms of kinship reinforce racism, as in Kincaid, Brand and Kay; instead, it demonstrates how diasporic cultures in general, but Caribbean and black Atlantic cultures in particular, are necessarily displaced not only from nation, but also from 'filiation', in Glissant's terms: that is, from claims of identity and legitimacy based on genealogy and lineage. The creole community, therefore, cannot be modelled on the nuclear family as its basic unit, nor coalesce around a shared (imagined) origin. If, as Povinelli argues, 'culture is conceived as an incrustation on the parent-child link' in western thought and particularly in anthropology, then Caribbean diasporas must formulate a new concept of culture.[138] *Texaco* undertakes this project via a gradual resignification and reorientation away from 'mother-France' towards 'blood siblings' and rhizomatic roots formed in communities of solidarity and anticolonial struggle, while also indicating the difficulty of this transition. Thus, even though the novel's characters and depicted sex acts are overwhelmingly heterosexual—without a whiff of Saint-Pierre's transgressive history[139]—the Glissantian concept of culture and relationality which the novel brings to life can be understood as a queering of nationalist norms of community, subjectivity and the social meaning of sexuality.

Jackie Kay's *Trumpet* is set after the death of a central character, and consists in large part of memories and mourning from those close to the deceased. Mourning is represented as a process of subjective undoing and remaking, and this 'permeable' mode of subjectivity, as Eve Sedgwick terms it, is shown to be a constituent feature of black diasporic *life*, as well as mourning.[140] This reflection on mourning and kinship is therefore not limited to questions of ethical love or relationality, but has broader implications for diasporic, postcolonial subjectivity and experience. Mourning becomes a mode of memory and historiography, as well as a way of creating powerful connections and interactions between bodies, experiences and histories for diasporic subjects. The text thus offer an alternative to the concern, voiced by Saidiya Hartman and Vijay Mishra, that although mourning and the recognition and memorialization of loss are essential to diasporic memory, cultures and political activism, it may be paralysing or perilous if mourning creates an idealized, irreplaceable homeland or promises to overcome the past.[141] In contrast to Mishra's claim that a diasporic focus on loss leads to

---

137 Édouard Glissant, *Poetics of Relation*, trans. Betsy Wing (Ann Arbor: University of Michigan Press, 1997).
138 Povinelli, 'Notes on Gridlock', p. 225.
139 Vanessa Agard-Jones, 'What the Sands Remember', *GLQ: A Journal of Lesbian and Gay Studies* 18.2–3 (2012), pp. 325–46.
140 Eve Kosofsky Sedgwick, *A Dialogue on Love* (Boston, MA: Beacon Press, 1999).
141 Hartman, 'The Time of Slavery'; Vijay Mishra, *The Literature of the Indian Diaspora: Theorizing the Diasporic Imaginary* (London: Routledge, 2007).

Introduction

'racist fictions of purity' and 'anti-miscegenation narratives of homelands', *Trumpet* represents mourning as a force not of preservation, but of transformation; the novel imagines diasporic subjects and spaces informed by their histories of migration and displacement, but defined *more* by their transnational aesthetics, cultural practices, political engagements and queered intimate bonds.[142] Furthermore, the text works against any fantasy of cultural purity preserved by heteronormativity through an emphasis on the queerness of these diasporic bonds and the queer textuality of their representation. In a similar way, while Benedict Anderson famously suggests that public mourning may create national sentiment by conjuring 'a combined connectedness, fortuity, and fatality in a language of "continuity"', Kay's novel both demonstrates the possibility and necessity of non-nationalist mourning and suggests that the temporality of this mourning would be less linear than that identified by Anderson.[143] In *Trumpet*, mourning works to alter kinship and subjectivity both retroactively and into the future, so that past, present and future are mutually enfolded in their becoming. Mourning in this sense is a force which creates queer diasporic bonds, affirming connections with the dead and transforming the living, enfolding the past into the future—that is, mourning is a key process of performatively generating kinship, and a key process of generating and perpetuating diaspora and of shaping diaspora space.

The modes of writing, of history, of community and mourning in these novels are distinctly black Atlantic, yet they are relevant not only to black, racialized, postslavery subjects in the New World. While the specificity of black Atlantic experience and culture must be acknowledged and not erased, nonetheless the experiences of such subjects—both their experiences of suffering and their creative resistance to oppression—might provide resources for rethinking global community and cosmopolitan relationality. As Chela Sandoval suggests, 'subordinated, marginalized, or colonized Western citizen-subjects [...] have been forced to experience the so-called aesthetics of "postmodern" globalization as a precondition for survival. It is this constituency that is most familiar with what citizenship in this realm requires and makes possible'.[144]

---

142 Mishra, *The Literature of the Indian Diaspora*, p. 16.
143 Benedict Anderson, *Imagined Communities: Reflections on the Origin and Spread of Nationalism* (London: Verso, 1991), p. 11.
144 Sandoval, *Methodology of the Oppressed*, p. 9.

Part I

Rewriting anthropology

CHAPTER ONE

Postcolonial sabotage and ethnographic recovery in Jamaica Kincaid's *The Autobiography of My Mother*

Despite its ambivalence, the title of Jamaica Kincaid's novel, although paradoxical, makes clear that it is concerned with kinship relations and with the possibility of writing kinship in a colonial language. As a family story and a reflection on the five-hundred-year history of contact and exchange between the indigenous, European and African inhabitants of Dominica, the novel suggests that kinship and colonial history are inevitably intertwined. It reveals the destruction and distortion caused to interpersonal relations by colonial rule and colonial racism, most of all in the realms of intimate relations, family life and kinship. Its tone, which ranges from bleak to sombre to despairing, might qualify it as a 'literature of recrimination and despair' (in Derek Walcott's phrase), yet the novel also seeks to inaugurate a new relationship to and between language and history.[1] In particular, it approaches and transforms the legacy of colonial rule via its rewriting of colonial and anthropological travel narratives, particularly James Anthony Froude's *The English in the West Indies* and Claude Lévi-Strauss's *Tristes Tropiques*, thereby exploring the possibility of writing as a postcolonial sabotage of imperialist ideology.[2]

By rewriting Lévi-Strauss and colonial–anthropological travel writing, the novel interrogates both colonized relationality and intimacy and the discipline of anthropology, where kinship has been studied, categorized, mapped out and written about most extensively, and where kinship studies

---

1 Derek Walcott, 'The Muse of History', in Alison Donnell and Sarah Lawson Welsh (eds.), *The Routledge Reader in Caribbean Literature* (London: Routledge, 1996), pp. 354–58.
2 James Anthony Froude, *The English in the West Indies, or the Bow of Ulysses* (London: Longmans, Green, and Co., 1888); Claude Lévi-Strauss, *A World on the Wane* [*Tristes Tropiques*], trans. John Russell (New York: Criterion, 1961).

long constituted one of the field's main and most sustained interests.[3] The structuralist analysis and approach of Claude Lévi-Strauss has had and, in some contexts, continues to have immense influence; his theory of writing, political power and cultural evolution, and his positing of the incest taboo as the fundamental threshold of all human cultures both continue to reverberate— particularly *outside* the discipline.[4] In recent decades, interrogations of the history and praxis of anthropology, usually from within the field itself, have excavated some of the epistemological implications and consequences of the discipline's foundations and methods. In addition to critiques of anthropological kinship studies, such as that from David Schneider, numerous scholars have analysed the relationship between anthropology and colonialism. Johannes Fabian insists that nineteenth-century anthropology 'contributed above all to the intellectual justification of the colonial enterprise' by providing colonialism with a concept of evolutionary time, and that a similar 'denial of coevalness' continues the same work in newer disciplinary forms, so that 'American anthropology and French structuralism [...] are potential and actual contributors to ideologies apt to sustain the new, vast, anonymous, but terribly effective regimen of absentee colonialism'.[5] In return, Talal Asad suggests, colonialism enabled anthropology by making 'the object of anthropological study accessible and safe'.[6] Elizabeth Povinelli's recent work joins these strands together: she argues that anthropology and (settler) colonialism have often had a symbiotic relationship, and that this had a particular impact on kinship and intimacy. Povinelli suggests that a binary understanding of possible modes of kinship and intimacy, which she terms 'the autological subject' and 'the genealogical society', 'emerged from European Empire as a mode and maneuver of domination and continue to operate as such'.[7] Thus, because supposed differences in kinship practices between cultures have often been mapped onto geographical and racial divides via European colonialism, an analysis of kinship, understood *both* as a potential tool of colonialism and a potential resource for anticolonial resistance, is crucial to a consideration of postcolonial and indigenous texts and contexts.[8]

---

3 For summaries of the history of kinship studies, see Schneider, *A Critique of the Study of Kinship*, pp. 97–112 (particularly on the Anglo-American anthropological tradition); and Povinelli, *The Empire of Love*, pp. 209–36 (for a longer and broader survey).
4 Including in ways that Lévi-Strauss distanced himself from. See for example the discussion in Butler, 'Is Kinship Always Already Heterosexual?', pp. 29–38.
5 Johannes Fabian, *Time and the Other* (New York: Columbia University Press, 2002), pp. 17, 69.
6 Talal Asad, 'Anthropology and the Colonial Encounter', in Gerrit Huizer and Bruce Mannheim (eds.), *The Politics of Anthropology: From Colonialism and Sexism Toward a View from Below* (The Hague: Mouton, 1979), p. 91.
7 Povinelli, *The Empire of Love*, pp. 16–17.
8 Simon During, 'Rousseau's Patrimony: Primitivism, Romance and Becoming Other', in Francis Baker, Peter Hulme and Margaret Iversen (eds.), *Colonial Discourse*

Jamaica Kincaid's The Autobiography of My Mother

Outside the field of anthropology, Derrida's analysis of 'The Writing Lesson' from *Tristes Tropiques* famously reveals Lévi-Strauss's approach to ethnography and to the Other as 'an ethnocentrism *thinking itself* as anti-ethnocentrism'.[9] Derrida rejects the division Lévi-Strauss makes between cultures with written language and those without, identifying in such a division not only an ethnocentrism pertaining to the definition of language and writing, but also a colonialist exploitation of anthropological Others, particularly indigenous peoples, to serve European desires—desires inherited from the eighteenth century and the work of Rousseau in particular, in which 'non-European peoples were [...] studied as the index to a hidden good Nature, as a native soil recovered, of a "zero degree" with reference to which one could outline the structure, the growth, and above all the degradation of our own society and our culture'.[10]

Kincaid's novel opens with the event which its narrator later calls the 'central motif' of her life, and to which her narration returns again and again: her mother's death in childbirth.[11] In the opening lines Xuela portrays her life as one bereft of any intimacy, kinship or care as a result of her mother's death: 'My mother died at the moment I was born, and so for my whole life there was nothing standing between myself and eternity; at my back was always a bleak, black wind' (*AM* 3). Set on Dominica in the early to mid-twentieth century, the novel is narrated by Xuela as an old woman. The story she tells of her life is dominated by two main causes of suffering: the death of her mother in childbirth and her lifelong sense of loss and abandonment resulting from it, and the racist dehumanization and dehistoricization she experiences over her lifetime—primarily as a black woman under British colonial rule, but also as the child of a Carib mother, othered and excluded by her black classmates in school. She becomes increasingly aware that she is expected to celebrate the same British colonial history that designates her as subhuman, and she realizes that colonial power is often reproduced in and exercised through the family and intimate sphere, leading to her attempt to reject and distance herself from both kinship and history entirely. Xuela is a contradictory character, and it is in these moments of contradiction that the limits of Xuela's chosen strategy of anticolonial and antipatriarchal resistance emerge. Through these contradictions, it becomes clear that the position outside of history, colonial power, and colonized intimacy that Xuela longs for is impossible, and that by refusing to acknowledge her complex position within colonialism she

---

/ *Postcolonial Theory* (Manchester: Manchester University Press, 1994), pp. 47–71; Rifkin, *When did Indians Become Straight?*

9 Jacques Derrida, *Of Grammatology*, corrected edition, trans. Gayatri Chakravorty Spivak (Baltimore: Johns Hopkins University Press, 1997), pp. 120, emphasis in original.

10 Derrida, *Of Grammatology*, pp. 114–15.

11 Jamaica Kincaid, *The Autobiography of My Mother* (London: Vintage, 1996), p. 225. Further references to the novel are given in the text as *AM*.

unwittingly reproduces certain forms of colonial oppression. In trying to resist colonialism, Xuela instead replicates aspects of its murderous violence, particularly when it comes to her reimagining of her indigenous Carib mother.

Kinship is crucial to this question, because Xuela asserts that biological reproduction is one of the key means by which colonialism and patriarchy are reproduced, and this anthropological discourse of the relationship between genealogy and culture remains unquestioned in the novel as a whole. If biological reproduction perpetuates colonial oppression, so too does cultural (re)production, or cultural creativity. J. Halberstam argues that the novel offers 'characters who can never thrive, never love, and never create precisely because colonialism has removed the context within which those things would make sense'.[12] This assertion of creative failure echoes the similar claim made by Xuela, and both resound within a long debate in Caribbean literature and historiography, most often in response to James Anthony Froude's claim of the impossibility of Caribbean creativity—although I argue that the position of Kincaid's novel within these debates is rather more ambivalent than Halberstam's reading. The discourse of defeat and failure adopted by Xuela as she partially re-enacts Froude's travels shows intriguing potential to sabotage colonial power and anthropological knowledge production, but this is a strategy with clear limits. This risks of this strategy, which can both sabotage and recuperate the ethnographic gaze, becomes clear in Xuela's imagining of her indigenous Carib mother and her (re)colonization of her mother's life and story. In part, this applies not only to Xuela, but to the text as a whole: despite its searing criticism of colonialism—particularly colonial racism and patriarchy and their effects upon racialized and formerly enslaved peoples—it continues to rely on some key elements of a colonial–anthropological logic, and in some respects remains trapped by the terms of the anthropological gaze, which thereby limits the scope and effectiveness of its rewriting project.

The connection made at the beginning of the novel between the death of Xuela's birth mother and her lifelong isolation, suffering and alienation simultaneously emphasizes the centrality of kinship—or the lack thereof—to her story, and defines what may be classified as kinship, or which bonds might provide shelter from the 'bleak, black wind' (*AM* 3): parent-child bonds predicated on biological relatedness, and nothing else. After her mother's death, Xuela's father places the infant in the care of another woman, and Xuela spends the next seven years living with this woman, whom she calls 'Ma Eunice'. Despite this familial signifier, however, she rigorously refuses to acknowledge Ma Eunice as kin or even kin-like; instead, she insists upon the impossibility of kinship between them on both physical and social grounds.

---

12 Judith [Jack] Halberstam, *The Queer Art of Failure* (Durham, NC: Duke University Press, 2011), p. 132.

Her recollection that 'in my mouth it [Ma Eunice's breast milk] tasted sour and I would not drink it' (*AM* 5) is the first of many assertions that kinship must be anchored in genealogical relations, as well as inscribed in and visible on the body.

At the same time, Xuela's understanding that Ma Eunice 'could not be kind because she did not know how' and Xuela 'could not love her because I, too, did not know how' (*AM* 6) and that 'in a place like this, brutality is the only real inheritance' (*AM* 5) demonstrates her awareness of the colonial burden upon kinship and intimacy in Dominica. When Xuela is punished by Ma Eunice for breaking a plate (the most treasured possession of Ma Eunice and a symbol of colonial cultural domination: the plate bears an idealized picture of the English countryside and the inscription 'HEAVEN' [*AM* 9]), she recognizes a continuation of colonial violence in her punishment, which she describes as 'redolent [...] in every way of the relationship between captor and captive, master and slave' (*AM* 10). Yet Xuela herself continues this cycle of violence and domination immediately afterwards. During her punishment, she sees several turtles: 'I fell in love with them, I wanted to have them near me, I wanted to speak only to them each day for the rest of my life' (*AM* 11). What begins as a professed desire for intimacy and communication soon becomes despotic: she captures the turtles, fashions an enclosure for them and brings them food and water so that they are 'completely dependent on me for their existence' (*AM* 11). When she discovers that, despite their material reliance upon her, she cannot entirely control the animals—they 'would withdraw into their shells when I did not want them to' (*AM* 11)—she seals up their shells as punishment and thus eventually kills them. In these two scenes, the potential tyranny of kinship, both in the sense of intimate attachment and material dependence, and its colonial burden—the historical echoes of slavery that Xuela hears in her punishment by Ma Eunice, and the further reverberations of a colonial discourse of paternalism in her own equation of control with care in regard to the turtles—are vividly apparent.

Upon her return to her father's house after his remarriage, Xuela becomes increasingly aware that the divisive rule of colonialism is replicated and carried out through the practices and values of colonized people, and through the family in particular. She is taught by her father not to trust the other children at her school, and she imagines that their parents tell them the same thing; Xuela understands this 'insistence on the mistrust of others' (*AM* 48) as both consequence and tactic of colonial rule. Significantly, colonial power is here exercised through intimate relations and the family, simultaneously constructing the respectable family—one like that of Xuela's father, structured by heteropatriarchy and sanctioned by legal marriage—and making kinship a tool of colonial rule and social division among colonized peoples. The material and social benefits conferred upon normative colonial kinship are again revealed when Xuela later attends a school which 'did not admit children born outside marriage, and this, apart from everything else, kept the school very small, because most children were born outside marriage' (*AM* 80). In this same period Xuela also experiences and witnesses the operations of patriarchy in intimacy. Her relationship with her stepmother is poisoned by her stepmother's patriarchal desire; that is, a desire to secure her own position by serving patriarchy, and her fear because she has not yet done so: 'she had not yet been able to bear my father a child' (*AM* 33). The poisoned necklace that the stepmother gives Xuela dramatically and literally signifies both the poisonousness of their relationship, indicating the stepmother's fear and hatred of Xuela as the child of another woman, and the poison of Xuela's burgeoning womanhood. The necklace thus symbolizes the dangers of patriarchy to women in the form of a beautiful, ornamental, and feminine object, while it echoes and twists the anthropological concept of the gift, suggesting that social bonds supposedly created by gift-giving are poisoned and dangerous. Following the motif of the gift from Mauss to Lévi-Strauss, who suggested that sociality and culture are formed through the exchange of women, the novel echoes the claims of feminist thinkers who insist that Lévi-Strauss's conceptualization of women as 'the most precious gifts' means that 'the world-historical defeat of women occurred with the origin of culture, and is a prerequisite of culture'.[13] Kincaid extends this insight to colonial contexts, suggesting that colonialism has poisoned intimacy, kinship, and culture as well.

The bind of Xuela's notion of kinship soon becomes clear: she recognizes the colonization of kinship and is therefore wary of it; she also recognizes the role of kinship in shaping subjectivity, and therefore the apparent necessity of it. She both desires kinship *and* defines it in such a way that it remains inaccessible for her—primarily through her insistence that only genealogical relatives can be kin. She writes of her time with Ma Eunice, 'I wished to see people in whose faces I could recognize something of myself. Because who was I? My mother was dead; I had not seen my father for a long time' (*AM* 16). In this passage, Xuela again defines kinship as specifically limited to her (biological) mother and father, as requiring corporeal legibility, and as a necessary condition of self-knowledge and subjectivity—without it, she cannot know who she is. Much later, she will repeat a similar sentiment: 'you are a child until the people who brought you into this world are dead; you remain a child until you understand and believe that the people who brought you into this world are dead' (*AM* 213), once again identifying a knowledge of and relationship to one's (biological) parents as a condition of adulthood, full subjectivity, and participation in culture. Yet with sad irony, Xuela's insistence on the genealogical basis of kinship in no way counters the colonial mutilation of kinship and intimacy and the colonial privileging of British metropolitan over local Caribbean culture that she has become aware of. Instead, it reinstates the link between physical reproduction, 'biology'

---

13 Marcel Mauss, *The Gift: Forms and Functions of Exchange in Archaic Societies* (New York: Norton, 1967); Lévi-Strauss, *The Elementary Structures of Kinship*; Rubin, 'The Traffic in Women', pp. 43, 46.

and culture, a foundational element of traditional western anthropology in which 'culture is conceived as an incrustation on the parent-child link'.[14] Furthermore, the link she posits between the knowledge of one's biological parents and adult subjectivity replicates the heteronormative imperative to kinship and culture implicit in models such as that of Lévi-Strauss.[15] Xuela thus cements the conditions for the continuation of the patriarchal forms of kinship and intimacy which she despises, and the text thereby shows that Xuela's awareness of the colonial and patriarchal dynamics which saturate kinship in Dominica does not prevent her replication of them. Just as she understood, but nonetheless pursued, the destructive tyranny of intimate control in the episode with the turtles, Xuela is keenly aware of the poison of patriarchy and its crushing effects on women's lives and she wishes to extract herself from such relations, yet she continues to reproduce patriarchal sexism in her understanding of *other* women's social roles. Of Madame LaBatte, a woman with whom she lives as a teenager, she writes: 'Her dress [...] was not in a stylish cut but loose, fitting her badly, as if her body was no longer of any interest to her' (*AM* 64). Xuela's assumption—that if Madame LaBatte chooses not to wear fitting clothes that show off her body, this must mean that her body is of no interest to her, because women's bodies exist solely for their attractiveness to the male gaze—is repeated, even more clearly, when she later writes of her sister: 'Her bosoms were large but without seductive appeal; they grew larger, but they did not invite caresses' (*AM* 118).

Rather than seeking alternative modes of relating to others and the world than those offered by colonialism and patriarchy, Xuela decides to reject dependence, intimacy and even community; she declares a desire to remove herself from the circulation of colonial power, to assume a position outside history and outside kinship, and she believes in the possibility of doing so. Encouraged by Madame LaBatte to pursue a sexual relationship with Monsieur LaBatte in order to produce a child for the couple, when Xuela does become pregnant she emphatically rejects the position Madame LaBatte imagines for her—and the position of mother offered by the broader culture—and procures the first of many abortions. This experience, including the refusal to become a mother, taking control over her own body and particularly its reproductive capacities, and the pain it entails, are considered by Xuela to be formative of her adult character and her independence, and they also mark a transition in her perception of and relationship to kinship. Rather than mourning her lack of kinship with her father and mother and focusing on her sense of abandonment and resulting lack of identity, she begins to actively renounce (genealogical) kinship: 'I had never had a mother, I had just recently

---

14 Povinelli, 'Notes on Gridlock', p. 225.
15 Butler, 'Is Kinship Always Already Heterosexual?'

refused to become one, and I knew then that this refusal would be complete' (*AM* 97). This renouncement of kinship and intersubjective dependence is linked by Xuela to her developing sense of herself as self-contained and autonomous, which soon becomes one of the chief markers of her public identity and subjectivity: she proudly describes herself as 'ruler of my own life' (*AM* 115) and relishes her status as an outsider—despite having recently moved back to her father's house.

Xuela also defines her rejection of kinship as a strategy of anticolonial and antipatriarchal resistance: by renouncing kinship, she claims to be removing herself from the damaging dynamics in intimate and family life that she identified earlier. She also claims to be withdrawing from shared identities such as race and nation; her decision not to bear children is defined as a refusal of both: 'I refused to belong to a race, I refused to accept a nation' (*AM* 226). Xuela's decision is described by Caroline Rody as one of 'refusing to bear more racialized history'.[16] Halberstam understands this strategy similarly: 'Where a colonized woman bears a child and passes on her legacy to that child, Kincaid insists, the colonial project can spread virus-like from one generation to the next'.[17] Yet Halberstam's metaphor is too broad, for unlike the horizontal transmission of most viruses, Xuela foresees only vertical transmission from mother to child. Both Xuela's claim and the readings by Rody and Halberstam imply that the reproduction of culture, including of colonial racism, is necessarily tied to biological reproduction, and that Xuela is able to remove herself from this cycle by refusing biological motherhood. Xuela's rejection of genealogical filiation as a strategy of antiracism is one of the most poignant ironies of the novel, for the concepts of biology and race that she thereby invokes are legacies and key techniques of colonialism.[18] Even her strategy of denying the importance of (genealogical) kinship—for herself—in search of an individual, non-filiative identity is a classic strategy of European Enlightenment and colonial thought, and this, together with Xuela's self-presentation as an original figure based on her exclusion from society, suggests an unexpected connection between Xuela and another famous autobiographer: Rousseau.[19]

It soon becomes apparent that Xuela's positing of clear boundaries between colonizers and colonized must necessarily fail, as must her attempt to position herself outside of colonial power and to deny her own implication or

---

16 Caroline Rody, *The Daughter's Return: African-American and Caribbean Women's Fictions of History* (New York: Oxford University Press, 2001), p. 129.
17 Halberstam, *The Queer Art of Failure*, p. 133.
18 Robert J. C. Young, *Colonial Desire: Hybridity in Theory, Culture and Race* (London: Routledge, 1995).
19 During, 'Rousseau's Patrimony'; Tobin Siebers, 'Ethics in the Age of Rousseau: From Lévi-Strauss to Derrida', *MLN* 100.4 (1985), pp. 758–79. Siebers also suggests that Rousseau's autobiographical works are his most significant contribution to anthropology.

complicity in complex colonial structures. This is evident in Xuela's language, which continually hints at the impossibility of her undertaking and indicates her imbrication in colonial structures and culture. Xuela decries the colonization of language, describing English as 'the language of a people I would never like or love' (*AM* 7), yet despite this implication that it is not and can never be her language or the language of anyone in the (post)colony, Xuela is also able to use English to her own advantage: 'I had, through the use of some words, changed my situation; I had perhaps even saved my life' (*AM* 22). Her language again reveals a more complex position than she herself chooses to admit when she claims that Christian belief 'signified defeat yet again' (*AM* 133) for colonized peoples, yet employs language suffused with Christian imagery, describing herself and the LaBattes as 'a trinity' (*AM* 93) and claiming that her father's skin is 'the color of bread, the staff of life' (*AM* 186). Xuela's presents her rejection of kinship as a matter of anticolonial resistance, yet when she writes, 'I felt I did not want to belong to anyone, that since the one person [her mother] I would have consented to own me had never lived to do so, I did not want to belong to anyone; I did not want anyone to belong to me' (*AM* 104), she imagines kinship via a discourse of possession; the bonds of kinship are rewritten as a matter of property and ownership. This language of kinship recalls the property relations of chattel slavery, demonstrating the crucial influence of colonialism upon Xuela's understanding of kinship, even as she seeks to distance herself from both. Similarly, her final claim, that she has removed herself from the circulation and reproduction of race and racism, is counteracted by her own use of a discourse of racial essentialism inherited from colonial racism, such as when Xuela employs and inverts, but does not undo, historically significant phenotypical markers to justify her dislike and distrust of her stepmother because her stepmother's lips are 'thin and ungenerous' and her nose is 'long and sharp' (*AM* 29).

The tragedy of Xuela's attempted denial of kinship is revealed in an episode that occurs when Xuela is a young woman and living once again in her father's house. Here, her refusal to acknowledge and *do* kinship results in the reproduction and continuation of the colonial violence which she ostensibly seeks to prevent. A woman delivers a baby to the house, claiming that it is the child of a man named Pacquet, the lover and future husband of Xuela's sister. Xuela writes:

> My sister and I took care of this child, though in reality it was I who did so, tending to its needs [...]. The child did not thrive, and after two years it died of a disease said to be whooping cough. The child's life passed unnoticed, as if it had never happened. My father forbade its burial in the same graveyard as his son, Alfred. (*AM* 127)

In her narration of this episode, Xuela seems critical of her father's refusal to let the child be buried with his son—that is, his refusal to recognize the child as kin—yet she, too, refuses to recognize this child as connected to her in any meaningful way. Although Xuela has complained many times that her father was not sufficiently loving towards her, and that she feels bereft at the loss of her mother, she seems equally indifferent towards this small child for whom she has taken over caring responsibilities. The performance of intimate care does not induce a bond between them, or at least Xuela's narration does not admit it, and her account emphasizes her detachment: She 'tend[ed] to its needs', a perfunctory performance of the absolute necessities without any emotional connection. The child dies of a disease 'said to be whooping cough': Xuela's disengagement is made clear by the uninterested 'said to be', which leaves Xuela's involvement and the extent of the medical care provided to the child vague. If this episode offers evidence of her rejection and refusal of kinship, it also demonstrates how that refusal of kinship facilitates the perpetuation of intimate violence, neglect and dehumanization which she herself suffered and for which she condemns her father. This symmetry is revealed when she describes the child upon its arrival as 'a small bundle' (*AM* 126), echoing her bitter recollection, at the beginning of the novel, that she too was once delivered into the care of Ma Eunice as one of 'two bundles' (*AM* 4), alongside her father's unwashed clothes.

The text thus demonstrates the failure of Xuela's strategy of anticolonial resistance through wilful denial, thus disproving Halberstam's premise—which is also Xuela's premise—that she can either 'become part of the colonial story or she can refuse to be part of any story at all'.[20] Even when, or perhaps even *particularly* when Xuela attempts such a refusal, she remains implicated in colonial oppression and its reproduction. Thus all of Xuela's claims which follow from her being 'alone in the world' (*AM* 223): including that she has freed herself from shared identities such as race and nation, that she stands outside the ongoing cycle of colonial oppression, or that she is not subject to patriarchal domination, must be contrasted by the reader (as Xuela fails to do herself) with her own implication in the colonial, national and patriarchal structures that she disavows. The novel makes clear that there is no way for colonized or postcolonial subjects to entirely remove themselves from colonial history, power and discourse, and it rejects that reversed ethnocentrism—us and them, colonizer and colonized as eternally distinct and separate populations—which Xuela endorses.

Despite the novel's undermining of Xuela's attempt to excise herself from colonialism, it does not question another key aspect of her understanding of kinship: its 'biological' basis and the inevitable or essential nature of such genealogical ties. Even as the text makes clear that Xuela's rejection of kinship cannot succeed as a strategy of anticolonial resistance, it also suggests that her denial of kinship, in particular with her biological father, is impossible per se. Despite Xuela's professed renouncement of kinship, or of all close personal bonds, and her refusal of any material inheritance from her father, the text suggests that she remains obsessed with, influenced and defined by

---

20 Halberstam, *The Queer Art of Failure*, p. 131.

her relationship with him for most of her life. Throughout the novel, Xuela is scathing in her criticism of her father—for his perceived neglect of her, for his complicity in colonial rule, his corruption, his greed, and his exploitation and mistreatment of others. Xuela's repetitive recounting of her father's crimes suggests her inability to separate herself from him, as does her behaviour (as opposed to her claims). During Xuela's youth, when he asks her to return and live with him again, she sets off immediately—within hours—and remains for at least the next seven years (during which time she also enjoys the material benefits of his ill-gotten wealth). Despite her repeated assertions that she is close to no one, she pays attention to every intimate detail of her father's life, noting for example when 'his skin then began to wrinkle, the folds were tiny, creases so minute that only someone as interested as I would have noticed' (*AM* 118). Years later, when her father dies, Xuela acknowledges his influence on her: 'It was at that moment [of his death] that I knew death to be a real thing; my mother's death in comparison was not a death at all' (*AM* 211). Finally it is Xuela, not her sister or stepmother, who chooses her father's burial clothes, thus performing a traditional rite of kinship.

Xuela paints her enduring bond to her father as an inevitability over which she has no control: 'I missed him when he died, and before he died I knew this would be so. I wished not to miss him, but all the same it was so' (*AM* 210). The text's portrayal of Xuela's relationship with her father, particularly her inability or failure to separate herself from him and his influence despite her professed desire to do so, seems to confirm Xuela's own belief in the inevitability of 'blood' ties. In the episode with the child, discussed above, although the text makes the reproduction of colonial oppression in this situation clear, it also simultaneously confirms the unimportance of Xuela's relationship with the child: the episode is recounted very briefly, comprising only a half paragraph, and despite the repetitive, cyclical style of Xuela's narration—numerous episodes are narrated multiple times, as she obsessively returns to her favoured themes—neither the child nor Xuela's experience of this period are ever mentioned again. In this way, the text again implicitly confirms one aspect of Xuela's claim: that the child meant little or nothing to her, the experience did not greatly affect her, and it was not and could not be kinship because they were not genealogical relatives. The consequences of this failure to interrogate this particular aspect of kinship later become enmeshed with the second major aspect of Xuela's chosen strategy of postcolonial identity and subjectivity—her embrace of failure and defeat through the story she tells of her Carib mother and the broader history of Caribbean indigeneity.

In addition to her refusal of kinship and attempt to position herself outside of colonial power, Xuela develops a second strategy of both anticolonial resistance and identity formation: she embraces the notion of defeat in an attempt to develop an alternative, postcolonial relationship to the island and its history. Xuela's embrace of defeat brings the novel into an intertextual debate with the work of James Anthony Froude and his numerous interlocutors since the late nineteenth century, as well as with the work of Claude Lévi-Strauss. Appropriately, this engagement with Froude and Lévi-Strauss is effected in part by taking up a narrative form used by both: the travelogue. The novel's contribution to the tradition of Froude scholarship and critique is an ambivalent one: one which offers intriguing potential, but which remains troubled and limited by the text's acceptance of some foundational tenants of colonial–anthropological discourse, even as it rewrites and challenges others. The novel reworks the genre of the travel narrative, adopting the form common to both Froude's *The English in the West Indies* and Lévi-Strauss's *Tristes Tropiques*, and effectively twisting the methods of colonial–anthropological knowledge production in order to expose some of their horrors and psychic effects. Nonetheless, I argue that the limits of this strategy are demonstrated when Xuela embraces defeat not only for herself, but also projects it onto the story of her mother, so that Xuela's rewriting of colonial forms and discourses becomes a repetition of colonial violence.

James Anthony Froude travelled around the West Indies in 1886–87 and spent two weeks on Dominica (a relatively long time, compared to the mere hours he spent in the ports of most other islands). His conclusion about the West Indies as a whole—that 'there are no people there in the true sense of the word, with a character and purpose of their own'—has been rebutted by Caribbean writers numerous times since.[21] It was first challenged, a short time after the original publication, by the Trinidadian historian J. J. Thomas, who argues that 'impartial history' and 'the actual facts of West Indian life' are alone sufficient to disprove Froude's racist assertions, and that a less biased examination of Caribbean history offers evidence of the essential similarity of white Englishmen and black West Indians.[22] Wilson Harris, however, suggests that Thomas's assertion of Caribbean rationality and civilization unwittingly shares a 'close rapport' with Froude's understanding of culture and history, and that both Thomas and Froude view 'primitive manifestations', which they understand as signs of degeneration or regression, with suspicion.[23] That is, Thomas's rebuttal of Froude's claim that Caribbeans were incapable of civilization or learning without white, ideally British, control and guidance nonetheless accepts the terms set by Froude, including Froude's definition of civilization and primitiveness, his concepts of progress and degeneration, and his understanding of culture. Harris champions a different approach: a celebration of specifically Caribbean creativity and hybridity and its 'limbo perspective'.[24] Furthermore, he deplores the fact that 'Froude was doing

---

21 Froude, *The English in the West Indies*, p. 306.
22 J. J. Thomas, *Froudacity: West Indian Fables by James Anthony Froude* (Philadelphia: Gebbie and Company, 1890), p. 13.
23 Wilson Harris, *History, Fable and Myth in the Caribbean and Guianas* (Wellesley: Calaloux, 1995), pp. 18–19.
24 Harris, *History, Fable and Myth*, p. 19.

on behalf of imperialism what many contemporary historians are doing in a protest against imperialism': both agree that 'the West Indies [has] no creative potential'.[25] In his dig at 'contemporary historians', Harris might also have been thinking of a writer like V. S. Naipaul, who quotes Froude in the epigraphs of the book and the first chapter of *The Middle Passage*, and ventriloquizes Froude when he writes of the Caribbean that 'the history of the islands can never be satisfactorily told. [...] History is built around achievement and creation; and nothing was created in the West Indies'.[26] In contrast to Naipaul's ambiguous mimicking of Froude, Derek Walcott has repeatedly written against Froude's pronouncements, endorsing a similar aesthetics and history of Caribbean creativity as Harris. In his poetic and dramatic works, Walcott repeatedly returns to this theme, referencing and rejecting Froude.[27] In his 1992 Nobel Prize lecture, Walcott rejects a Froudian understanding of Caribbean history and culture as 'fragments and echoes of real people, unoriginal and broken', in favour of a celebration of the 'love that reassembles our African and Asiatic fragments, the cracked heirlooms whose restoration shows its white scars'; this reassembling of broken pieces, this remaking of culture is, he suggests, 'the exact process of the making of poetry'.[28]

Kincaid's novel, which is dedicated to Walcott, takes up this question once again. Xuela's description of the population of Dominica as 'people who had never been regarded as a people at all' (*AM* 177) resounds with Froude's dismissive characterization, just as she echoes Froude when she writes, 'The population of Roseau, that is, the ones who looked like me, had long ago been reduced to shadows; the forever foreign, the margins, had long ago lost any connection to wholeness, to an inner life of our own invention' (*AM* 132–33). This reworking of Froude is not a direct criticism or rebuttal; rather, Xuela offers a different response to Froude than those from Thomas, Harris and Walcott. She seeks neither to counter such a claim by asserting the contrary, that is by insisting on her own or others' 'wholeness' or the existence of an 'inner life', neither does she champion impure, vital creativity. Instead, Xuela accepts and embraces the defeat diagnosed by Froude, but endows it with the potential for creating renewal, endowing it with a historical force which

---

25 Harris, *History, Fable and Myth*, p. 22.
26 V. S. Naipaul, *The Middle Passage: Impressions of Five Societies—British, French and Dutch—in the West Indies and South America* (New York: Vintage, 1981), p. 29. Graham Huggan suggests that this particular 'mimicking' of Froude is difficult to define as either support or rejection, and that 'although Naipaul "mimics" Froude in *The Middle Passage*, the cameo appearance made by Froude in the later novel *The Mimic Men* is obviously ironic'. See Graham Huggan, 'A Tale of Two Parrots: Walcott, Rhys, and the Uses of Colonial Mimicry', *Contemporary Literature* 35.4 (1994), p. 644.
27 Paula Burnett, *Derek Walcott: Politics and Poetics* (Gainesville: University Press of Florida, 2000).
28 Derek Walcott, 'The Antilles, Fragments of Epic Memory: The 1992 Nobel Lecture', *World Literature Today* 67.2 (1993), p. 262.

Froude did not foresee. Towards the end of the novel she predicts a future in which her story will write history: 'for me the future must remain capable of casting a light on the past such that in my defeat lies the seed of my great victory, in my defeat lies the beginning of my great revenge' (*AM* 215–16). In these passages, Xuela takes on the Froudian accusation of cultural failure and begins to turn her claim to be 'of the vanquished, of the defeated' (*AM* 215) into a strategy of anticolonial resistance.

Froude's claim of 'no people' is both a historical and anthropological claim, and Kincaid's novel—again alongside the work of Wilson Harris and Derek Walcott—grapples with key elements of the anthropological tradition, particularly the work of Lévi-Strauss, and demonstrates the close relationship between colonial domination and anthropological inquiry. Once again, Kincaid's text differs substantially in its approach to those of the other writers. Paula Burnett details how Walcott takes on Lévi-Strauss, 'repeatedly ironizing' the nostalgic tone of *Tristes Tropiques*, which 'sums up for him the melancholic and essentially disparaging view of the Caribbean'.[29] She suggests that Walcott shows Lévi-Strauss 'to be the Rousseau of contemporary thought, who reinscribes in scientific codes the old, damaging binarism by which societies regarded as radically different are marginalized by being construed as primitive—however nostalgically or romantically so—in relation to the center's appropriation of the civilized'.[30] Burnett's analysis thus portrays Walcott's work as a critique, in poetic form, with many similarities to Derrida's reading of Lévi-Strauss.[31] Walcott writes, 'A culture, we all know, is made by its cities. [...] To be told you are not yet a city or a culture requires this response. I am not your city or your culture. There might be less of *Tristes tropiques* after that'.[32] He thus offers a transition from the arguments of Froude to those of Lévi-Strauss, from 'not a people' or 'not a culture' to 'not yet a culture', suggesting that the two are closely related and should be equally rejected.

Kincaid's novel again takes up this refrain, and Xuela's rewriting of it is typically defeatist:

> Roseau could not be called a city, because it could not embody such noble aspirations—center of commerce and culture and exchange of ideas among people, place of intrigue, place in which many plots are hatched and the destinies of many are determined; it was no such thing as a city, it was an outpost, [...] and there were many places like Roseau, outposts of despair; for conqueror and conquered alike these places were the capitals of nothing but despair. (*AM* 61)

Xuela's gloomy pronouncement undoes colonial power in a different way: by asserting its failure even in the place—a colonial capital—of its apparent

---

29 Burnett, *Derek Walcott*, p. 80.
30 Burnett, *Derek Walcott*, p. 57.
31 Derrida, *Of Grammatology*, pp. 101–40.
32 Walcott, 'The Antilles', pp. 263–65.

triumph. It also undermines the notion of progress and evolutionary temporality which anthropology of the late nineteenth and early twentieth centuries shared with colonialism.[33] Through Xuela, the novel offers an alternative challenge to colonial power which is neither the claim of essential, universal sameness of J. J. Thomas nor the celebration of creole creativity of Walcott and Harris. Instead, Xuela's response sabotages Lévi-Strauss and Froude by apparently agreeing with or accepting their terms, only to redirect the resulting tristesse from the *tropiques* to colonial Europe, thereby suggesting that 'nothing but despair', rather than 'noble aspirations', undergirds supposed colonial glories and civilizational achievements. Xuela's strategy of radical passivity, of accepting the denigrating terms of colonial–anthropological discourse, thereby works to undermine colonial power and its claims of cultural and political achievement and knowledge.

The text simultaneously offers another response to Froude's accusation of creative failure, for Xuela's defeatist admission of her own lack of creative force and lack of agency—such as when she disavows the power of her own language, claiming that she is 'not in a position to make my feeling have any meaning' (*AM* 137)—is obviously contradicted by the text as a whole, which is above all a record of Xuela's effective, even if not always intended, interventions in the world and of her rich 'inner life of her own invention'. While Xuela does not specify the medium through which the future might '[cast] a light on the past' (*AM* 215–16), the text shows that writing and narration, including its own rewriting of colonial–anthropological forms, can play this role. Yet the novel's rewriting of colonial and anthropological discourse, despite generating the subversive potential discussed above, nevertheless fails to fulfil its own promise in some key ways: in particular, it casts no 'new light' on the indigenous past—or indeed present—of the island, and instead reinforces colonial–anthropological discourses of indigenous purity and extinction.

The relevance of anthropological discourses and the work of Lévi-Strauss to Kincaid's novel has occasionally been recognized by scholars. Terri Smith Ruckel argues that the text 'moves beyond the imperialist methods of a classic ethnographer like Lévi-Strauss' because, rather than the ethnographer's efforts to 'explain "foreign" cultural systems to the cultural center', Kincaid's work instead 'translates the polyphonic voices of decentered postcolonial subjects for a "foreign" audience', thus becoming a 'tour guide' to diverse diasporic experiences.[34] I concur with Ruckel that Xuela's story and particularly her language work—to some extent—to deconstruct 'the European-engineered dichotomies that depict us versus Other';[35] the text thereby works against

---

33 Fabian, *Time and the Other*.
34 Terri Smith Ruckel, '"To Speak of My Own Situation": Touring the "Mother Periphery" in Jamaica Kincaid's *The Autobiography of My Mother*', *Anthurium: A Caribbean Studies Journal* 3.1 (2005), unpag.
35 Ruckel, 'To Speak of My Own Situation'.

the 'ethnocentrism *thinking itself* as anti-ethnocentrism'[36] of Lévi-Strauss, just as it works against what might be termed the reproduction of colonial racism *thinking itself* as anticolonial antiracism of Xuela herself. However, I do not share Ruckel's conclusion that the novel 'celebrat[es] heterogeneity and plurality', nor that it effectively 'counter[s] an appeal to essence and purity'.[37] Although the text makes clear that a 'pure' or essential cultural identity, unsullied by colonialism, is impossible for Xuela herself, it does not contradict such claims of purity or cultural essence when they are made about the figure of Xuela's indigenous mother, and it thereby risks installing a nativist claim to belonging at the expense of all others, as well as the perpetuation of colonial violence against indigenous peoples.

Ruckel's reading is revealing, for it exposes the difficulty of challenging anthropological discourse from within the terms of that discourse—the same difficulties which confront and eventually limit Kincaid's novel. The difference Ruckel proposes between explaining foreign cultures to the metropolitan centre and making diverse diasporic experiences available to a foreign audience is primarily one of tone, didactic or enterprising; both are, after all, oriented to a presumed Euro-American audience. The description of Kincaid as a 'tour guide'—beholden, in the end, to her tourist customers—is similarly revealing. Rather than overturning, exceeding, or effectively deconstructing anthropological classifications, I suggest that Ruckel's reading and, to some extent, the novel itself remain trapped within them. Xuela transfers the burden of essentialism, purity and absolute Otherness to the figure of her indigenous Carib mother, who is constructed, true to the Lévi-Straussian tradition, 'as a model of original and natural goodness'.[38] This construction of her m/other, alongside the relegation of her mother to a past inaccessible except through Xuela, results in Xuela adopting rather than subverting the role of the Lévi-Straussian ethnographer. In this way, Xuela's rewriting of colonial–anthropological exploitation is *also* a continuation of colonial violence. Yet in contrast to the text's implicit critique of Xuela's strategy of denying colonialism and its impact, discussed above, the text offers no such critique of her reconstruction of her mother, and such a critique can only be generated extra-textually. Indeed, the text's unquestioned acceptance of genealogical kinship *enables* Xuela's appropriation of her mother's indigeneity: her proclaimed right and ability to narrate her mother's story relies on her claim of an essential, biological connection between her unknown mother and herself, just as her claim to be 'of the defeated' is based in part on her genealogical connection to supposedly defeated, vanquished indigeneity.

Xuela's quest to reclaim the story of her mother is an attempt to access a 'native', pre-Columbian and precolonial identity and sense of connection to Dominica. This appeal to indigeneity, far from refusing colonial structures,

---

36 Derrida, *Of Grammatology*, p. 120.
37 Ruckel, 'To Speak of My Own Situation'.
38 Derrida, *Of Grammatology*, p. 114.

employs and reinforces them, in that it not only naturalizes the biological link between Xuela and her mother as the only possible source of cultural identity and path of cultural transmission, but also relies upon colonial tropes of indigenous primitivism and indigenous extinction. April Pelt argues that Xuela thus 'reclaim[s] the inheritance of her mother [...] based on a primary attachment to the island and its history' and that this 'provides her with the agency to resist her own victimization by using her "inheritance"—namely defeat and brutality—to take a moral stance against the forces of racism and colonization'.[39] Yet this process depends upon and reinstantiates elements of colonial racism and the colonial discourse of indigenous extinction, so that Xuela's claim to connect to the land via the indigenous heritage of her mother is a process of appropriation and exploitation, putting into question its purported antiracist and anticolonial workings.

Xuela's reconstruction of her mother's life and the history of the Carib people of Dominica begins at the moment when Xuela claims to have renounced kinship after terminating her first pregnancy. In a dream, Xuela travels around the island, exploring its landscapes and history. Xuela's narration of this dream is a travel narrative which rewrites colonial texts such as Froude's. The colonial claim of territorial control via discourses of property ownership and racial entitlement is rewritten by Xuela, who describes her dream as a walk 'through my inheritance' and a means to 'claim' 'all the things that were mine' (*AM* 89). That which she claims as her inheritance is not, as in Froude's narrative, the economic potential of the island or the political prestige of colonial possessions. Rather, her travel narrative records a series of tangential visits or evasive moves: 'I passed through Mahaut crawling on my stomach, for I was afraid I would be recognized'; 'I passed by the black waters of the Guadeloupe Channel; I was not tempted to be swallowed up whole in it [...] I passed by the black waters of the Martinique Channel; I was not tempted to be swallowed up whole it in' and minor touristic defeats: 'I could not see the top of Morne Diablotin; I had never seen it it any case, even when I was awake'; 'It was raining in Merot, it was raining in Coulibistri, it was raining in Colihaut' (*AM* 87–88). Here, her admission of minor failures—it is raining everywhere, she cannot see major landmarks, she is hampered by fear and self-doubt—rewrites the colonial claim to see, survey and judge all in travel accounts such as Froude's, and Xuela's embrace of her own failure works to undermine Froude's claims, throwing doubt upon his professed experiences and knowledge. The fact that her 'travel' around the island takes place in a dream, rather than in the sense of physical travel, also subtly ridicules Froude's account—and a significant portion of all European colonial travel narratives—which also involved very little physical travel: often he did not even leave the ship to go on land, so his book is based mostly on his

---

39 April Pelt, '"Weary of Our Own Legacies": Rethinking Jane Eyre's Inheritance through Jamaica Kincaid's *The Autobiography of My Mother*', *ARIEL: A Review of International English Literature* 41.3–4 (2011), pp. 85–86.

own preconceived ideas about the West Indies or conversations with other European travellers on board.

Another aspect of Xuela's dream, however, mirrors colonial discourse *without* effectively undermining it. The dream contains two references to the island's indigenous people that indicate her attitude towards both the role of indigeneity in her own narration and the role of indigenous people in her telling of history, and which invoke long-standing colonial–anthropological claims about the indigenous inhabitants of the New World. First, she retells a storied event of Dominican history:

> It was at Massacre that Indian Warner, the illegitimate son of a Carib woman and a European man, was murdered by his half brother, an Englishman named Philip Warner, because Philip Warner did not like having such a close relative whose mother was a Carib woman. (*AM* 87)

Xuela's narration of this incident from the seventeenth century reaffirms her obsession with colonial kinship and genealogy, emphasizing not only Warner's parentage and 'half' brother, but also his status in colonial kinship discourse as 'illegitimate'; she also chooses to use the colonial nickname 'Indian Warner'. The murder is framed by her retelling as a matter of intimate racism, a murderous discomfort with racially other kin of which Indian Warner becomes the passive victim. Among the many things which Xuela's narration of this episode neglects to mention are Thomas 'Indian' Warner's trans-Caribbean migration, his powerful position as British Governor of Dominica, his complex role as a mediator and negotiator between various European colonial powers and Carib peoples on multiple Caribbean islands, and finally his murder by Philip Warner as—among other things—an act of war due to deteriorating relations between the British and Caribs.[40] Xuela's narrative, while it eschews some of the markers of colonial power which undoubtedly shape the alternative account presented here, nonetheless also denies the history of Carib sovereignty, the struggle over sovereignty in the Caribbean, Carib involvement in colonial government, Carib resistance to colonization, and transregional Carib political organization. Instead, Xuela's depiction of Carib peoples, both in the twentieth century in which she lives and in the centuries of colonization before, is of a people always 'defeated and exterminated, thrown away like the weeds in a garden' (*AM* 16). Her description of Indian Warner as the passive victim of racist violence (without mention of any other aspects of his history) thus fits well with the second, contemporary, mention of indigenous people in her dream: 'somewhere between Marigot and Castle

---

40 Peter Hulme and Neil L. Whitehead (eds.), *Wild Majesty: Encounters with Caribs from Columbus to the Present Day: An Anthology* (Oxford: Clarendon, 1992), pp. 89–106; Peter Hulme, *Remnants of Conquest: The Island Caribs and their Visitors, 1877–1998* (Oxford: Oxford University Press, 2000), pp. 206–07; Philip P. Boucher, *Cannibal Encounters: Europeans and Island Caribs, 1492–1763* (Baltimore: Johns Hopkins University Press, 1992), esp. pp. 49–86.

Bruce lived my mother's people, on a reserve, as if in commemoration of something no one could bring herself to mention' (*AM* 88). In Xuela's narration of the twentieth-century history of Carib people, they are still living, but only as a 'commemoration' of an unspeakable history (which remains equally unspoken by Xuela), so insubstantial or spectral that even their location remains geographically indistinct and colonized ('somewhere between' two colonial-era place names). The reference to 'something no one could bring herself to mention' recalls Jean Rhys's *Wide Sargasso Sea*: there, Antoinette says of the town of Massacre, 'Something must have happened a long time ago. Nobody remembers now'.[41] The unwillingness to remember with which Rhys's text grapples is thus bitterly referenced in Kincaid's novel—yet it too demonstrates a large measure of this unwillingness.

Later in the novel, Xuela returns to the figure of her mother, who emerges in Xuela's imagination as a contrast and counterbalance to Xuela's colonial–hybrid father. Xuela describes her father as someone in whom 'there existed at once victor and vanquished, perpetrator and victim' and who chose 'the mantle of the former' (*AM* 192). Xuela recalls her father's enthusiasm about the grapefruit, a hybrid fruit 'natural to the West Indies', and she believes that her father 'wanted the grapefruit and himself to be One' (*AM* 102). Her father embraces a hybrid identity, both European and African, yet native to the Caribbean, that she despises. (Ironically, Xuela's language again undermines her own rejection of hybridity and colonial influence, with numerous botanic metaphors that recall the history of colonial plant-breeding that in turn influenced thinking on human racial 'mixture' in the colonial Caribbean, and which also echo Froude's use of similar imagery.)[42] In contrast, her depiction of her mother emphasizes her supposed racial purity and, just as in Xuela's narration of Indian Warner, her powerless, helpless, doomed victimhood. She writes:

> the color of her skin—brown, the deep orange of an old sunset—was not the result of a fateful meeting between conqueror and vanquished, sorrow and despair, vanity and humiliation; it was only itself, an untroubled fact: she was of the Carib people. (*AM* 197)

The contrast to Xuela's father is made clear: while he represents colonial history and the meeting and mixture of 'victor and vanquished, perpetrator and victim', her mother is defined as precolonial: 'not the result of a fateful meeting between conqueror and vanquished'. Xuela thus imagines her mother (and all Caribs) as unchanged—culturally and racially pure—since the arrival of European colonists five hundred years ago, and thus effectively

---

41 Jean Rhys, *Wide Sargasso Sea* (London: Penguin, 2001), p. 36.
42 Froude, *The English in the West Indies*, p. 307. On plant breeding and colonial racism, see Young, *Colonial Desire*; Ramón E. Soto-Crespo, 'Death and the Diaspora Writer: Hybridity and Mourning in the Work of Jamaica Kincaid', *Contemporary Literature* 43.2 (2002), pp. 342–76.

confined to the distant past. Xuela's claim of racial purity for her mother is not only historically unlikely (Xuela's own story of Indian Warner, a Carib man of mixed heritage in the seventeenth century, is enough to throw doubt on any such claim for someone in the twentieth century), but it relies upon a notion of 'pure' race closely allied to the concept of blood which underpinned scientific racism in the nineteenth and early twentieth centuries, which was often invoked in slave codes, and on which much colonial discourse rested.[43] It also problematically restores skin colour as proof of both 'racial' and cultural affiliation. Xuela's claims that her mother's identity as a Carib woman is 'untroubled', despite noting that she grew up in the care of Catholic nuns, confirms her essentialist, racializing understanding of cultural identity, while the description of her mother's skin as the colour of 'an old sunset' positions Carib people as archaic and on the brink of sinking into oblivion.

Xuela's claim that her mother's identity as a Carib woman was 'an untroubled fact' makes the figure of her mother ripe for Xuela's appropriation, but it once again relies on heavy-handed editing of the history of the Caribs of Dominica: far from being 'untroubled', some scholars have suggested that the term 'Carib' should be considered a colonial category, as well as an identity both strategically shed and assumed as an act of anticolonial resistance; others have suggested that Dominica may have been uninhabited by indigenous people prior to 1492 and that 'Carib' or other indigenous groups may have migrated to the island to escape persecution from the Spanish elsewhere.[44] Whether or not such speculations are correct, they make clear that the interrelated history of indigenous, colonizing and transported populations in the Caribbean is likely far more complicated and 'troubled' than the version of history offered by Xuela.

This simplistic, one-dimensional imagining of her mother enables Xuela to project both her own sense of failure and defeat onto her mother and to project her own construction of her mother as a passive victim onto others, assuming for example that it is these attributes of suffering and helplessness that attracted her father: 'no doubt to him her beauty would have lain not in the structure of her face […] no, it would have lain in her sadness, her weakness, her long-lost-ness, the crumbling of her ancestral lines, her dejectedness, the false humility that was really defeat' (*AM* 200). Her mother's

---

43 See for example Anderson, *Imagined Communities*; Anthony Appiah, 'The Uncompleted Argument: Du Bois and the Illusion of Race', in Henry Louis Gates, Jr. (ed.), *"Race," Writing, and Difference* (Chicago: University of Chicago Press, 1986), pp. 21–37; Robert F. Berkhofer, Jr., *The White Man's Indian: Images of the American Indian from Columbus to the Present* (New York: Alfred A. Knopf, 1978), esp. pp. 55–61; Ann Laura Stoler, *Race and the Education of Desire: Foucault's* History of Sexuality *and the Colonial Order of Things* (Durham, NC: Duke University Press, 1995).
44 Stephan Lenik, 'Carib as a Colonial Category: Comparing Ethnohistoric and Archaeological Evidence from Dominica, West Indies', *Ethnohistory* 59.1 (2012), pp. 79–107.

'defeat', that is, Xuela's *construction* of her mother as defeated and weak, provides the basis for Xuela's own claim of the right to narrate her mother's story and to appropriate it for herself. She justifies this move by asserting the Carib population's supposed cultural degeneration and imminent extinction, claiming that the Carib people 'had lost not just the right to be themselves, they had lost themselves' (*AM* 198). Thus, in a double move, she projects her own sense of defeat onto her mother, then claims her mother's defeat as justification for assuming her mother's voice. In this moment, as Xuela asserts the right to her mother's story and voice, effectively (re-)colonizing Carib peoples through the figure of her mother, the autobiography of Xuela becomes the autobiography of her mother. To be sure, this is a move which subverts fundamental assumptions about the nature of autobiography—in which, as in Rousseau's *Dialogues* (the 'autobiographical text *par excellence*') the subject is expected to be the 'self and nothing else'[45]—but Xuela shows that this is a move which recovers autobiography for the purposes of ethnography, rather than decolonization.[46] It bears comparison to the phenomenon identified by Jossiana Arroyo in literary and ethnographic writing from Cuba and Brazil that she names 'cultural transvestism', in which identification with an Other functions as a strategy of power *and* its disavowal.[47]

When Xuela writes that it would have been better if her mother had never lived—'to say it makes me feel sad not to have known her would not be true at all; I am only sad to know that such a life had to exist' (*AM* 201)—she extends the trope of indigenous extinction upon which her appropriation of her mother's identity is founded to actively wish death upon living Caribs, further advancing her claim to speak for her mother, and also extending her mirroring of colonial domination. Critics such as Kathryn Morris, who identify and celebrate Xuela's Carib mother as a mythical, voiceless figure who must be ventriloquized through her daughter, neglect to consider how this mythologization and silencing is complicit in colonial discourses of indigenous peoples.[48] When Xuela describes the Caribs of Dominica as 'remnants of a vanishing people' (*AM* 80), she uses a word, 'remnant', common to almost all modern European accounts of the Caribs; in both Xuela's story and those other accounts it indicates a belief that Carib peoples are 'doomed to extinction, usually soon after the moment of writing'.[49] The trope of indigenous extinction

---

45 James F. Jones, Jr., *Rousseau's* Dialogues*: An Interpretive Essay* (Geneva: Librairie Droz, 1991), p. 47.
46 For more on the relationship of autobiography to ethnography and the ethnographic use of the 'autobiographic past', see Fabian, *Time and the Other*, esp. pp. 87–97.
47 Jossiana Arroyo, *Travestimos culturales: literatura y etnografía en Cuba y Brasil* (Pittsburgh: Instituto de Literatura Iberoamericana, 2003).
48 Kathryn E. Morris, 'Jamaica Kincaid's Voracious Bodies: Engendering a Carib(bean) Woman', *Callaloo* 25.3 (2002), pp. 954–68.
49 Hulme, *Remnants of Conquest*, p. 5.

has long held sway in the Caribbean, in which, according to some accounts, indigenous people have been extinct for almost five hundred years.[50] Yet rather than describing the actual extinction of indigenous peoples, it generally functions, as in Xuela's account, in the way described by Scott Morgensen: Xuela's narrative imagining of her mother and the indigenous community from which she came reinstantiates a Caribbean version of a 'colonial necropolitics' in which indigenous populations are 'marked for death'.[51] Xuela's appropriation of her mother's story and her depiction of the extinction of Caribbean indigeneity, even the *desirability* of that extinction in the wake of colonialism, cannot be understood as an attempt to 'revive the Carib heritage as a founding discourse for Carib(bean) identity', as Morris argues.[52] Rather, it is a repetition and reenaction of colonial violence which claims, through its appropriation of indigeneity, to be the opposite.

Therein lies the central ambiguity of the text, and, I suggest, its key limitation in decolonizing writing. Xuela's assertion of defeat as a historical force, capable of 'casting a light on the past' (*AM* 215–16), depends on her colonialist imagining of her mother as both 'pure' and authentic *and* defeated and vanquished, and on her construction of all Carib people as doomed to extinction. Xuela's answer to Froude's assertion of Caribbean ahistoricity and cultural–civilizational failure depends upon not only an acceptance and rewriting of those terms for herself—a strategy of failure, defeat and radical passivity which generates the potential for anticolonial sabotage—but also a violent imposition of them upon (m)others, in a recolonizing gesture that demonstrates the limits of this particular rewriting strategy. Despite the text's relentless criticism of colonialism and its rewriting of colonial discourses and forms, its perpetuation of two other key elements of colonial–anthropological thinking, namely the extinction of indigenous peoples and the necessarily genealogical basis of kinship, limits its ability to imagine an anti or postcolonial otherwise. As for Xuela, her identification with colonial–anthropological discourse becomes clear at the end of the novel, when she embraces a concept of 'nature' as 'outside history' (*AM* 218) and outside colonial or any human influence—a notion of intrinsically 'good' nature that echoes

---

50 Maximilian C. Forte, 'Extinction: Ideologies Against Indigeneity in the Caribbean', *Southern Quarterly* 43.4 (2006), pp. 46–70. For more on the history of the tropes of disappearance and racial purity in colonial writings about Dominica specifically, see Hulme, *Remnants of Conquest*. For more on the history of the trope of disappearance in a North American context, see Berkhofer, *The White Man's Indian*.
51 Scott Lauria Morgensen, 'Settler Homonationalism: Theorizing Settler Colonialism within Queer Modernities', *GLQ: A Journal of Lesbian and Gay Studies* 16.1–2 (2010), p. 106. See also Andrea Smith, 'Queer Theory and Native Studies: The Heteronormativity of Settler Colonialism', *GLQ: A Journal of Lesbian and Gay Studies* 16.1–2 (2010), pp. 42–68.
52 Morris, 'Jamaica Kincaid's Voracious Bodies', p. 956.

through Lévi-Strauss and back to Rousseau. While the destructiveness of Xuela's renouncement of kinship is made clear, there is little suggestion in the text that there might be alternative ways of defining kinship than as limited to genealogical relations. Similarly, Xuela's rewriting of her mother's story and her appropriation of the figure of her mother as a means of accessing a precolonial history and link to Dominica remains uncriticized by the text. In this way, when Xuela says of Carib people: 'they were no more, they were extinct, a few hundred of them still living [...] like living fossils, they belonged in a museum, on a shelf, enclosed in a glass case' (*AM* 197–98), she enables and perpetuates precisely the forms of colonial knowledge which lead to indigenous people becoming museum specimens, and the text thus—albeit unwittingly—creates the conditions of possibility for the scene in Pauline Melville's *The Ventriloquist's Tale* when Beatrice visits a museum in Montreal 'to see the shrunken Indian head preserved in spirits' in a glass case.[53]

---

53 Pauline Melville, *The Ventriloquist's Tale* (London: Bloomsbury, 1998), p. 273.

CHAPTER TWO

Destabilizing structuralism in Pauline Melville's *The Ventriloquist's Tale*

Like Kincaid's novel, Pauline Melville's *The Ventriloquist's Tale* offers a rewriting of colonial and anthropological discourses, but with a very different tone, and with more optimism about the potential of anti and postcolonial writing. Unlike the despairing tone of Kincaid's text, Melville's novel is narrated, at least in part, by a rambunctiously cheeky ventriloquist and trickster, and even in its more sober and 'realist' sections it never slips into despair even in the face of tragedy. Instead of a life narrated from birth to old age, it is structured in five parts, shifting backwards and then forwards again over several generations before a twist which throws both its narrative structure and apparent realism into doubt. Melville's novel also grapples with an anthropological—particularly and specifically Lévi-Straussian—and, by extension, Derridean legacy, by addressing the intersection of kinship, anthropology and colonialism. Despite their differences, the two novels also both address the question of writing and language as such—not only because they both feature female characters who are inveterate masturbators, thereby simultaneously recalling and resignifying the fact that for Rousseau, in many ways the forefather of modern anthropology and a strong influence on Lévi-Strauss, 'it was difficult to separate writing from onanism'.[1] Melville's novel, however, exemplifies more the other style of postcolonial writing described by Derek Walcott in 'The Muse of History': more interested in integrating the past into a syncretized present than in the crimes of the past, and understanding language as endowed with creative potential by its colonial history, rather than burdened by it.[2] *The Ventriloquist's Tale* features a structural anthropologist who seems to be a latter-day version (and parody) of the Lévi-Strauss

1 Derrida, *Of Grammatology*, p. 165.
2 Walcott, 'The Muse of History', pp. 354–58.

himself, and it offers an exploration of the relationship between myth and reality. It also offers an interrogation of two of Lévi-Strauss's key themes: writing, language and cultural change, and incest, sexuality and kinship. Set mostly in a Wapisiana Amerindian community in the central savannahs of Guyana, not far from the Brazilian Amazon where Lévi-Strauss did the fieldwork described in *Tristes Tropiques*, Melville's novel directly addresses the relationship between indigenous peoples and western knowledge production, and between knowledge, narration and colonial violence.

Another key difference between Melville and Kincaid's novels lies in their approach to and representation of indigeneity in their writing of the twentieth-century Caribbean, the temporality to which indigeneity is assigned, and the role assigned to or demanded of indigeneity as a founding force of contemporary Caribbean identity. Despite the changes that have occurred in the discipline of anthropology, from its eighteenth-century or earlier foundations, to its establishment as a science in the nineteenth century, to the development of cultural and structural anthropology in the twentieth century, there are many continuities in the field's understanding of indigenous peoples: at least until the 1950s, the majority of anthropological work in the Americas ignored or slighted contemporary Indian cultures, 'as if the only true Indian were a past one'.[3] The resulting discourses of indigenous extinction, disappearance and degeneration remain widely accepted and influential today—including in some postcolonial writing and theorizing.[4] Melville's text insists on Amerindian survival via its rewriting of anthropology, which includes questioning the category and limits of the human and challenging structuralist understandings of kinship and the supposed connection between the incest taboo and culture.

The novel follows several generations of an Amerindian family in Guyana, shifting from the late to the early twentieth century and back again in order to consider both the contemporary conditions of indigenous Caribbean identity and survival and the relation of that present to its past(s). After an impresario introduction from an unnamed, but apparently mythical narrator, part one of the novel sees Chofy McKinnon, a Wapisiana man from the inland savannahs, move to the capital Georgetown, accompanied by his elderly aunt Wifreda. In Georgetown, Chofy begins a passionate affair with a British literary scholar, Rosa Mendelson, garnering an accusation from his cousin that relationships between Indians and non-Indians will be the death-knell of Wapisiana culture. The intellectual enquiries of Rosa and the Czech structural anthropologist Michael Wormoal collide with Chofy's own worries and questions about the nature and future of indigenous identity, prompting Wifreda to tell him a long—and long repressed—family story. The flashback which forms part two of the novel takes place on the Rupununi savannahs during Wifreda's

---

3 Berkhofer, *The White Man's Indian*, p. 67.
4 Forte, 'Extinction'; Peter Hulme, *Remnants of Conquest*; Morgensen, 'Settler Homonationalism'; Smith, 'Queer Theory and Native Studies'.

childhood in the early twentieth century and tells the story of the incestuous affair of her siblings Beatrice and Danny.

The prominence of this storyline means that the topic of kinship has not gone unnoticed in the critical literature. Most scholars' approach to the novel's thematization of hybridity and indigenous survival politics, however, has been to construct those politics as a choice between 'endogamy' and 'exogamy', whereby the incestuous affair between Danny and Beatrice symbolizes 'ultimate endogamy' and the interracial affair between Rosa and Chofy figures as 'trans-racial exogamy'.[5] In doing so, these scholars replicate the schema, proposed by Lévi-Strauss, in which miscegenation is posited as the opposite of incest; and they anchor kinship in genealogy and tied closely to a concept of 'race'.[6] Analyses structured in this way thus accept key tenets of western anthropology which the novel *challenges* and in part overturns, and thus this premature acceptance of anthropological, particularly Lévi-Straussian, terms prevents an appreciation of the full force of the novel's interrogation of anthropological discourse. Far from acceding to an anthropological framework, the text refuses to choose between the positions commonly available to Amerindian people in colonial and anthropological discourses, in which indigenous subjects have value either as 'savages'—archaic specimens required to display cultural 'purity'—or as 'civilized' assimilated subjects identifiable in particular by their conforming to Euro-American norms of kinship. The link between genealogy and culture on which much anthropology rests, and upon which Lévi-Strauss particularly insists, is undone as one important aspect of a thorough interrogation of colonial–anthropological discourse: not only about indigeneity and indigenous peoples, but extending to temporality, reality, and the potential of writing itself.

The novel opens with a series of epigraphs, the second of which reads, 'There shall be no more novels about incest. No, not even ones in very bad taste'.[7] This quotation, from Julian Barnes's novel *Flaubert's Parrot*, is framed by two others: the first from Lévi-Strauss, describing Amerindian eclipse mythology, the third a 'fifteenth-century Portuguese proverb': 'Beyond the equator, everything is permitted'. All three epigraphs function less as frames which enclose the novel than as points of rupture and overflow. The quoted

---

5 Paula Burnett, '"Where Else to Row, but Backwards?" Addressing Caribbean Futures through Re-visions of the Past', *ARIEL: A Review of International English Literature* 30.1 (1999), p. 25. Other critics also use this terminology, including April Shemak, 'Alter/natives: Myth, Translation and the Native Informant in Pauline Melville's *The Ventriloquist's Tale*', *Textual Practice* 19.3 (2005), pp. 353–72; Albert Braz, 'Mutilated Selves: Pauline Melville, Mario de Andrade, and the Troubling Hybrid', *Mosaic* [Winnipeg] 40.4 (2007), unpag.; and Elizabeth DeLoughrey, 'Quantum Landscapes: A "Ventriloquism of Spirit"', *interventions* 9.1 (2007), pp. 62–82.
6 Lévi-Strauss, *The Elementary Structures of Kinship*.
7 Melville, *The Ventriloquist's Tale*, unpag. Further references to the novel are given in the text as *VT*.

passages constitute claims to know, understand, categorize, regulate, forbid and allow—and the novel subjects each of them to scrutiny, revealing in the process how anthropological knowledge, kinship discourses and (neo-)colonial excess are linked together—but also how other forms of writing may displace, undermine or overturn them all. The epigraph from *Flaubert's Parrot* references another novel concerned with the possibility of access to the past and the power and possibilities of fiction.[8] Like Barnes's novel, Melville's text questions the notion of realism in fiction, explicitly exposing the constructedness of its own apparent realism via the narrator's prologue and his later phantom reappearance.[9] Unlike Barnes's narrator Braithwaite, however, who believes fiction should 'make sense of life' (a claim nonetheless undermined by Barnes's novel), Melville's narrator embraces uncertainty.[10] He suggests that 'variety [is] much more important than truth' (*VT* 3) and exults in the power of storytelling to *create* worlds—not explain them—in which chaos and randomness are life-generating.

In the prologue the narrator both introduces many of these themes and already begins to deconstruct them, himself working like the 'glorious spirit of rot' (*VT* 3) which he claims as the hallmark of the tropics. Even as he describes a debate and disagreement between himself and his grandmother about written and oral literature, for example—his grandmother 'distrusts writing' (*VT* 2) and 'flew into a rage when she heard I was going to write the stories down' (*VT* 8)—the terms of this debate are already undermined by his destabilization of other categories, including his own ontological classification. Is the narrator mythological and timeless, as suggested by his guarded hint that he might be Macunaima, or is he all-too-human and set firmly in the twentieth century, as might be indicated by his choice of clothes and cars, his knowledge of the 'BBC's World Service' and the linguistic particularities of a 'London hoodlum' (*VT* 8)? In a similar way, the narrator introduces and already begins to dismantle the importance of kinship: he claims that his ancestry is 'impeccable' and that 'any one of us can recite our ancestry back for several hundred generations', only to interrupt the anthropological notion of kinship as the foundational basis of human culture by proclaiming, 'I will have you know that I am descended

---

8 William Bell, "Not Altogether a Tomb: Julian Barnes's *Flaubert's Parrot*', in David Ellis (ed.), *Imitating Art: Essays in Biography* (London: Pluto, 1993), pp. 149–73.

9 Berlatsky argues that *Flaubert's Parrot* offers a 'metafictional denaturalization of the realistic plot'. See Eric Berlatsky, '"Madame Bovary, c'est moi!": Julian Barnes's *Flaubert's Parrot* and Sexual "Perversion",' *Twentieth Century Literature* 55.2 (2009), p. 175.

10 Julian Barnes, *Flaubert's Parrot* (London: Jonathan Cape, 1984), p. 168. Scott suggests that Braithwaite's rules for literature—of which Melville's epigraph is one—are constantly undermined by Barnes's novel, which reveals reality, truth and identity to be 'mercurial consequence[s] of discourse'. See James B. Scott, 'Parrot as Paradigms: Infinite Deferral of Meaning in *Flaubert's Parrot*', *ARIEL: A Review of International English Literature* 21.3 (1990), p. 58.

from a group of stones in Ecuador' (*VT* 2). Is this an earnest claim which introduces the novel's posthumanist reflections, or a joke which pokes fun at anyone who takes genealogy too seriously? This kinship claim also hints at the text's undoing of the link—proposed by Lévi-Strauss and accepted by Derrida—between writing and genealogy, or writing as a guarantee of genealogy: the narrator's claim that he is able to recite his ancestry initially seems to fit with Lévi-Strauss's note of 'communities who can recite straight off family trees involving dozens of generations', but the notion that these generations involve only genealogical relatives is immediately undermined by the claim of kinship with stones.[11] Finally, he offers a virtuoso performance as a narrator, even as he suggests that language and words exceed his use of them. He describes himself as a tool of language, rather the other way around: he claims to have been 'chosen' as the narrator by a 'throng of words', an 'incessant chattering from the past' which emerged from a lake, swept him up in their midst, and designated him their ventriloquist vessel (*VT* 5). This passage both upsets the notion of language as a purely human characteristic and one of the chief markers of the human even as it affirms the power, and the joy, of language and narration. The narrator then announces that he 'must appear to vanish' in order to tell the story, because 'realism is what is required these days' (*VT* 9). And vanish he does, more or less, until the epilogue of the novel. As promised, his characteristic narratorial voice disappears—or almost disappears—as part one of the novel begins and the main body of the text is narrated in a (seemingly) realist style.

As part one begins, the key themes of indigenous survival politics, kinship, mythology and anthropology are introduced through the figure of Chofy, at home in the savannahs, followed by a series of conversations after he moves to Georgetown to find work after a disastrous loss of cattle on his in-law's farm. The threat of poverty in his savannah home has caused Chofy to become distrustful and resentful towards those he views as 'alien': 'coastlanders and Brazilians who were invading the region to settle there' (*VT* 14). Although vaguely dissatisfied with his life, he is hampered by his internalization of a discourse which constructs tradition and cultural identity as static; he has the feeling that 'any change was the beginning of disintegration' (*VT* 15). A short time later, after moving to Georgetown—a change he finds both bewildering and refreshing—he discusses the situation with his cousin Tenga:

> [Chofy:] 'I think we have to mix: otherwise we have no future. We must get educated.'
> [Tenga:] 'Let them get educated our way.'
> [Chofy:] 'We can't go backwards. Guyana has to develop.'
> [Tenga:] 'I'm not Guyanese. I'm Wapisiana.' [...]
> [Tenga:] 'We're destroyed if we mix. And we're destroyed if we don't. [...] The worst thing is when they come and marry us.' (*VT* 54–55)

---

11 Lévi-Strauss quoted in Derrida, *Of Grammatology*, p. 125.

The European visitors to Georgetown, Rosa and Wormoal, repeat a remarkably similar, if somewhat more abstract, version of this conversation a short time later:

> [Wormoal:] 'It is a shame [...] how rapidly Indian culture is disintegrating these days – contaminated mostly by contact with other races.' [...]
> [Rosa:] 'I'm an internationalist, I suppose. I believe in a mixture of the races.' [...]
> [Wormoal:] 'I believe in the purity of the nation.' (*VT* 78–79)

Despite their differences in perspectives—Chofy and Tenga are concerned primarily with their own cultural survival, while Wormoal and Rosa speak with the authority of science or political ideology—both conversations link questions of cultural continuity and change explicitly to intimate and sexual relations—that is, to matters often, although not necessarily, linked to kinship—and to questions of nationalism, including both indigenous and postcolonial nations in Guyana and European nation-states. The novel, however, will go on to reject all of these overly simple positions: the belief in progress or development within neoliberal and neoimperial capitalism, which Chofy suggests; the easy internationalism of Rosa; the claims of ethnically pure nationhood endorsed by both Tenga and Wormoal, and most of all Tenga's dispirited suggestion that indigenous peoples are 'destroyed' either way. In particular, all claims of ethnic purity are quickly undone: Tenga's ethnocentrism and Wormoal's notion of Amerindian 'purity' will soon be dismantled in the story to come; in the case of Wormoal's cherished Czech national identity his name betrays him immediately: the letter 'W' is used exclusively for foreign, not yet naturalized words in Czech.

The introduction of Wormoal marks the beginning of the novel's explicit engagement with anthropology. Wormoal is a Czech structural anthropologist who is visiting Georgetown to give a paper at the local university and continue his research into Amerindian mythology. The title of his proposed paper, a long passage of which is included in the novel, is 'The Structural Elements of Myth', and a clear play on Lévi-Strauss's 'The Structural Study of Myth', while his Czech nationality hints at a reference to the Prague School.[12] Wormoal is something of a combination of the two, transported from mid-century to the 1990s through the wormhole which his name conjures. Although the Prague School understood structuralism 'as an anti-western strategy, directed against the hierarchical cultural and racial assumptions of imperialist European thought', and Lévi-Strauss claimed his posited structural equivalence of mythological and rational scientific thought as a project of anti-ethnocentrism, the rewriting of Lévi-Strauss and of structuralism enacted by Michael Wormoal in the text

---

12 Claude Lévi-Strauss, 'The Structural Study of Myth', *The Journal of American Folklore* 68.270 (1955), pp. 428–44.

makes explicit the violent potential of Lévi-Strauss's Eurocentrism, as criticized by Derrida.[13]

In Wormoal's formulation, the relationship between myth and science and between 'man' and nature is a question of dominance, overthrow and rule, phrased in metaphors of war, and invoking a clear linear chronology:

> [S]cience is the *winning strategy* of the *modern* world. Science and reason are now invoked in every field, including areas which have *previously evaded* them such as mythology.
> There is nothing that cannot be *tackled* by reason. [...]
> It has only to be decoded and the world *surrenders*. It used to be thought that by obeying nature we *commanded* it. [...] Now, however, it is generally understood that man has become the *master and possessor* of nature. The need to obey has disappeared. (*VT* 81, emphases added)

Wormoal's essay positions 'science and reason' as both superior to, and incompatible with, both 'myth' and 'nature'. Robert Ness describes Wormoal's position as the 'western view' and suggests that the novel instead offers a world in which 'disaster as a sort of agentless principle, fate perhaps' is at work.[14] Yet such a reading, which assigns rationality and autonomous human agency to the West and agentless, irrational fatalism to the indigenous world, simply replicates Wormoal's categorization without recognizing the novel's critique and deconstruction of precisely the opposing categories of (irrational, Indian) myth and (rational, western) science. In the course of the novel, Wormoal will find that he is far from the master of nature, and the ramifications of quantum mechanics and astrophysics—which Wormoal invokes to support his argument when he quotes Stephan Hawking: 'We live in a universe governed by rational laws' (*VT* 81)—prove to be rather different than he imagines.

The relationship between anthropology, as represented by Wormoal, and colonialism or neocolonialism is made apparent through Wormoal's own admission: 'My knowledge of the Indians is a way of owning them—I admit it. We fight over the intellectual territory. But it's better than stealing their land, isn't it?' (*VT* 80). This makes clear that knowledge production may be as much a method of colonial exploitation as territorial domination or resource exploitation (despite Wormoal's claim of a 'better', gentler colonialism), and the devastating consequences of Wormoal's—and, for that matter, the postcolonial literary scholar Rosa's—intellectual pursuits become clear at the end of the novel. At the same time, however, Wormoal's claim to

---

13 Robert J. C. Young, *Postcolonialism: An Historical Introduction* (Oxford: Blackwell, 2001), pp. 67–68; Jacques Derrida, 'Structure, Sign and Play in the Discourse of the Human Sciences', *Writing and Difference*, trans. Alan Bass (London: Routledge & Kegan Paul, 1978), pp. 278–93; Derrida, *Of Grammatology*, pp. 101–40.
14 Robert Ness, '"Not His Sort of Story": Evelyn Waugh and Pauline Melville in Guyana', *ARIEL: A Review of International English Literature* 38.4 (2007), p. 59.

'knowledge' of the Amerindians undermines itself, for Wormoal is fantastically unknowing. The text mocks Wormoal, suggesting that he is unable to achieve the totalizing knowledge he seek, or indeed any knowledge at all: for most of the novel, he remains in his hotel in Georgetown, seemingly as blind as a worm or a mole, both comically and tragically unaware of the events unfolding around him. Rosa's project—to research Evelyn Waugh's visit to the country in the early 1930s—is equally unsuccessful due to the crippling Eurocentrism of her supposedly postcolonial project.[15] Rosa too remains oblivious to much of what happens in the novel, and to her own part in it; like Wormoal, she is handicapped by her categories of knowledge, particularly a strict opposition of 'mythology' to 'rationalism'. Yet although the text suggests that Wormoal and Rosa are blinded by their preconceptions—a condition that the novel suggests has always affected colonialists in the region—that does not prevent them from causing damage: at the end of the novel Chofy's young son, Bla-Bla, dies after his father's full name is discovered first by Rosa, told to Wormoal, then passed on to American oil prospectors in the savannahs. The violent, deadly consequences of anthropology—for the episode is, once again, an echo of Lévi-Strauss, who boasted in *Tristes Tropiques* of his success in extracting the secret names of the Nambikwara—are evidently still with us.[16]

It is Rosa's desire to meet Chofy's aunt Wifreda (because Rosa knows that Waugh stayed with members of the McKinnon family during his visit to the country and hopes Wifreda might be able to tell her something about him) that prompts the long flashback that forms part two of the novel. This, too, is introduced by an episode of blindness: beset by anxiety caused by Rosa's visit, the elderly woman suddenly goes blind and begins to hear the voice of her sister Beatrice, recalling their childhood. Yet the story she remembers, then later recounts to Chofy, helps Chofy to see and understand his own situation more clearly. Although it contains much that would be of interest to Rosa and Wormoal, neither of them ever gets to hear it; nonetheless it can be understood as a response to their conceptions of indigeneity and culture, to Chofy's uncertainties about his own future, and to Chofy and Tenga's debate around indigenous identity and cultural survival. Although it is not directed at, and remains unknown to, the European characters, it is not a call for isolation or segregation; rather, the introduction of part two of the novel, much like the story recounted within it, notes the necessity and creativity of cultural interaction, and Wifreda's story enables Chofy to reconsider the consequences of cultural stasis, the meaning of tradition and the basis of his identity as an Amerindian and his connections to others. Chofy's encounter

---

15 Waugh recorded his experiences in his travel diary, published as *Ninety-two Days: The Account of a Tropical Journey Through British Guiana and Part of Brazil* (New York: Farrar & Rinehart, 1934), and fictionally reworked them in his novel *A Handful of Dust* (New York: Dell, 1934).

16 Lévi-Strauss, *A World on the Wane [Tristes Tropiques]*, p. 270.

with his own family history *and* with cultural otherness in the overtly diverse environment of the city bring to light both the multiple pressures facing Amerindian peoples in the novel, the dangers of appealing to either ethnic purity or the postcolonial nation-state for help or redress, and the necessity of interrogating anthropological thinking about identity, kinship and culture in order to imagine, and to write, contemporary indigeneity anew.

In the Guyanese hinterlands portrayed in part two of the novel, which takes place from around 1900 to 1920, centuries of colonialism and slavery on the coast initially appear to have had little impact on the savannahs where the Amerindian population lives. Somewhat like an intrepid anthropologist carrying out fieldwork, Alexander McKinnon arrives in the early years of the century and has the impression that the Indians 'cut cassava farms for themselves and carried on hunting and fishing as usual' (*VT* 98). McKinnon's perception, signalled by that 'as usual', that Indian life in the savannahs is one isolated from outside influences and unchanged for centuries, is soon revealed to be a dual construct. On the one hand, it is a claim made *about* Amerindians by Westerners, like McKinnon, seeking exoticism, escape or 'savagery'; McKinnon himself arrives in the savannahs in an attempt to 'get as far away from civilisation as possible' (*VT* 96). On the other hand, it is simultaneously a claim made *by* the Amerindian community, which insists on recognizing their own continuity *through* change. It soon becomes clear that the Amerindian community is not shielded from cultural change or the impact of colonialism, but their discourse of self-definition emphasizes continuity. McKinnon's belief that the Amerindians 'laughed at the idea of progress, despised novelty' (*VT* 99) is contradicted by his observation, a few lines later, that 'people welcomed anything he brought back from town that proved useful' (*VT* 100). Clearly, novelty is not the problem, although there is certainly a difference between the Amerindian characters' tendency to determine the value of innovations by their usefulness, while McKinnon values newness for itself as a mark of 'progress'. McKinnon's steadfast belief in Indian cultural stasis is the pendant to Wormoal's claim, decades later, that 'Indian culture is disintegrating *these days*—contaminated mainly by contact with other races' (*VT* 78, emphasis added). Both comments can be understood as part of a colonial–anthropological discourse of primitiveness, or what April Shemak terms 'colonial reinventions of the primitive', which defines Amerindian cultures in terms of their supposed purity and historical position on the brink of extinction.[17] This (neo)colonial discourse, however, becomes entangled with the claim made numerous times by various Amerindian characters that their culture *is* unchanging, *despite* constant alteration, adaptation and innovation.

---

17 Shemak, 'Alter/natives', p. 353. See also Smith, 'Queer Theory and Native Studies', pp. 42–68 for a discussion of how many *postcolonial* discourses *also* imply that indigeneity is always already disappearing.

In the prologue, this paradox intersects with the narrator's discussion of oral and written literature. His grandmother is enraged that he plans to write down stories that have otherwise been passed on orally: 'She is a stickler for tradition. All novelty or innovation is a sign of death to her' (*VT* 9). Yet in preferring the oral tradition, described as a support for 'tradition' and opposed to 'innovation', she ensures and *generates* newness in another sense: via the continual reinvention and retelling of stories, rather than the (apparent) stasis of written record. Furthermore, as the novel's own contribution to this debate emerges, this binary breaks down further as it becomes apparent that writing, too, is unstable, indeterminate, and capable of generating newness. The novel challenges not only the colonial–anthropological discourse of primitiveness, cultural purity and stasis, but also questions the meaning of terms such as innovation, cultural change or continuity, and how, or by whom, they might be defined. Among the many forms of cultural contact represented in the novel is the savannah tradition of hospitality: the novel records visits by prominent figures like Charles Darwin (*VT* 3), a 'German man' (*VT* 133), and Evelyn Waugh (*VT* 286–89).[18] The presence of these visitors, all of whom are in the savannahs to conduct research of various kinds, is a reminder both of the indigenous peoples' potential exploitation by western knowledge production (foreshadowing the work of Wormoal many years later), and simultaneously an insistence upon the Amerindian sovereignty and their resulting ability to offer hospitality to such visitors. The text's representation of these visitors and their hosts refuses the binary of rapacious western intellectuals and their victimized objects of study: the 'German man', for example, remains unnamed, thus the text refuses him any status or enduring fame as an explorer or scientist; furthermore he is sick, injured and entirely dependent on the Indians for his survival.

McKinnon originally arrived in the savannahs in a similar way: lost, sick and disoriented, he happened upon an Amerindian village. His wife Maba later recalls:

> He wanted to stay. [...] Everyone in the village discussed it and Daddy gave him permission to hang his hammock next to mine in the big house, which meant that we were married.
>
> Another man in the village wanted to marry Zuna but our father said that McKinnon must have first choice because it was the tradition amongst Wapisiana people that if a man marries one sister he has first choice of the next one. Your father accepted both of us, so here we are. (*VT* 97)

This story introduces the topic of marriage, kinship, and the cultural specificity and meaning thereof in part two of the novel. At first glance, the polygamous

---

18 According to Elizabeth DeLoughrey, the 'German man' is a reference to the German ethnologist Teodor Koch-Grundberg (also spelt Theodor Koch-Grünberg), although as I argue below, the figure's namelessness is an important element of the text's representation of him. See DeLoughrey, 'Quantum Landscapes', p. 72.

marriage, cast here as Wapisiana 'tradition', appears to confirm the radical cultural difference between Europeans and Amerindians and to confirm the authenticity of the Indian culture. Certainly McKinnon himself picks out kinship as a key matter of cultural difference: for him the 'family structure was entirely different from anything [...] [he] had known' (*VT* 103). When another European arrives in the area, the Catholic missionary-priest Father Napier, he describes the McKinnons' marriage as an 'intolerable arrangement' (*VT* 110) and makes convincing—or forcing—the Indians to accept monogamy one of his chief concerns. This focus on kinship as a key marker of cultural identity and indigenous cultural difference might be understood as confirming elements of the anthropological tradition of kinship, particularly Lévi-Strauss's positing of kinship (which for him means rules pertaining to marriage and reproduction) as the basis of all human culture and society, that is, that 'the ties of marriage represent the very warp and woof of society, while other social institutions are simply embroideries on that background', as well as the conclusion that changes to kinship forms and traditions necessarily lead to the erosion or alteration of the culture built upon them.[19]

Yet there are soon reasons to question various aspects of this interpretation. Although the polygamous marriage of a man and two sisters is described as a Wapisiana tradition, the text notes that the two women were, initially, unhappy with the arrangement and jealous of one another, suggesting that tradition can be and is questioned even by those upholding it. Furthermore, even its status as a tradition is somewhat in doubt: it is striking that it is the only such relationship to be found in the novel. Of all the other marriages that are described, some are monogamous, some are polygamous, but no others involve two sisters. If there is a 'Wapisiana tradition' of marriage, an empirical consideration of the text might lead to the surprising conclusion that the most widespread marriage practice is to marry cultural outsiders: marriages between Wapisiana Indians and various 'others' constitute the majority of the relationships featured in part two of the novel.[20] Indeed, kinship defined in the Lévi-Straussian sense—as particular, culturally specific rules defining permitted and forbidden marriage partners, and as the most important and

---

19 Claude Lévi-Strauss, *Race and History* (Paris: UNESCO, 1958), p. 27. This idea is developed in much greater detail, but rarely stated so succinctly, in Lévi-Strauss, *The Elementary Structures of Kinship*. Povinelli offers an extensive background on the development of this idea in the field of anthropology from Victorian scholars up to and including Lévi-Strauss's work. See Povinelli, *The Empire of Love*, pp. 215–22.
20 In addition to Maba and Zuna's marriage to the ethnic Scotsman McKinnon, other examples include: Beatrice and Danny's maternal grandmother is a Macusi Indian (104), Wifreda later marries Sam Deerschanks, who is a 'part Sioux Indian from Texas' (177), Danny (after the end of his affair with his sister Beatrice) marries Sylvana, a Brazilian woman 'descended in a direct line from Portuguese shopkeepers' (234), while Beatrice moves to Montreal and marries the white Canadian Horatio Sands.

fundamental structure of a culture—does not seem to exist in the Amerindian community depicted. The novel's engagement with kinship in part two does not repeat the anthropological conflation of kinship and culture (a conflation that was also to be heard in Tenga and Wormoal's pronouncements about the dangers of cultural deterioration through mixed marriages in part one); rather, it points to precisely such an amalgamation as an error of understanding caused by colliding myths of the meaning of kinship and the definition of the human: anthropological, Catholic and Wapisiana.

This anthropological inheritance—the link between kinship and culture and associated categories such as human and non-human, nature and culture, writing, time, progress and stasis—is taken up quite literally when Beatrice and Danny, the two eldest children of Maba and McKinnon, begin a sexual relationship as teenagers. Although their initial motivations remain unclear, not least to themselves, vague concerns about the preservation of Wapisiana identity seem to play a role. Danny becomes jealous when Beatrice begins flirting with a young black man from the coast; Beatrice soon discovers in the relationship a means to return to cultural practices she views as more authentic, to recapture a 'pure' or undefiled indigeneity. After the two run away together and journey through the jungle, they appear to travel out of western influence, gradually discarding their clothes and eating only what they can hunt and gather. Yet because their relationship is in part a reaction to cultural changes wrought by colonialism, it remains bound to the very cultural influences they reject. They are responding to social changes such as the labour migration which brings workers like the young black man, Raymond, to work in the savannahs, or to experiences such as their years spent at Catholic boarding schools in Georgetown—in which racism and the accusation of cultural betrayal lead Beatrice to understanding cultural alterity as a matter of 'hostile territory' in which she must struggle to stay 'intact' as a Wapisiana (*VT* 138)—and this means that their quest for 'pure' indigeneity, free of any such influences, grows ever more elusive. An incestuous relationship between siblings is tolerated by the Amerindian community—'it was [not] unheard of for a brother and sister to live "close" as it was known' (*VT* 176)—and this might appear to support Beatrice's belief that she is refusing western, colonial norms and the Catholic morality represented by Father Napier in favour of a more authentic indigenous model. She makes a fundamental mistake, however, in conflating Wapisiana culture with a particular kind of sexual relationship. She thereby aligns herself with an anthropological understanding of kinship and culture which is generally *not* to be found in the Amerindian community. Indeed, the way in which Danny and Beatrice's journey into the forest echoes the journey of Dante—a jaguar marks the entrance to the forest, they are attacked by biting insects and must travel along the River of the Dead—hints at the extent of the Catholic influence upon the couple.

During a period of introspection during their journey through the jungle, Beatrice concludes that her desire for Danny comes from a wish to 'stop the

Pauline Melville's The Ventriloquist's Tale

passage of time' (*VT* 197). Whether in the sense of a return to a pre-colonial state of Amerindian culture or in the sense of mythical timelessness, the novel suggests that she is mistaken both in her desire for cultural purity and in her perception that time flows only in one direction, like the river that she and Danny are travelling on at that moment. Indeed, surrounding her on the river is the first indication of Beatrice's mistake, although she remains unaware of it: the river is known to another tribe as the River of the Dead due to the ancient petroglyphs on its banks; it is said to be 'by means of those marks [...] that the dead were still able to speak to the living' (*VT* 196). As the marks are said to be 'older than the great flood' (*VT* 195), that is, to date to before the creation myth of the Wapisiana and thus to come from another world, they are a wormhole through spacetime to alternative universes. This is not the first indication that the linear time of both empire and anthropology, described by Adam Barrows as 'a river with one source, one outlet, and one even rate of flow', is not infallible—as will soon be confirmed by the approaching eclipse.[21]

The solar eclipse of May 1919, which occurs during Danny and Beatrice's time in the jungle, carries enormous symbolic weight for multiple characters. Maba is initially comforted by the news of the approaching eclipse, as it confirms to her that Danny and Beatrice are reenacting elements of a widespread Amerindian eclipse myth that is recounted multiple times in the novel.[22] The myth records how a brother and sister who had an incestuous relationship rose into the sky and became the sun and the moon. The eclipse is eagerly awaited by McKinnon, who has read about the planned scientific observations to verify Einstein's theory of general relativity by measuring the bending of light from the stars by the gravity of the sun, and who plans to try to photograph the eclipse himself: he is excited at the prospect of taking part, albeit as an amateur, in another mark of 'progress'. Maba, Zuna and the other Indians are more apprehensive, as they regard the eclipse as harbouring chaotic and transformative potential:

> An eclipse is a disgrace. It brings chaos. [...] Even the dead rise up to see what is happening. And everything can change into something else.

---

21 Adam Barrows, *The Cosmic Time of Empire: Modern Britain and World Literature* (Berkeley: University of California Press, 2011), p. 71. Similarly, Johannes Fabian writes that 'anthropology contributed above all to the intellectual justification of the colonial enterprise. [...] It promoted a scheme in terms of which not only past cultures, but all living societies were irrevocably placed on a temporal slope, a stream of Time—some upstream, others downstream'. See Fabian, *Time and the Other*, p. 17.

22 The myth is referenced in the epigraph from Lévi-Strauss and related in various versions numerous times in the novel, including being recorded in several versions in Wormoal's paper (*VT* 82–83), acted out by Wario in the communal hut of the Wai-Wai (*VT* 191–93), with a slightly different version offered by the Taruma men (*VT* 194), and reported with a mix of derision and fear by Sister Fidelia, who has found herself implicated in what seems to be a latter-day recurrence in Mexico (*VT* 146–47).

> Animals into people. People into animals. The dead and the living all mix up. (*VT* 180–81)

This transformative potential is again evident in a story told to Danny as a child by his uncle Shibi-din, according to which it was also during an eclipse that people became separated from animals and plants: when the sun returned to normal, the Wapisiana had lost their immortality and their ability to speak to plants and animals, and 'everywhere there was a dreadful stink. That's why they say the loss of immortality has to do with a bad smell' (*VT* 123).

This collection of myths, beliefs and stories contains myriad challenges to the Lévi-Straussian understanding of human culture represented by Wormoal. Zuna's representation of the eclipse, that is, a cosmic, 'natural' phenomenon, as 'a disgrace' and an instigator of 'chaos' contests the anthropological vision of nature as a realm of 'order and natural peace' (at least prior to the entrance of the anthropologist or western civilization) or Rousseau's claim of nature as inherently good.[23] From the guiding 'spirit of rot' (*VT* 3) of the tropics, which works against stasis and classification, to the vampire bat attack which opens part one of the novel, the 'natural' world, inasmuch as it can be isolated as such, is inconstant and rarely peaceful. In the eclipse myth recounted by Shibi-din, the eclipse seems to mark the beginning of human culture, including the emergence of human language and a cultural understanding of death. But this change is described as a loss rather than a gain: humans *lost* their ability to speak the language of plants and animals, and *lost* their immortality. (In the prologue, language was already posited as a posthuman force which exceeds human 'culture', countering Rousseau's claim that writing is a 'dangerous supplement' that 'destroys nature'.)[24] As the eclipse is a recurring event, not a singular threshold, the border between human culture and nature remains porous and subject to chaotic change or reversal. Non-human objects, even the stars, sun and moon, are revealed to be historical actors, further smudging any clear delineation of a realm of human culture, and the dead rise up to overturn linear, continuous time once again.

The novel does not simply offer this Amerindian cosmology as an alternative to, for example, the worldview of Wormoal; the text not does not replicate Lévi-Strauss's claim of *equivalence* (but difference) between myth and 'science', such as when he writes that 'the kind of logic which is used by mythical thought is as rigorous as that of modern science […] man has always been thinking equally well'.[25] This supposed equivalence rigidly separates myth and science, assigns one to the West and the other to the non-West, one to the present and one to the past. Rather, the novel's retelling of these 'myths' alongside the events of the 1919 eclipse demonstrates, first, that

23 Derrida, *Of Grammatology*, p. 113.
24 Derrida, *Of Grammatology*, p. 151.
25 Lévi-Strauss, 'The Structural Study of Myth', p. 444.

the time of anthropology has long been out of joint, and secondly that the so-called 'rational laws' (*VT* 81) of Stephen Hawking may not be what Wormoal and others like him think they are. The time of anthropology and the anthropologist—not only linear and continuous, but also permanently removed from the discipline's objects of study—is a pre-relativity time. As Johannes Fabian argues, 'anthropology achieved its scientific respectability by adopting an essentially Newtonian physicalism [...] at a moment near the end of the nineteenth century when the outlines of post-Newtonian physics [...] were clearly visible', and this was, he suggests, '*anything but* historically or politically neutral'.[26] Rather, it served to enable and preserve what Fabian terms the 'denial of coevalness', or *Gleichzeitigkeit*: one of the key conceptual means through which anthropology has supported colonialism, from the age of high imperialism in the late nineteenth century to today.[27] The novel's endorsement of a post-relativity or even quantum time must therefore also be understood as a political intervention into indigenous 'survival politics'.[28]

Quantum time in the novel is not a property of the 'rational' or 'scientific' West; rather, it disturbs, upsets, and overturns many of the western tradition's foundational assumptions and categories. In many ways, the novel shows it to be a better fit with cultures of the savannahs than those of their European visitors. Barrows reads a similar scene from a classic colonial novel as follows: 'In *King Solomon's Mines* (1885) Allen Quartermain and crew represent themselves as "men from the stars" and, in an often-imitated scene, predict a solar eclipse to shock and awe the natives'.[29] Yet although the 'natives' in Melville's novel are anxious about the coming eclipse, they are not overawed by McKinnon's foreknowledge of it. Rather, his wife Maba is frustrated at his failure to understand the multiple meanings of cosmic events; to her he 'seemed to be completely unaware of what was happening' (*VT* 208). In a similar way, the landscape of Guyana has long disturbed colonists because, 'the non-Euclidean waters which in some rivers ran backwards were [...] incomprehensible to them' (*VT* 36). If, as Michael Whitworth suggests, Euclid functioned in nineteenth-century Europe as 'a byword for infallibility and for self-evident truth [...] his geometrical axioms as the very foundation of civilization',[30] the novel puts these 'self-evident' truths and certainties into question—not only for or in Guyana or the colonized or postcolonial world, but especially for Europeans and European societies as well. In a similar way, the novel's insistence on non-Newtonian time undermines the certainty and infallibility of the colonial–anthropological mission and throws doubt upon its longevity, even if it cannot ward off its most violent effects.

26 Fabian, *Time and the Other*, pp. 16, 17, emphasis in original.
27 Fabian, *Time and the Other*, p. 31.
28 'Survival politics' is taken from Burnett, 'Where Else to Row, but Backwards?'.
29 Barrows, *The Cosmic Time of Empire*, p. 79.
30 Michael H. Whitworth, *Einstein's Wake: Relativity, Metaphor and Modernist Literature* (Oxford: Oxford University Press, 2001), p. 199.

Indeed, relativistic spacetime is not, in itself, enough to prevent colonial exploitation and destruction. The Catholic priest, Father Napier, is sent to look for Beatrice and Danny by their father; when he finds the couple in the jungle, Beatrice smells him before she sees him: Napier's black soutane 'exuded a damp, gaseous aura like the smell of rotting cassava or a secreted compost heap. To Beatrice the stench was overwhelming' (*VT* 221). The parallel with one of the eclipse stories suggests that Napier's intervention, his imposition of Catholic morality and Catholic kinship discourse, is a kind of 'loss of immortality' (*VT* 123), and that the increasing influence of Catholicism in indigenous communities is a kind of death, the beginning of the end for indigenous cultures and peoples. The 'loss of immortality' smelled by Beatrice manifests as a sudden turn to Catholicism in Danny: when he hears Father Napier approaching, he declares, 'God has sent him here' (*VT* 221). Yet this influence, as undeniable as it is, is also ambivalent and unpredictable. When Danny responds to Father Napier, the spell of Beatrice upon Danny is abruptly broken; he follows Father Napier back to the ranch and puts an end to the affair as Father Napier instructs him to do. In this way, the narrative echo of Dante and Beatrice is diverted, suggesting that the eclipse, although it heralds the end of Danny and Beatrice's relationship, also inaugurates the end of a narrative tradition that might be traced back to Dante and Catholic Europe.

Father Napier, the representative of Catholicism and thereby one of the chief arms of colonization in the text, occupies an ambivalent position in the novel: often represented as a figure of ridicule and scorn, but also one who brings death and destruction. In his black soutane he is described as 'a black crow on the landscape' (*VT* 149), capturing this twin sense of foreboding and derision. Although the tone of the narration remains generally light-hearted, the text's contempt for his missionary undertakings is suggested by his paedophiliac predilection for some of the young boys in his tutelage and his increasingly egotistical and extravagant visions of glory and papal reward. His dreams of glory are also paradigmatic visions of industrial British 'modernity': above all, he dreams of building a railway to transport the Pope from the coast to the inland savannahs. In a rare moment of harsh criticism, Father Napier is described as working 'subtly, like a cancer virus mimicking the workings of a cell it has entered' to 'destroy Indian beliefs' (*VT* 150). The tone of the novel is unusually critical in this passage, and indeed Napier's actions do lead to tragedy, yet the image of a 'cancer virus mimicking the workings of a cell it has entered' also reveals that it is not only Amerindian culture that is changed by the encounter with Catholicism, but that the religion, too, has changed, adapted, mutated, and become part of the Amerindian culture and landscape—something that both Father Napier and Beatrice emphatically deny. Beatrice is enraged by Napier's interference in her relationship with Danny, and some time later carries out her revenge, arranging for him to be poisoned by another woman. (She thereby employs both indigenous knowledge—the poisonous beans from the piaiwoman, Koko Lupi—and Father Napier's own kinship politics against him: the woman whom Beatrice convinces to poison him, Aro, fears for her position as a second wife if Father Napier's policy of monogamy is enforced.) During Napier's subsequent descent into madness he sets fire to many of the churches he has built in his years in the savannahs, but with some irony, Catholicism cannot be eradicated so easily: the Indians now seek to protect the churches from Napier's insanity. Both Napier and Beatrice are forced to leave the savannahs: Napier is sent back to a monastery in Britain, while Beatrice leaves after her actions identify her as a 'kanaima', a 'spirit of revenge', which—unlike her incestuous relationship with Danny—the community is unable to tolerate: 'vengeance attacks were more terrifying than incest' (*VT* 266). This symmetry points to a certain similarity between Beatrice and Napier: in seeking to reject all foreign influences, Beatrice has actually drifted *away* from the communal sovereignty and rule which has long defined and protected Amerindian communities like her own. The difference between her individually planned revenge and the mode of governance described by Maba years before, talking about her own marriage—'everyone in the village discussed it' (*VT* 97)—demonstrates that this communal sovereignty is more important to the community and their cultural survival than any particular mode of kinship.

In Montreal, Beatrice reconsiders her previous desire to 'stop the passage of time' (*VT* 197). Visiting the museum with friends, Beatrice, like them, is fascinated by the exhibition of a 'shrunken Indian head preserved in spirits' (*VT* 273). Although the exhibition of the head is a reminder of the colonial claim that indigenous peoples are both remnants of the past and worthy objects of scientific examination, dissection and display, as well as possible evidence of murderous colonial violence, Beatrice sees instead in the head signs of life—in the present—in the savannahs, in the 'ruddy brown' complexion and 'cheeks [...] rouged with annatto'; the head 'reminded Beatrice of her grandmother' (*VT* 273–74). The 'preserved' head echoes Beatrice's ongoing pondering of the question of whether it is 'better for her own people to preserve themselves within their traditions or to allow change' (*VT* 281), but it soon becomes clear that this dichotomy—and its temporality of freeze or flow—is a false one. One day, at the circus, she watches a Native American stunt woman trapped in a glass coffin, and as she watches she 'lapsed into a state that felt like eternity without passage of time' (*VT* 277). When the woman emerges from the icy tomb, Beatrice 'felt as though she herself had been freed' (*VT* 277): freed not only from the coffin, but from a state of timeless eternity or frozen time, which she now experiences as a terrifying, rather than desirable. Filled with relief, she realizes that it is 'possible to survive the ice coffin and emerge unscathed' (*VT* 278). Not only is it possible to survive as an Amerindian in a different landscape and climate, but her culture and identity, together with Amerindian traditions, do not need to be 'frozen': they too can survive being thawed out, warmed up and brought into a different spacetime.

The child whom she leaves behind in the care of her younger sister, Wifreda, indicates the 'exorbitant'[31] effect of the orbits of the eclipse on the text. Sonny is the child of Beatrice and Danny, conceived during the solar eclipse. He is never given a name other than his position as a 'son', and thus seems to symbolized the weight that kinship is expected—by anthropology and for a time by his mother—to carry. Nevertheless, he seems to reject kinship in the sense of intimacy: he 'did not seem particularly attached to anybody' (*VT* 268), and also in the sense of relationships which shape subjectivity: he 'didn't know who he was or where he came from' (*VT* 285). Eventually, still a child, he disappears from Wifreda's farm and is never seen again. Never again *seen*—but in this text, the unseen has only *appeared* to vanish. When Sonny disappears into the bush, most of the other characters assume that he wishes to escape from the burdens of kinship and social bonds. He has, however, not quite disappeared, and he has certainly not abandoned his connections to others. Rather, his apparent disappearance mirrors another apparent vanishing: that of the narrator at the end of the novel's prologue. It soon becomes clear that Sonny has become—or has been all along—the original narrator of the story, identifiable by his matching clothes (found abandoned by a waterfall), his ventriloquist abilities and the sound of his laughter. Sonny's disappearance and reemergence as the narrator has obvious consequences for the story's chronology: the twist messes up the spacetime of the story entirely, wrenching apart linear chronology as Sonny enters a wormhole which allows him to become both be part of Wifreda's narrative from the early twentieth century and to narrate the story as a semi-timeless figure decades later. Sonny's transformation links the excess generated by the eclipse, the exorbitance of those intersecting orbits, to the much discussed question of the novel's narratorial form, and reveals another challenge to colonial–anthropological discourse: the puncturing and twisting of its evolutionary, linear time and of the 'denial of coevalness', to use Fabian's term, which would arrest indigenous peoples in the pre-modern past.

Sonny is portrayed as the personification of the (indigenous) quantum spacetime which becomes apparent in the text through him. He is described by Wifreda as being like a black hole, 'a walking event-horizon' and 'a singularity' (*VT* 283), with a large degree of ontological indeterminacy: 'he managed to be there and not to be there at the same time' (*VT* 285). These descriptions, in terms taken from astrophysics and popularized by the work of Stephen Hawking, reclaim this field from Wormoal and simultaneously demonstrate Wormoal's lack of understanding of quantum 'rationality', thus placing his entire knowledge production on shaky ground. In fact, the narratorial and stylistic implications of Sonny's exorbitant position are foreshadowed early in the text, in an episode narrated in part one, long before his disappearance, during his encounter with Evelyn Waugh (then currently staying at Wifreda's

---

31 Derrida, *Of Grammatology*, p. 161.

house during his travels through Guyana). Waugh is carrying with him a copy of Dickens's *Dombey and Son*, a novel which records the upheavals in British life caused by the building of the railways—a pervasive literary symbol of the standardized time which would become the 'cosmic time of empire' in the late nineteenth century.[32] (Dombey thereby again echoes *Flaubert's Parrot*, in which the narrator, Braithwaite, says of Flaubert, 'Gustave belonged to the first railway generation in France; and he hated the invention'.[33]) The standardized time of *Dombey's* England and the age of imperialism it represents is incompatible with Sonny's quantum era, and he is violently repelled by Waugh—a hint that the novel, despite its *apparent* similarities to nineteenth-century realist fiction and its rewriting of Waugh's *A Handful of Dust*, is actually pursuing a very different narrative strategy.

Sonny disappears, he enters a black hole and emerges again, transformed or 'scrambled'.[34] After his transformation, the text describes him in religious terms: 'Sonny's apotheosis' (*VT* 291), or his 'numinous laughter' (*VT* 292). This might be read as a self-glorification and -deification by the hardly humble original narrator in this description of Sonny/himself, or as an acknowledgement of the true god of this story: narration and storytelling, and its power to create new worlds. Sonny's apparent rejection of intimacy and kinship is nothing of the sort, for—in the guise of the narrator—he has followed this family for generations; it is perhaps better understood as a refusal to be bound by genealogy, by the position denoted by 'Sonny', just as the text refuses to be bound by the demand for 'realism'. For Sonny's disappearance and reemergence as the narrator of the novel also demonstrates the limits of those readings which discern clear boundaries between the 'magic realist' prologue and 'realist' parts one to three of the novel.[35] Sonny makes the inadequacy of these

---

32 Barrows, *The Cosmic Time of Empire*.
33 Barnes, *Flaubert's Parrot*, p. 114.
34 In another remarkable twist, the novel thus seems to anticipate recent developments in theoretical astronomy, such as Stephen Hawking's recent announcement that his well-known theory of black holes, as a region from which light and information can never escape, may be incorrect. See S. W. Hawking, 'Information Preservation and Weather Forecasting for Black Holes' (Preprint, submitted 22 January 2014, http://arxiv.org/abs/1401.5761). In more accessible terms: 'If Hawking is correct, there could even be no singularity at the core of the black hole. Instead, matter would be only temporarily held behind the apparent horizon, which would gradually move inward owing to the pull of the black hole, but would never quite crunch down to the centre. Information about this matter would not destroyed, but would be highly scrambled so that, as it is released through Hawking radiation, it would be in a vastly different form, making it almost impossible to work out what the swallowed objects once were'. See Zeeya Merali, 'Stephen Hawking: "There are no black holes",' *Nature*, 24 January 2014, http://www.nature.com/news/stephen-hawking-there-are-no-black-holes-1.14583. As the novel presciently declares, 'Which came first, the equation or the story? The story, of course' (8).
35 John Thieme, 'Throwing One's Voice? Narrative Agency in Pauline Melville's *The*

categories clear, just as his quantum time travel—which seems to make him somewhat mythical—displays the dislocation of clear distinctions between 'myth' and 'science'. In the indigenous quantum spacetime of Melville's novel, one can be both, and in the singularity which Sonny both represents and makes apparent, just as in a black hole, the 'equations' of colonial–anthropological discourse no longer adequately describe reality.

At the beginning of part three of the novel, after this long flash-back, Wifreda repeats this family history to Chofy, who thereby hears it for the first time. The radical undermining of western knowledge production offered by the indigenous quantum spacetime of part two of the novel shows immediate effects: Chofy first chooses *not* to pass on the story, including the information about Waugh, to Rosa, thereby refusing to become subsumed by the terms she, as a 'complete rationalist' (*VT* 298), offers, including her belief in an unimpeachable divide between myth and reality. Soon afterwards, further reverberations of the destabilization of western knowledge become clear at Wormoal's long-planned lecture. Wormoal's work and writing tries to effect another kind of wormhole: one which would turn back time to a day in which his discourse had authority, backed up by colonial power and the reassurances of 'science'. Instead he is defeated by natural forces he imagined he could control; he loses the ability to write and the certainties of his knowledge are obliterated by torrential rain:

> The piece of chalk Wormoal held slid across the wet surface of the blackboard as he tried to write the words "Eclipse – a Rational Analysis of Myth". Water leaked from the ceiling directly above his head. Chofy watched the words disintegrate. Wormoal shook his head in annoyance. He tried again and the chalk skidded off the board. (*VT* 308)

Back in the savannahs, Chofy's wife Marietta considers the unequal power of indigenous and non-indigenous people during a tug-of-war at a rodeo. As she watches the group of Wapisiana vaqueiros win against the larger, stronger, but less unified team from the coast, this victory seems to offer hope for indigenous material survival in the contemporary world as well. Yet soon it becomes tragically clear that alone the subversion of colonial–anthropological discourse cannot protect Chofy or his family from harm (echoing Jonathan Goldberg's criticism of Derrida).[36] A few days later, Chofy's young son Bla-Bla is seriously injured by an explosive charge set by the Hawk Oil company, and he later dies in hospital in Georgetown. Chofy's cousin Tenga blames Chofy for the death: according to Tenga, Chofy's careless

---

Ventriloquist's Tale', *The Literary Criterion* 35 (2000), pp. 170–92; Braz, 'Mutilated Selves'.

36 Jonathan Goldberg, 'The History that Will Be', in Louise Fradenburg and Carla Freccero (eds.), *Premodern Sexualities* (New York: Routledge, 1996), pp. 3–21.

talk—too much bla-blaing—and his affair with Rosa led to the accident. By his logic, the answer is cultural, geographical and intimate isolation in order to prevent future tragedies. Yet Tenga's call for isolation, echoed by critics such as Braz, is shown to be no option for Amerindian peoples, and Tenga's is most certainly not the voice of the text.[37] Rather, the ethnocentrism he calls for would be a capitulation to the colonial–anthropological claims about indigenous people—that they are primitive and soon to be extinct—that *also* led to Bla-Bla's accident: causing, for example, the communicative breakdown between the oil prospectors and Bla-Bla because the prospectors 'didn't even realise he spoke English' (*VT* 343–44). Instead, it is clear that survival depends on a refusal to accept the terms of cultural identity and the limits of humanity dictated by colonialism and its assistant knowledges, whether discourses of primitivism, blood or genealogy. In this way, the tragedy of Bla-Bla's death can also be understood as an anti-genealogical turn in the novel—for the text insists on indigenous futurity despite the fact that the only child of the main protagonists is dead.

When Chofy and his wife Marietta return to their farm after Bla-Bla's death, Chofy rediscovers a sense of being at home in the savannahs which he lacked at the beginning of the novel. This sense of belonging has been made possible by his experience of finding a place of belonging in the city and his multiple encounters with cultural otherness there, so that Chofy's movement symbolically counters that described by Shona Jackson, in which non-indigenous residents of Guyana effectively banish indigenous people to the interior in order to 'indigenize' themselves on the coast.[38] He also feels reassured by the fact that 'there was a lot of work to be done on the house' (*VT* 349). In this short phrase the text reveals both an enormous change in Chofy's relationship to identity, landscape and belonging, and an alternative to the essentialism of Tenga: he has rediscovered the value of working together as a tie to the land and a means of generating community, rather than feeling threatened by 'aliens' (*VT* 14) defined in racial or ethnic terms, as he did at the beginning. In this, he has returned to a logic of kinship that can be found throughout part two of the novel, although it is mostly overshadowed by more spectacular events. Although part two of the novel does not uphold the Lévi-Straussian logic which ties kinship to culture, that is not to say that there are not significant differences between the indigenous and Euro-American understandings of kinship presented in the text. They are not, however, primarily differences in kinship structure, in the sense of, for example, polygamous marriages, but rather in the meaning and scope of kinship, and the ways in which kinship is created and maintained. Maba's original account of her marriage points not only to polygamous practices, but also to kinship as a network enveloping a whole

---

37 Braz, 'Mutilated Selves'.
38 Shona N. Jackson, *Creole Indigeneity: Between Myth and Nation in the Caribbean* (Minneapolis: University of Minnesota Press, 2012).

community and sovereign political entity: '*everyone in the village* discussed' her impending marriage (*VT* 97, emphasis added). Over the course of part two, alongside the relationship obsessed with the formal boundaries of permissible kinship in a Lévi-Straussian sense—the incestuous relationship of Danny and Beatrice—another concept of kinship emerges, based neither on 'blood', race or ethnicity, nor on the formal structures of a genealogical chart, but on the ties generated out of shared labour. Working together is crucial to the establishment and maintenance of close relationships in the Amerindian community, offering a different perspective on McKinnon's initial observation that the Indians 'cut cassava farms for themselves and carried on hunting and fishing as usual' (*VT* 98): the constancy of cultural practices may not be crucial, but the constant recreation of kinship bonds which bind together the whole community through working together certainly is. In the early years of their marriage, Maba and Zuna overcome their jealousy of one another through the realization that 'there was too much work for one woman' (*VT* 93). The alienation from her family experienced by Beatrice when she arrives back in the savannahs after years at boarding school is described in terms of her having 'forgotten how to work' (*VT* 158). When outsiders and cultural others arrive or wish to become part of the Amerindian community, it is never questioned whether their integration is possible or desirable in cultural or ethnic terms. Rather, it is a matter of usefulness and labour: Sam Deershanks, Wifreda's husband, is welcomed because he 'had a gift for handling cattle' (*VT* 177), while Sylvana, Danny's wife, is approvingly described as having 'the air of a sensible, strong young woman, outward-looking and practical' (*VT* 233).

In the epilogue of the novel, the original narrator returns (again)—not that he ever really left—and he, too, acknowledges that the power of storytelling alone, its power to overturn colonial categories and to undo anthropological claims about indigeneity—including the 'denial of coevalness' which confines them to the past, predictions of degeneration and demise, or the mandate of cultural 'purity'—may not protect indigenous peoples from the perils of neocolonial exploitation in the form of deforestation or resource extraction. But the novel suggests that to focus *only* on this would be to submit to colonial time and thus colonial domination once again, to be ruled by 'narratives of colonial victimization [that] are themselves a kind of world standard time'.[39] The narrator's refusal of this victim status, noting that indigenous people are at times complicit in their problems, asserts an alternative spacetime—a shared spacetime—opposed to what Wilson Harris terms the 'time of conquest'.[40] When the narrator claims that, 'unable to decide whether we should stick to ourselves or throw ourselves on the mercy of the wide world, […] I decided to return and take up residence once more in the stars' (*VT* 357), he is at his

---

39 Barrows, *The Cosmic Time of Empire*, p. 152.
40 Harris, *History, Fable and Myth in the Caribbean and Guianas*, p. 28.

Pauline Melville's The Ventriloquist's Tale

ventriloquist and trickster best. To begin with, he has already suggested that 'we Indians [...] are brilliant at divining what you would like to hear and saying it, so you can never be really sure what we think' (*VT* 354), thereby twisting the colonial stereotype of the inscrutable Indian into a devastating—for the certainties of colonial knowledge—reminder of the uncertainty and instability of the text. Secondly, the text has made clear that a 'residence in the stars' is no withdrawal from history, but rather a cosmic intervention *in* history that leads to the chaos which enables storytelling again. And thus the novel's final promise of indigenous futurity is a narrative one: the promise of another story from the narrator, 'another time' (*VT* 357).

In both Kincaid and Melville's novels, the narrators work by appearing to accept the terms of colonial discourse or European narrative conventions, only to twist and sabotage them. Yet while Xuela's endorsement of colonial 'defeat' and her writing of autobiographical ethnography in *The Autobiography of My Mother* tends to confirm at least some aspects of anthropological discourses, particularly around indigeneity, and to deny the possibility of significant anticolonial rewriting, the ventriloquist fiction offered by Sonny in Melville's novel is *almost* realist, but not quite, just as the text's representation of indigenous culture and kinship seems, in some moments, to confirm colonial–anthropological expectations, only to perform a quantum leap which wrenches the (Euclidean) ground out from beneath the feet of Wormoal and his anthropological claims, and which reclaims the potential of storytelling to imagine 'alter/native' futures.[41]

---

41 'Alter/native' is taken from Shemak, 'Alter/natives'.

Part II

Historiography and the afterlife of slavery

CHAPTER THREE

'As constricting as the corset they bind me in to keep me a lady': colonial historiography in Andrea Levy's *The Long Song*

The potential for literature to imagine what *might have been*, and to thereby negotiate and rework tensions between categories of history and fiction, gains particular relevance in a black Atlantic, postslavery context. Wendy Walters argues that writers of fiction can influence historiography in such cases not only by imagining otherwise, with an interest in 'imagining the possible [rather than] explaining the evidence', but also by showing and challenging the limits of 'the master's violent, scandalous archive'.[1] In interviews, Andrea Levy has spoken both of her sense of a lost history *and* of learning to rediscover and re-imagine that history by reading archival materials against the grain. On the one hand, she notes that 'three hundred years of history—the history of the enslaved people of the Caribbean—are missing from the record. Just a big black hole'.[2] On the other, she has described her archival research and the process of learning to read the nineteenth-century Jamaican materials, including books and journals from white residents and visitors, between the lines, in order to 'stare back at these testimonies from the point of view of the people they were describing'.[3] In other words, she suggests that at least *some* of the history of enslaved peoples can be extracted from the 'black hole' of the colonial archive through a reading that is both careful and creative. Levy's description of her own research and creative process thus parallels the two trends which Walters identifies in contemporary historical

---

1 Wendy W. Walters, *Archives of the Black Atlantic: Reading Between Literature and History* (New York: Routledge, 2013), pp. 105, 112.
2 Andrea Levy quoted in Jane Ciabattari, 'Giving Voice to Slaves' (Interview with Andrea Levy), *The Daily Beast*, 8 June 2010, http://www.thedailybeast.com/articles/2010/06/08/the-long-song-by-andrea-levy-interview.html (last accessed Mar. 2017).
3 Levy quoted in Ciabattari, 'Giving Voice to Slaves'.

85

research on and literary responses to slavery: noting 'the gaps, silences, and missing pieces of the archives' and reading 'the masters' own archive for a paper trail of resistance'.[4] Levy again demonstrates her attunement to current historiographical debates when she notes the limitations of available nineteenth-century Caribbean slave narratives: because they were produced or mediated by the British abolitionist movement, they are 'tailored to a political cause aimed at changing white public opinion'.[5] Similarly, Anita Rupprecht argues that white abolitionist movements avoided depicting slave resistance in order to maintain the image of enslaved Africans as 'innocent, and more importantly, passive victims'; thus they ensured the inscription of the trope of slave passivity within the archive.[6] These archival limitations underscore the important work that fiction, with its comparatively greater freedom to imagine otherwise, might do.

Levy's novel, like other contemporary neoslave narratives, can also be read as a challenge to the genre of the historical novel. Although Levy herself has stated that she does not consider *The Long Song* to be a historical novel, because 'what I wanted to explore isn't in our history books',[7] I suggest that the text can productively be read within that generic tradition, albeit as a novel simultaneously engaged in both demonstrating the limits of the genre and expanding and rewriting those limits. Levy's novel makes particularly visible the mediation and editorial process involved in historiography, with a high-degree of the self-reflexivity which Linda Hutcheon ascribes to postmodern 'historiographic metafiction' (although other scholars suggest that this self-reflexivity may not be new at all, but rather a feature of historical novels since the nineteenth century).[8] It demands a place for black Jamaicans within colonial history, writing them into a history from which they were formerly excluded as actors, and thereby significantly altering the scope and focus of colonial historiography, but largely retaining its form. It simultaneously makes visible the exclusions and omissions which form a necessary part of this writing of history: even as the novel narrates some of the stories that were excluded from the colonial account of Caribbean slavery, it also makes apparent other stories which must again be excluded, in order for the narrator, July, to tell the kind of story that she wishes to tell and create the kind of history she desires. In *The Long Song*, these historiographic

---

4 Walters, *Archives of the Black Atlantic*, p. 108.
5 Levy quoted in Ciabattari, 'Giving Voice to Slaves'.
6 Anita Rupprecht, 'Excessive Memories: Slavery, Insurance and Resistance', *History Workshop Journal* 64.1 (2007), p. 14.
7 Andrea Levy, 'The Writing of *The Long Song*', AndreaLevy.co.uk, p. 9, http://www.andrealevy.co.uk//content/Writing%20The%20Long%20Song.pdf (last accessed Mar. 2017).
8 Linda Hutcheon, *The Politics of Postmodernism*, 2nd edition (London: Routledge, 2002); Mariadele Boccardi, *The Contemporary British Historical Novel: Representation, Nation, Empire* (Basingstoke: Palgrave Macmillan, 2009), p. 8.

interventions are largely enacted and shaped by its representation of kinship, for it is, above all, a family story.

The Long Song takes place in nineteenth-century Jamaica and it begins, true to the style of a Bildungsroman, with the conception of its protagonist July. This act of procreation is barely over—'it was finished almost as soon as it began', as the opening line observes—before the first narratorial interruption occurs, thus introducing the struggle for narrative authority in the novel that accompanies the story: 'Reader, my son tells me this is too indelicate a commencement of any tale'.[9] The historiographical questions about the validity of narrative fiction and memory and their relationship to more traditional modes of history discussed by Walters, as well as related questions about literary style, thus form a crucial theme of the novel, played out dramatically in the struggle for narrative authority between the storyteller and her son. Indeed, it is the son, Thomas, whom we read first, for his Foreword and Afterword bracket the text, thereby framing and containing it. As Thomas introduces his mother's narrative, he emphasizes both its role both in cementing a certain family form and in materializing the desire to surmount the lingering shame of slavery in post-emancipation Jamaica: according to Thomas, his mother's story

> lay so fat within her breast that she felt impelled, by some force which was mightier than her own will, to rely this tale to me, her son. Her intention was that, once knowing the tale, I would then, at some other date, convey its narrative to my own daughters. And it would go on. The fable might never be lost and, in its several recitals, might gain a majesty to rival the legends told whilst pointing at the portraits of busts in any fancy great house upon the island of Jamaica. (*LS* 1)

Thomas implies that the aim of a story of slavery should not only be remembrance, so that the story is 'never [...] lost', but also that it should aim to rival the family stories of wealthy, white colonial Jamaicans, suggesting that colonial historiography and even colonial family legends define the playing field of this story. It is not only that Thomas himself intervenes in and tries to control his mother's story—generally to be met with her sometimes fierce, sometimes sly resistance. In addition, this installation of colonial narratives as the only worthy and valid models for history will prove constraining. In order to overcome her lingering shame at her own enslavement, July endorses the ideal of progress and champions capitalist enterprise as means of healing the historical wounds of slavery. It becomes clear that this requires her to also endorse linear, genealogical descent and the nuclear family as essential elements of appropriate kinship—and to banish all hints of other intimate bonds from her narration.

This struggle for narrative and historical authority between July and Thomas continues throughout the novel, and their disagreements are at

---

9 Andrea Levy, *The Long Song* (London: Review, 2010), p. 7. Further references to the novel will be given in the text as *LS*.

times so great that they threaten to damage their relationship—in this text, not only does kinship shape history, but the definition of history can shape kinship. Their arguments demonstrate the intimate linkage between these two topics, which form the joint focus of my analysis: the definition of history and validity of memory and imagination, and the definition of family and kinship. By endorsing and naturalizing one model of kinship, the novel naturalizes its associated mode of history—linear, teleological, and liberal capitalist—while other possibilities are marginalized or unimaginable. And vice versa: the novel makes clear that a certain mode of historiography may demand a certain definition of kinship. Hints of alternatives—both other forms of kinship and other histories—remain, surfacing occasionally within the narrative, and these make visible the editorial work performed by July as she chooses what to remember and what to forget, what may become part of her story and what may not. At times, when other voices briefly crowd the text, it becomes clear that other stories could be be told, but that such stories are deemed by July to be external to or even unsuitable for her chosen history. As July's family story functions allegorically as her proposed story of the emerging Jamaican nation, the marginalizations and omissions which attend the writing of a national narrative are also exposed.

Immediately after July's first narrative salvo with her interfering son, she continues with the tale of her own birth, a story of which there appear to be multiple versions: born upon a cane field in a rain storm, or under the hot sun, or in a high wind, or even while being menaced by a six-legged tiger. This multiplicity is identified as a specifically Afro-Caribbean form of creativity connected to the mythical storyteller Anancy (*LS* 10), but July—the elderly narrator, as opposed to the young protagonist—soon puts a stop to it:

> I cannot allow my narrative to be muddled by such an ornate invention, for upon some later page you may feel to accuse me of deception when, in point, I am speaking fact [...]. Although you may deem your storyteller humdrum for what hereinafter follows, it is, with no fear of fantasy, the actual truth of July's delivery into this world. (*LS* 10–11)

The initial celebration of multiplicity, storytelling and creative invention is halted in the interest of credibility to a hostile audience; fantasy and 'actual truth' installed as each other's binary opposites, with 'truth' clearly privileged. The split that the novel offers between the older, bourgeois July and the younger enslaved character emphasizes both the class position required for successful narration and history writing and once again makes the enslaved only the object of others' histories, rather than the authors of their own histories. The younger July's various tales of her birth are not history, but 'fantasy', and they must be excluded from the text in order for the older July's story to be acceptable.

The story which follows is perhaps more 'humdrum' and less fantastic, but it is also noticeably more patriarchal: while in the first set of stories, the 'mighty black woman that was her mother' (*LS* 9) gives birth alone and otherwise dominates the various scenes, in the 'true' version it is Tam Dewar, the plantation overseer and erstwhile rapist of July's mother Kitty who features prominently. Dewar towers over the prostrate Kitty and her diminutive midwife Rose during her painful and protracted delivery in her hut in the field slaves' village, although his interest in the child is a purely financial one: he orders the women to 'be careful with that wee baby—it will be worth a great deal of money' (*LS* 14). The 'actual truth' of July's delivery into this world is thus focused upon her status in the world of colonial slavery as human chattel and the property of the plantation owner, and it gives primacy to her biological paternity.

The bulk of July's narrative focuses on her experiences during slavery and in the period immediately following the abolition of slavery in 1838, when she was a young woman. Her story recounts the daily life of a plantation house, including the culture of New World slavery and the cultures generated by the enslaved, and it shows how both of these contributed to the society and culture which emerged after emancipation in nineteenth-century colonial Jamaica. It is the status of July's story as a *family* story, however, which shapes the text in crucial ways. What does and does not count as kinship for July is closely tied to the form of the story she tells—the jumps and omissions in the narrative are often closely tied to the formation and breaking of various kinship bonds—and to the kind of history she tells. As narrated by the older July, young July's life is one marked primarily by various kinds of destroyed, failed or perverse kinship. The correlation of history and family in the early chapters of the novel effectively works to highlight how the institution of slavery and the racist discourse it fostered operated in part through discourses of kinship, simultaneously destroying enslaved families *and* claiming that poor parenting was a sign of the degeneracy of so-called negro nature, which in turn was called upon as a justification for slavery. When July is forcibly separated from her mother as a small child, their owner remarks, 'She would be taken soon enough anyway. It will encourage her [Kitty] to have another. They are dreadful mothers, these negroes' (*LS* 35). In return for this destruction of kinship, the culture of New World slavery offers a racist paternalism in which the white slave owner is portrayed as a long-suffering father-figure and educator to his enslaved 'children': 'these blacks be like children—all must be shown how is good and how is bad' (*LS* 29), claims the owner's wife.[10] July's narrative shows clearly that the apparently 'childlike' behaviour of the slaves is a strategy of resistance to their forced labour, but it also suggests that the possibilities for resistance, particularly for the house slaves of the novel, are conditioned and limited by the vexed intimacy generated between house slaves and owners.

In slavery, where people become property, the language of ownership collides with and coincides with the language of kinship. A linguistically

---

10 On slave owner paternalism and other ways in which the institutions of slavery produced the Lack which they attributed to racialized and enslaved subjects, see Sylvia Wynter, 'Sambos and Minstrels', *Social Text* 1 (1979), pp. 149–56.

conjured equivalence between the bondage of chattel slavery and kinship bonds of care and responsibility sometimes leads to a perverse form of belonging in which property and kinship are blurred together.[11] When Caroline Mortimer, the sister of the plantation owner Howarth, says to July, whom she has recently taken from her mother in order to train her as a maid, 'you are mine now!' (*LS* 51), the claim of possession as property is overlaid with a sense that she is also claiming July as a daughter. In the sense of legal chattel, July's status has not changed—she was and remains the property of Caroline's brother in the eyes of the colonial law—yet Caroline insists that July is 'mine *now*', thus implicitly accepting that she was previously someone else's: she 'belonged' to Kitty, that is, she was Kitty's daughter. Caroline's words create a symmetry between herself and Kitty, both acknowledging the validity (albeit now abrogated) of the bond between Kitty and July, and positioning herself as a substitute mother—a position of perverse maternity further underscored by Caroline's attempts to rename July. The effectiveness and insidiousness of such a colonial discourse upon those it oppresses is seen clearly in July, who vacillates between her scorn for her mistress (inspiring endless schemes to escape from her duties, undermine Caroline's authority, and effect petty acts of resistance) and her feelings of genuine, if complex, attachment to the woman with whom she has spent much of her life in close contact. The extent to which July's bond to Caroline involves an internalization of the racism of colonialism and slavery is made clear during the uprisings shortly before the end of slavery: July simultaneously entertains a fantasy of revenge against Caroline *and* feels a sudden urge to protect her mistress from a vision conjured straight from the pages of white colonial terror-fantasies: she fears 'her missus's ravishment' by a 'rabble of black men' (*LS* 89).

July's narration of a gathering of house slaves from different plantations demonstrates that bonds of identity and attachment between slaves and owners are widespread, but suggests that these may have at least as much to do with perceived status as with the intimacy discussed above. She writes that these bondspeople insist that they are 'house servants' (*LS* 68), *not* slaves, and shows them competing with each other via the status and wealth of their owners. July and Clara, a 'house servant' from a neighbouring plantation, use the wealth of their masters and the perceived attractiveness of their mistresses—that is, two gendered forms of status in white colonial society— as proxies in tussling with each other: 'Your massa have no money for white muslin for you'; 'Me massa have plenty money'; 'your missus does have an ugly face'; 'your missus has a big-big batty' (*LS* 70–71). July's years as Caroline's maid are thus shaped by both the strange intimacy between them *and* July's desire for social status, both of which generate a treacherous equipoise and

---

11 Hartman argues that the two are necessarily linked: 'owning persons and claiming kin are one and the same'. See Saidiya V. Hartman, *Lose Your Mother: A Journey Along the Atlantic Slave Route* (New York: Farrar, Straus and Giroux, 2007), p. 87.

hinder her in substantial acts of resistance.[12] She happily steals small items of clothing from her mistress or pilfers alcohol from the dining room in order to supply the slaves' party, but she is equally willing to assist Caroline in extracting the maximum amount of forced labour from the field slaves. Together they 'inspect those field slaves that hoped sickness might relieve them from their work' and July, although more than practised in the art of deceiving her mistress, chooses to side with her owners and reveal the tricks of the field slaves: 'That black tongue not be sickness, it can be wipe off', she declares (*LS* 54–55).

July's depictions of relationships between the slaves on the plantation, particularly among the house slaves with whom she works, and her own lack of solidarity with the field slaves (one of whom is her birth mother), suggest that relationships of mutual support, let alone intimate bonds of lived kinship, do not or cannot exist among the enslaved. Echoing her owner's contention that negroes are 'dreadful mothers' (*LS* 35), July often describes relationships between black subjects (including both enslaved and free people) in terms of failed or inadequate kinship. July writes of two antagonistic acquaintances that they 'believe themselves to be like brothers. As few at Amity had any notion of how brothers behaved to each other, [...] being a brother had come to mean two men in constant, bloody fight' (*LS* 88). July's double implication is that there is a proper definition of kin—the two men '*believe* themselves to be *like* brothers', are thereby defined as *non-brothers*—and a proper way for kin to behave, and that slavery has destroyed both. July's descriptions of the house slaves both ridicule the notion that kinship might be possible between non-genealogical relatives, and yet they also suggest that even 'blood' ties do not generate lasting bonds or solidarity between slaves.

These failed non-kin stand in contrast to those kinship relations in the text which *are* seemingly recognized by July, if sometimes belatedly, as legitimate. These kinship bonds can be determined in part by examining the structure of the text: After narrating July's birth, the novel then skips over July's first eight or nine years, which she spends with Kitty. It attends in great detail to her relationship with Caroline Mortimer. It notes in short the birth of her son and her subsequent abandonment of him, then again skips several years until emancipation and the beginning of her relationship to Robert Goodwin, a white overseer. That relationship is recalled in detail, including the birth of their daughter Emily, and the narrative then comes to a penultimate close after July's loss of her second child. It omits the several decades that July then spends in a free negro camp and resumes once again, at least thirty years later, only when July is reunited with her son (whom she now recognizes as

---

12 The novel thus offers a Caribbean version of the influential thesis of Eugene Genovese, who—writing about slavery in the US South—argued that slave owner paternalism and small-scale wins through slave resistance hindered more radical or successful slave revolts. See Eugene D. Genovese, *Roll, Jordan, Roll* (New York: Pantheon Books, 1974).

such). The narrative is thus structured by the formation and breaking of July's kinship bonds, which is to say, by those relationships which she retrospectively, at the time of writing, considers worthy of the name.

The common factor which unites July's recognition of these bonds as kinship is not the common western formulation of kinship as 'blood or law' (although July certainly employs this discourse at times), but is a question of status: kinship is recognized only if doing so grants July higher status—as the almost entire exclusion of her birth mother Kitty and the inclusion of her mistress Caroline makes clear. She is proud of her relatively privileged position as a house slave, considering herself superior to field slaves like her mother. She abandons her son Thomas as a baby, considering him worthless because his skin is dark. As this point, July's narrative briefly ventriloquizes Thomas's story, recounting the early years of his life as the adopted son of a white Baptist minister and his wife. But July refuses to narrate this period of her own life, because these are years in which July loses her position as a ladies' maid; she is severely punished for her small part in the chaos of the uprising, and she narrates that *one* July, 'that mischievous girl that you have come to know [...] departed. And a withered and mournful girl stumbled in, unsteady, to take her part' (*LS* 147). This *other* July is to have no part in the story: the narrative continues only once July's status as Caroline's maid is restored, which is soon followed by emancipation and the start of her relationship with Robert Goodwin, the new white English overseer of the plantation, then the birth of their light-skinned daughter Emily: all circumstances which grant July higher status, in her own eyes, and all narrated in detail.

Certainly July employs the language of institutionalized kinship in her relationship with Robert: 'husband was July's favoured name for Robert Goodwin—for every time she said it [...] he responded obediently by calling her wife' (*LS* 225). But the word 'wife' is not desired because it indicates an intimate relationship of reciprocal love or care, nor a place in a wider network of kinship and community, nor because it designates certain legal rights, of which July has none. Robert, after all, has legally married Caroline Mortimer, July's former owner, in order to 'have' July (*LS* 211), which both suggests that their relationship is analogous to chattel slavery and serves as a reminder of the role of legal marriage (or in this case, the perceived impossibility of a legal marriage between Robert and July) in creating and enforcing racial difference.[13] Rather, the promise of the word 'wife' for July lies in the social status and financial benefits that she hopes a white lover can provide to her in the emergent world

---

13 Nancy F. Cott, *Public Vows: A History of Marriage and the Nation* (Cambridge, MA: Harvard University Press, 2000), see in particular pp. 59–70. Cott also suggests that in the Southern US by the 1830s, the relationship between slave and master was often described using a marital analogy (replacing the previous popular parent–child analogy), suggesting a possible additional layer of meaning which would build upon and combine the other two.

of postslavery Jamaica. The post-emancipation experience of her erstwhile competitor, Clara, clearly demonstrates to July the two-fold social advancement offered by a white lover. There are immediate and financial benefits, such as the lodging house which Clara's 'husband' buys for her, enabling her to become a business woman (*LS* 191), and future-oriented and genealogical 'benefits': Clara's motto, 'Only with a white man, can there be guarantee that the colour of your pickney will be raised' (*LS* 187) is eagerly adopted by July. According to this logic, increasingly light skin through successive generations explicitly marks the march of progress, and a dark-skinned child takes one 'back down' (*LS* 187), marking one as a degenerate who no longer moves forward through teleological history.

July's idealization of whiteness in these years has brutal consequences: her light-skinned daughter Emily is stolen by Caroline and Robert Goodwin when they leave Jamaica to return to England in the wake of worker uprisings. Bereft of her daughter, abandoned by her lover and betrayed by her owner/employer of many years, July has lost everything she valued and everything which granted her social status—and, once again, her narrative breaks off, resuming again only when July meets her son Thomas some thirty years later. July's reconciliation with the child she once abandoned as 'the ugliest black-skinned child she had ever seen' (*LS* 143) might seem to signal a renouncement of the desire for whiteness which resulted in, among other things, the tragic loss of Emily, and might seem to represent the reversal of the privileging of relationships with white subjects prevalent in July's youth. The name he now bears, Thomas *Kinsman*, emphatically underscores his role in the text's representation of acceptable and authentic kinship forms. But July's son, once abandoned as an inferior child, is now able to grant many of the same benefits that July once hoped to gain through her attachments to white subjects: he is highly educated, a successful business man, a property owner, and he lives in a legal marriage with his wife and three daughters. Most significantly, July recognizes him as her son and becomes interested in a relationship with him *only once she realizes this*. Her narration of the moment of recognition is imprinted with images of Thomas's wealth and bourgeois respectability, indicated by his corporeal grooming, adornment and clothing: 'His breath was faltering, his fingers fidgeting—with the curve of his nails, his marriage band, his cuff' (*LS* 304).

Although July's narrative appears to be divided into times of lacking kinship (most of her life) and proper kinship (her later years with Thomas and his family), July's acknowledgement of kinship with Thomas is actually contingent upon the social status and the material comforts he is able to provide, and thus represents far more continuity in July's understanding of kinship than a decisive break. For July, Thomas personifies the possibility of overcoming the injustice and lingering shame of slavery, and her narrative suggests that her integration into recognized bourgeois kinship relations is an important aspect of this recovery. Indeed, July's recognition of her son only after she becomes aware of his wealth and status again makes clear the extent to which July's narrative is driven by—and attempts to erase—the shame she feels for her own history of enslavement. Through her recognition of Thomas, July suggests that the joint bourgeois values of private property and a private life organized by marriage are the most effective antidote to the oppression of enslavement. Thomas Kinsman's own story seems to highlight the promise of 'possessive individualism'; his future status as a propertied individual is foreshadowed when he begins to 'possess himself', that is, when he begins to attend the 'club for mutual improvement' run by his employer in England, at which 'his mind steadily opened' and he read literature, philosophy and political theory (*LS* 297–99).[14] Yet this concept of self-possession and its standing at the basis of liberal individualism and liberal citizenship rights is based upon 'a prior assumption that selves are *possessable objects*—an assumption that was generated, before and alongside liberal political theory, in the practice of Atlantic slave capitalism'.[15] Saidiya Hartman's suggestion that we should seek 'the routinized violence of slavery and its aftermath' not only in scenes of overt violence and suffering, but also others such as 'slaves dancing in the quarter [...] and the fashioning of the self-possessed individual', suggests a critique not only of Thomas as a figure of hope and progress, but of July's undertaking as a whole.[16]

As a black man, Thomas Kinsman's accession to liberal individual subjecthood is complexly situated: his financial success, the business acumen it demonstrates, and his marriage and nuclear family signal, on the one hand, his acceptance of the colonial culture which, just a few years earlier, justified the enslavement of his mother, as well as the racism he experiences in both England and Jamaica. The possibility of his success, and his acceptance of the (begrudged) social position he thereby acquires, can be read as an early example of a transformation described by Grace Hong: 'Racial capital transitioned from managing its crises entirely through white supremacy to also managing its crises through white liberalism, that is, through the incorporation and affirmation of minoritized forms of difference. This meant normalizing racialized populations once positioned as entirely nonnormative'.[17] By imagining Thomas's success and emphasizing the possibility of black middle-class Jamaicans in the nineteenth century, the novel might be read as implicitly shifting the blame for ongoing poverty away from imperialism and racism to the marginalized sections of those racialized populations. Nonetheless, Thomas's success can *also* be read as a form of resistance to racist colonialism, which demands economic success and bourgeois marriage

---

14 C. B. Macpherson, *The Political Theory of Possessive Individualism: Hobbes to Locke* (Ontario: Oxford University Press, 2011).
15 Jennifer Rae Greeson, 'The Prehistory of Possessive Individualism', *PMLA* 127.4 (2012), p. 918, emphasis added.
16 Saidiya V. Hartman, *Scenes of Subjection: Terror, Slavery and Self-Making in Nineteenth-Century America* (New York: Oxford University Press, 1997), p. 4.
17 Hong, 'Existentially Surplus', p. 89.

as proof of emancipated people's humanity and civilization, but invests enormous resources to prevent black subjects from actually achieving them.[18] Thomas Kinsman's upsetting of racist colonial expectations precisely by fulfilling the demands of colonial culture is, however, a very different kind of resistance to the one represented by the free negro community in which July lives for many years. The limits of Thomas's resistance-by-success are hinted at in the stories of his daughters: the patriarchal nuclear family of Thomas, which July understands as a mark of status for the formerly enslaved—what Hortense Spillers calls 'the mythically revered privilege of a free and freed community'[19]—demands training in extremely constricting gender roles for his small daughters, indicating that the burden of the link between middle-class status and sexual 'respectability' is born primarily by women. It is one of the ways, as Michelle Wright has argued, that 'Black Studies and Black Diaspora Studies'—or in this case black Atlantic fiction—'reproduce gender and sexual hierarchies not only in their contemporary theorizations on blackness and diaspora, but also their (re)narration of that Diasporic past'.[20] Unlike earlier forms of postcolonial and black diasporic rewriting associated with pan-Africanism or Negritude, Levy's text does not call on Africanness to rebut claims of diasporic black inferiority, but on heteronormativity.

As July constructs her own story of hope and progress, promising that slavery can be left behind, she also reveals what must be excluded from her narrative to make this story possible—or what becomes unimaginable in this optimistic imagining. At least two key exclusions are necessary to inaugurate the upbeat, progressive and national narrative that July presents: the disavowal of alternative kinship forms, and of radical, transnational, anti-capitalist resistance. At the time of writing, July lives with and is materially supported by Thomas, and his material support (in the form of food and housing, and in the supply of paper and ink) is necessary for her story to be told at all. This support, however, is not unconditional: Thomas tries to shape and control July's story in various ways, and her narrative explicitly struggles against his patriarchal interventions. Her story is bracketed and conditioned by the Foreword and Afterword which he, as his mother's editor and printer, has appended to her text, while his other demands are thematized by July's narrative as she attempts to tell her story in the way

---

18 For more on the role marriage and the bourgeois family played in the construction of newly emancipated black subjects in the Caribbean, see Catherine Hall, *Civilising Subjects: Metropole and Colony in the English Imagination, 1830–1867* (Cambridge: Polity Press, 2002). On the final point and the possibility of reading the fulfilment of this colonial ideal as a form of resistance I am indebted to Ira Berlet, whose paper, 'Henry Bibb and the Detroit–Windsor Border as a Path to Manhood', at our shared panel at the Mid-America Conference 2013 suggested the possibility and necessity of this reading.
19 Spillers, 'Mama's Baby, Papa's Maybe', p. 218.
20 Wright, 'Can I Call You Black?', p. 7.

of her choosing. Sometimes his interventions are moralistic, claiming that certain scenes are inappropriate, sometimes historical, berating his mother for leaving out historical events or figures or claiming that her narrative is historically incorrect. His Foreword positions July as an inexperienced and nervous narrator who needs her son's professional, British-educated skill as a printer to 'find meaning in the most scribbled of texts' (*LS* 2). She should feel no shame at this editorial assistance, he writes, as it is standard practice 'at some of the best publishing houses in Britain' (*LS* 3), thus again positioning July's narrative as an aspirant to these colonial traditions. July attempts to assert herself and her own voice beyond her son's framing, slyly poking fun at his attempts to control her story and sometimes openly arguing back against his interventions or defying his instructions. In some cases she is successful—as Thomas himself acknowledges, his 'advice often fell on to ears that remained deaf to it' (*LS* 3)—but in others, she accedes to his demands.

While at the very beginning of the novel the narrator July decried fantasy and committed herself to factual truth, later this question re-emerges in the struggle for narrative authority between July and Thomas, whereby the text again stages a debate between mother and son that mirrors the historiographical questions in which the novel as a whole intervenes. After a passage in which the young July recounts how the news of a slave uprising arrived at her plantation, a new chapter reverts to July's other narratorial voice—that of the older July at the time of writing—to note the protests of her son. Thomas claims that July has mixed up two separate uprisings, or that she has made a mistake in her dating of events—whatever it is, she's in the wrong. July writes that Thomas 'then commenced to blast me with fierce commands' (*LS* 77), creating an uneasy equivalence between the fierce commands of July's son to his elderly mother and the fierce commands of July's previous owner, John Howarth, to a younger, enslaved July, narrated on the previous page. Thomas orders his mother to include certain things in her story: where and why the fighting started, what she knows of a certain rebel leader, that she should 'make it clear how every negro believed themselves to have been freed by the King of England' (*LS* 77) and more. July becomes defensive and addresses her audience: 'Now, reader, it is not that your storyteller is indolent and idles about when there is work that must be done' (*LS* 77). Just as the symmetry between Thomas's 'fierce commands' and those of the slave owner Howarth suggests, Thomas's demands have reduced July to a caricature figure from the colonial archive: the negro (slave) who is too lazy to work, and she is thus implicitly compared to Thomas himself, a model of the protestant work ethic. Thomas's insistence that the rebellious slaves must have been under the mistaken impression that they had 'been freed by the King of England', rather than determined to free themselves, further underscores his investment in colonial and patriarchal power. Rather than asserting the validity of her memory against the potted record of the colonial archive which Thomas understands to be truly historical, July instead retreats into apologies, claiming that 'the reason I have little to advise upon these truths is within the nature of these olden times; for news did not travel as it does today' (*LS* 77–78). The difference between July's story and the colonial record is no longer a historiographical one about the validity of different forms of memory and evidence, but is reduced to a problem of inadequate communication technology preventing her access to 'these truths'. After her browbeating, July accepts her son's account as more 'true' than her own, and accepts that his version of history represents omniscience, rather than an equally limited, but more powerful, version of events. Humbly acknowledging the shortcomings of her narrative, she recommends an alternative: a pamphlet written by a white Baptist minister about the uprising and recently given to, or imposed upon, July by her son. July continues to demand a place for her story, but only as personal memory, not historical truth, and thus she no longer explicitly challenges colonial historiography. This struggle for control of historical memory again makes clear that only certain forms of memory, and certain truth claims, can play a role in both officially recorded history and in the story July wishes to tell—whether it would be possible to write history in another way, however, remains unclear.

This confrontation between mother and son also reproduces the traditional gendering of knowledge and history: Thomas speaks for and with the force of fact, truth, rationality and universality, while July can defend only the domain of the personal and domestic, which is eventually reinstated as outside proper history by this exchange. While the novel exposes this gendering, it seemingly cannot be overturned without jeopardizing the status of July's story. This is further emphasized by another confrontation between Thomas and July, a few chapters later, when they argue over the status of July's narrative as fiction or fact. July insists, 'This tale is of my making. This story is told for my amusement. What befalls July is for me to describe' (*LS* 142), claiming the protagonist July as a fictional character of her own creation. Thomas, however, answers that 'this is the story of your own life, not of your creating' and that July must 'speak true' (*LS* 142–43)—recalling July's promise to relate the 'actual truth' (*LS* 11) at the beginning of the novel. July experiences Thomas's denial of her narrative and creative freedom as an extension of the gendered strictures which apply to her new position within his wealthy family: 'sometimes his demands upon me are as constricting as the corset they bind me in to keep me a lady' (*LS* 143). This conflict between July and Thomas can also be understood as a debate over the object of historical writing: the elderly July's claim that young July is a character of her own making underscores the productive function of historical discourse and the process by which historiography constructs the historical figures which are its object, whereas Thomas's insistence on the conflation of July the narrator and young July as the 'truth' obscures this historiographic production.[21] This conflation

---

21 Jennifer Terry, 'Theorizing Deviant Historiography', in Ann-Louise Shapiro (ed.), *Feminists Revision History* (New Brunswick: Rutgers University Press, 1994), pp. 276–303.

does not abrogate the separation of July-as-bourgeois-narrator and young, enslaved July, but rather reduces even the adult July to a memoirist, at best, or fantasist, at worst—precisely that fate, in other words, which she tried to avoid by renouncing creativity for 'humdrum' (*LS* 11) history.

In this case, July criticizes her son's authoritative and controlling tendencies, but eventually submits to them because, she argues, her material well-being depends upon her obedience: 'I must do as my son bids. Else I may wake to find my valise […] placed outside the gates of this house, and my aging nagging bones cast out to join [it]' (*LS* 143). Yet although July claims that her cooption into colonial historiography is coerced by the threat of renewed homelessness and starvation, in other scenes July is more than willing to integrate herself into the emergent black elite in colonial Jamaica, including participating in the oppression of other, less wealthy, black subjects. July struggles against Thomas's control of her own writing, but, having achieved a comfortable position within colonial capitalism and the Jamaican class hierarchy, she is no longer opposed to the economic oppression and exploitation of others that it entails. She passionately rejects *for herself* the idea of working again as a servant, but she does not object to being served by the household employees of her son. These passages suggest that July largely accepts both the constraints upon herself and the colonial–capitalist social order as the conditions of her becoming an agent of history—but also that it is not an anticolonial history that she writes.

July protests lightly against her own 'corset', both in the literal sense and in the sense of Thomas's curbing of the occasional unorthodox excesses of her narrative, but she regularly scolds her granddaughters to school them in the rigid gender norms of wealthy, upper-middle-class women. The metaphoric and literal corsets worn by both July and her young granddaughters make clear that the projection of July and the children into a (better, happier) future also requires their adherence to heteronormativity; heteronormativity is another condition of their becoming-historical. With great irony, however, while the class position and gender norms which determine July's suitability as a narrator are made clear, and July accepts these limits in order to tell her story, this acceptance of the standards of colonial historiography simultaneously devalues July's contribution, so that her story can never claim the status of history. In a similar way, the gendered norms to which July and her granddaughters adhere, because they promise 'progress', are the same racialized norms which were once employed to degender and dehumanize Kitty—of whom Caroline Mortimer once asked, 'Is it a woman?' (*LS* 33)—as well as to justify her exploitation in the cane fields and the removal of her daughter July, making it questionable how emancipatory they can truly be for July or others. In order to assume the position of the narrator of her story and a teller of history, July has adopted key elements of colonial discourse, demonstrating a growing confluence between her work and the colonial historiography from which her story originally diverged, yet without gaining the authority of the colonial voice.

Andrea Levy's The Long Song

In the middle of the novel, a short interlude temporarily upends the dominance of patriarchal authority and desire for whiteness which otherwise dominates July's narrative, and it briefly gestures towards alternative modes of both kinship and history. At the time, July is on the run for her life. For a few pages, the story returns to the plantation's negro village, the field slaves and July's birth mother, Kitty, as it narrates Kitty's attempt to save her daughter from the wrath of the plantation overseer, Tam Dewar—who is, not incidentally, July's biological father. July's status as Kitty's daughter is first recognized not by Kitty herself, but by Rose, the elderly midwife. Her crucial role in this incident suggests the importance and endurance of the bond between both midwife and mother and midwife and child, suggesting a kind of triangular kinship between Kitty, July and Rose—and an alternative to the triad of Dewar, Kitty and July.[22] Featuring a multitude of voices and conflicting versions of events, this section marks a clear stylistic break from July's usual style of narration. This momentary overthrow of colonial patriarchy, as the maligned figure of the enslaved woman and mother Kitty surges to the fore, upsets colonial historiography in the story more than any of the squabbles between July and Thomas. While July's narrative makes clear the concessions she is forced to make in order to shape her story to the demands of the history she wishes to tell, Kitty's actions are able to unsettle the terms of colonial history in a different way, smudging the separation between those deemed the proper actors of colonial history and those, like Kitty, usually erased from the record. As Kitty rushes to save July from the overseer, one resident of the field slaves' village

> was convinced that it was Kitty's passing footfall that had shaken his house to trembling. But his wife, Peggy, swore that the rumbling of the earth that had so rocked their feeble dwelling that night was started as the militia began advancing upon them. (*LS* 126)

The two versions of events offered here—was it Kitty's powerful gait which shook the ground, or the advancing colonial militia?—suggest a certain momentary equivalence between Kitty's actions, and the consequences of her actions, and those of the white colonial militia. For a brief moment, Kitty overturns the tendency in representations of Atlantic slavery to depict white Europeans—or those, like July and Thomas, who strive to conform to white norms—as the only 'makers of history'.[23]

A fleeting reference, and one that is almost lost in the tumble of chaotic action in these scenes, makes clear that Kitty's actions should be

---

22 The importance of midwives in slave societies and their enduring bonds to the women and children they attended is discussed in the US context by Deborah Gray White, but White does not entertain the possibility that these bonds could be understood as a form of kinship. See her *Ar'n't I A Woman? Female Slaves in the Plantation South* (New York: Norton, 1985), especially pp. 91–118.
23 Barnor Hesse quoted in Walters, *Archives of the Black Atlantic*, p. 108.

read not only as a personal mission to save her daughter, but as overtly political acts of resistance and war as well: Kitty is as 'bold as Nanny Maroon' (*LS* 128). This comparison to the eighteenth-century Jamaican rebel leader, ties Kitty's actions into a longer history of (female-led) slave resistance, revolts and free communities. This reference to Nanny Maroon and her history *could*, and momentarily does, provide a counterweight to the power of colonial authorities, but this alternative mode of narration quickly subsides, and July's text refuses to narrate Kitty's final revenge. She frees her daughter and kills the overseer, whose body she is found beside, and for whose murder she will soon be hanged—or so we are left to assume, for, although 'what happened next has been told in so many ways by so many people' (*LS* 130), the text shies away from narrating any version of this scene of triumph and self-sacrifice. Kitty's killing of Dewar, which is also Kitty's revenge on white patriarchy—she kills her rapist and the white father of her daughter—is suggested by the narrative only in somewhat coy rhetorical questions. 'Did she bash his head upon a stone until it split like a ripe coconut?' asks July; 'Reader, we will never know' (*LS* 131). July's claim that she cannot narrate this with certainty because 'not one soul saw' (*LS* 131) is less a protection of Kitty, a refusal to testify to her crimes, than a denial of her her agency; her actions, the force of which was compared to the power of the colonial militia a few pages earlier, are now semi-erased; her momentary status as a 'maker of history' rendered uncertain or unknowable. The final scene of Kitty's execution returns her to passivity and inaction. Despite her resistance to colonial power in the style of Nanny Maroon, and the knowledge and awareness of colonialism this implies, she is now unable to understand the workings of colonial power: appearing before the court she 'carr[ied] a look of puzzlement' (*LS* 133); she does not understand that her case has already been heard and judged. She is hung immediately afterwards, and July's final image is of her hanging 'small and black as a ripened pod upon a tree' (*LS* 135)—her distinctive height and prodigious strength finally erased.

After this brief episode, the trace of radical anticolonial resistance and female leadership in the novel is largely lost, and July refuses to take up this role herself, in effect refusing this cultural inheritance from Kitty. A few years later, she resurrects Tam Dewar when she begins to speak of him often as her 'much cherished papa' (*LS* 188) in order to claim the status of a mulatto, thereby also accepting and integrating, or ingratiating, herself into the colonial logic of blood quantum. Later, although she lives three decades of her life in a free negro community (perhaps like the ones founded by Nanny Maroon a century and a half earlier) she refuses to narrate this time, claiming that to do so would be to 'dwell upon sorrow' (*LS* 305)—with the disturbing implication that the horrors of enslavement, including the many scenes of suffering, exploitation, mutilation, rape and torture which she *has* narrated in detail, were less sorrowful. Thomas, once again, interferes, insisting that a narration of these years is required. July refuses and acquiesces at once; thus her brief reference to these decades entails only a list of the many causes of suffering in the community:

> Must I show you the trouble those free negroes had to endure? Should my reader feel the fear of the harassment from planters that came upon that place almost daily? [...] Would you care to face a loaded pistol with a machete and hoe? [...] Should I let the earthquakes rattle and the floods pour? [...] Must I find pretty words to describe the yellow fever that took so many? (305)

Purporting to be a refusal to narrate that which it thereby describes, this passage again makes explicit the forces which determine the contours and contents of July's narrative. First, her attempts to resist her son's control of her story are never entirely successful, illustrating the patriarchal and material pressures on July's story. Secondly, July's designation of this period of her life as unworthy of remembrance, undeserving of a place in her history, again demonstrates the extent to which July determines her story based on her own social status—a status that, even after emancipation, continues to be largely determined by colonial power. It is a dramatic example of the way in which racialized communities 'have always policed and preserved the difference between those who are able to conform to categories of normativity, respectability, and value, and those who are forcibly excluded from such categories'.[24]

Indeed, the text also includes occasional scraps of evidence that suggest that the story of the free negro community, had July been willing to tell it, might have substantially altered the story she does offer about the afterlife of slavery, nationalism and anticolonial resistance. Tantalizing hints of trans-Caribbean links and the influence of revolutionary Haiti on the black population of Jamaica are to be found in the statements of the court prosecutor, who reveals at one stage that a 'crowd of negroes were singing and making threats that they will see Jamaica become another San Domingo and run all white men from the island' (*LS* 286). When the same prosecutor says disparagingly, 'these negroes, as always, seem to fear that slavery is being brought back, that this island will be sold to the Americas and they will then find themselves again slaves' (*LS* 286), he unwittingly reveals that the free negroes, who refuse to work for the planters, are aware of North American and Caribbean geopolitical manoeuvrings and that, despite their geographical isolation, they have an astute awareness of international politics in the late nineteenth century.[25]

---

24 Hong and Ferguson, 'Introduction', p. 2.
25 This line might suggest an awareness, for example, of the imperialist plans of some Southern US slaveholders and politicians in the first half of the nineteenth century for the annexation of parts of Central America and the Caribbean—especially Cuba, but potentially also Jamaica—to the USA. See Walter Johnson, *River of Dark Dreams: Slavery and Empire in the Cotton Kingdom* (Cambridge, MA: Belknap Press of Harvard University Press, 2013), especially pp. 303–29.

Thus the text offers hints that such free negro communities might have had cultural and political links outside of the colonizer–colonized binary which dominates the story, but the fact that these hints do not come from July, but are instead voiced by figures of white, patriarchal colonial government, symbolically contains them within the scope of colonial authority.

Apart from her indication of the suffering experienced there, July's own experiences in the free negro community remain obscured. In particular, nothing at all is said of the forms of intimate or social life there. Hints of the forms of kinship, family life or community structures that might have been practised in the community, or which July herself might have been part of, are completely absent. Although in numerous other cases the novel makes July's exclusions and omissions explicit, such as in her brief description of suffering in the free negro community above, the omission of these more intimate experiences is not signposted. They are not only deemed unsuitable for the family history which July wishes to craft, but are also excluded from the novel's exploration *of* that crafting, and the inclusions and exclusions, rememberings and forgettings which it involves. The counter-narrative of anticolonial resistance which can be traced from Kitty's comparison to Nanny Maroon to the resistance and trans-Caribbean political organization of the free negro community becomes part of the text *through* its visible exclusion from July's story, and, by extension, the marginal position of these stories in the narrative of nascent Jamaican nationalism which July offers also becomes clear. But there is no trace of non-patriarchal, perhaps non-genealogical kinship, to be found. Instead, July crafts a narrative which retrospectively arranges her life and experiences into a heteronormative chronology, suggesting that the 'narrative coherence' of a heteronormative life is a condition of her narrative authority and the cultural intelligibility she hopes to achieve by it.[26]

The question of genealogy and its meaning is taken up in the final pages of the novel, in the Afterword written by Thomas and appended to July's text. He notes a remaining gap in his mother's story: the fate of her second child, Emily, of whom 'all trace has been lost' (*LS* 307). He writes that, at times, his mother has pondered Emily's fate—that is, her racial and social status: 'She has asked me, for example, whether Emily lives as a white woman in England? Does she reside within a fancy house or is she used as a servant?' (*LS* 307). Thomas, too, is curious: 'Perhaps she is in England, unaware of the strong family connection she has to this island of Jamaica. She may have children of her own, who have no understanding that their grandmama was born a slave' (*LS* 308). Thomas's logic links together genealogy, nation and history: for Thomas, Emily's genealogical tie to her mother should also entail a connection to the emerging nation, Jamaica, and to her mother's history of

---

26 Judith [Jack] Halberstam in Dinshaw et al., 'Theorizing Queer Temporalities', p. 182.

slavery and the overcoming of slavery. His final words offer a slight twist on this logic of blood kinship: after asking readers for any news of Emily to be sent to him, he adds 'one word of caution [...]. In England the finding of negro blood within a family is not always met with rejoicing', so the news of Emily's genealogy 'may prove to be unsettling' (*LS* 308). Thomas's final words here take up the trope of genealogy as 'blood' to suggest the potential 'unsettling' of a European or English myth of racial purity by Emily's 'negro blood', thereby utilizing the colonial concepts of blood, race and kinship to destabilize both English racial purity and genealogical certainty.[27] The history of July, Thomas suggests, her shame and her suffering, might also be the personal, family, 'blood' history of unknowing English people. This application of the colonial discourse of 'negro blood' unsettles the boundaries between English and Jamaican populations, both in the nineteenth century of the novel and the present, but it also reaffirms a colonial logic of kinship as 'blood or law' as the only imaginable alternative to the logic of status employed by July throughout her narrative.

July's story, which is her means of overcoming the lingering shame she feels for her own enslavement, and the historiography she proposes—for herself, for Jamaica, and by extension for other black diasporas—is one which offers the same teleological journey from shame to pride, and from enslavement to middle-class comfort, that she carefully crafts in her narrative. July's narrative, as the story of a woman and a former slave, does much to both overturn and make visible the strictures of colonial historiography and to fill the blind spots or invisible gaps of the colonial archive. July's narrative makes visible and vibrant some of the stories excluded from the colonial account, but also performs multiple excisions of its own. For July to tell the story which she wishes to tell, much must be excluded, and some of these omissions, these forgotten or ignored stories, crowd the margins of July's narrative. Although July's story is one marginalized within, indeed almost completely erased from, the colonial archive, her mode of historiography in many ways in conforms to the demands of colonial historiography—perhaps because the wish to fill in the gaps and create a more complete history is, as Grace Hong suggests, 'fundamentally nationalist and colonial'.[28] Levy's novel makes those demands visible, and thereby denaturalizes them, just as the voices of the stories excised by July remain, if only barely, accessible. These other voices, whispering in the wings of July's narrative performance of progress and success, lead to the question—not answered by Levy's novel—whether history might be written yet another way. A history which

---

27 On the myth of racial purity and homogeneous whiteness, see Gloria Wekker, *White Innocence: Paradoxes of Colonialism and Race* (Durham, NC: Duke University Press, 2016).
28 Grace Kyungwon Hong, '"A Shared Queerness": Colonialism, Transnationalism, and Sexuality in Shani Mootoo's *Cereus Blooms at Night*', *Meridians: feminism, race, transnationalism* 7.1 (2006), p. 76.

might not demand, for example, the deliberate forgetting and erasure of the culture and society of the free negro community, or which not require a model of kinship, gender and sexuality 'as constricting as the corset they bind me in to keep me a lady' (*LS* 143)—would that still be a history at all? It is this self-shattering of history which Dionne Brand's novel *At the Full and Change of the Moon* proposes.

CHAPTER FOUR

Shattering the flow of history: Dionne Brand's *At the Full and Change of the Moon*

At the Full and Change of the Moon chronicles a family story with no pretensions to completeness or continuity, but rather one which 'bursts forth in snatches and fragments'.[1] Rather than exploring and exposing the shortcomings of colonial historiography in order to demand a place for enslaved peoples and their descendants within an expanded version of that history, the novel highlights the continuities between past colonial violence, including the violence contained within the gaps of the colonial archive, and the violences and silences of contemporary social and economic relations. Brand's novel starts from the margins of the colonial archives, but it suggests that colonial historiography, while still powerful, is neither an adequate recourse for the injustices of the black Atlantic past nor a vehicle for the diasporic longings of black Atlantic subjects today. Rather than 'yearning for a different past',[2] in the sense of erasing the shame and suffering of slavery, the novel charts multiple desires for a new mode of relating to the past and thus new ways of being in the present and alternative futures for black diasporic subjects. Containing only fragments of each character's life story and thus working against the 'narrative coherence'[3] of the temporality of a normative life, this is a queer family history in which the lives sketched in the fragments rarely follow the prescribed sequences of national heteronormativity. Refusing the logic which allows 'heterosexuality [...] to masquerade [...] as History itself',[4]

---

1 Glissant, *Poetics of Relation*, p. 69.
2 Klaus Neumann, 'But Is It History?' *Cultural Studies Review* 14.1 (2008), p. 29.
3 Judith [Jack] Halberstam in Dinshaw et al., 'Theorizing Queer Temporalities', p. 182.
4 Eve Kosofsky Sedgwick, 'Gender Criticism', in Stephen Greenblatt and Giles Gunn (eds.), *Redrawing the Boundaries: the Transformation of English and American Literary Studies* (New York: Modern Language Association of America, 1992), p. 293.

the text offers a diasporic queerness which results in a representation both of 'modes of being [...] that refuse the consequential promise of "history"'[5] *and of the transformational challenge posed by, and transformational potential promised by the narration of those lives to that history.*

The novel's insistence that memory shapes, and indeed confounds, the past and future—that slavery means that 'every turning stood still [...] every stillness turned to motion [...] what she was about to do she had imagined done already, like a memory'[6]—suggests first the ways in which memory might work to 'displace the developmental temporality that constitutes this [individual] subject as wilful and self-possessed',[7] or a colonial hierarchy which accords such self-possessed subjectivity a superior position. It also exposes and renegotiates contemporary black Atlantic historicity, in the sense developed by Michel-Rolph Trouillot. For Trouillot, the relationship between *what happened* and *what is said to have happened* must be constantly renegotiated in order to understand how the present moment shapes and punctures the representation of the past.[8] Rather than considering the spectral hovering of the past over the present in the novel as a traumatic phantom, an 'inexplicable' remnant of the past in the present, as some readings using trauma theory suggest—that is, as a form of atypical and pathological temporality which deviates from the linear time presumed of proper history—it can be understood as a sign of a different kind of interaction between past and present.[9] Trouillot insists that we are neither prisoners of the past nor is history simply whatever we make of it. Rather, the interaction between past and present produces us as subjects and confounds linear, progressive temporality: any collective's 'constitution as subjects goes hand in hand with the continuous creation of the past. As such, they do not succeed such a past: they are its contemporaries'.[10] Trouillot further insists that 'what we often call the "legacy of the past" may not be anything bequeathed by the past itself': neither the original impact of an event, nor the mode or importance of the historical recording of that event determines its relevance, but rather the relation between a past event and

---

5 Annamarie Jagose in Dinshaw et al., 'Theorizing Queer Temporalities', p. 186.
6 Dionne Brand, *At the Full and Change of the Moon* (Toronto: Alfred A. Knopf Canada, 1999), p. 9. All further references to the novel are given in the text as *Moon*.
7 Grace Kyungwon Hong, *The Ruptures of American Capital: Women of Color Feminism and the Culture of Immigrant Labor* (Minneapolis: University of Minnesota Press, 2006), p. 68.
8 Trouillot, *Silencing the Past*.
9 Erica L. Johnson, 'Unforgetting Trauma: Dionne Brand's Haunted Histories', *Anthurium: A Caribbean Studies Journal* 2.1 (2004), unpag; Maureen Moynagh, 'The Melancholic Structure of Memory in Dionne Brand's *At the Full and Change of the Moon*', *The Journal of Commonwealth Literature* 43.1 (2008), pp. 57–75; Julia Grandison, 'Bridging the Past and the Future: Rethinking the Temporal Assumptions of Trauma Theory in Dionne Brand's *At the Full and Change of the Moon*', *University of Toronto Quarterly* 79.2 (2010), pp. 764–82.
10 Trouillot, *Silencing the Past*, p. 16.

the present.[11] The past is continually recreated within the context of the present, and that context determines the meaning and relevance of the past in that moment. It is *the way in which* the present is haunted by slavery that shows that we live in a racist global present of economic oppression, labour exploitation and racialized incarceration, but also a present characterized by resistance and determination to imagine otherwise. Brand's novel offers just such an exploration of the afterlife of slavery—one that not only remembers the past of slavery, but also calls attention to the racist present in which this past is remembered. It does so by reflecting on the black Atlantic diaspora's loss and recreation of kinship and the strangulating normative pressures of contemporary kinship discourses.

The novel opens on a cocoa plantation in Trinidad in the 1820s, where a rebellious slave, Marie Ursule, is preparing a mass suicide—the last of her many revolts. The suicide is simultaneously an act of desperation and one of decisive action: Marie Ursule and the other slaves, who call themselves the San Peur Regiment, seize control over their lives by ending their lives; they wish to escape the enslavement of the body by destroying the living body. This gesture against futurity is also an escape from the past, for the plans of the rebels are described as a desire to go somewhere 'dark and empty of things that had happened and dark and empty of failure and dark and empty of history' (*Moon* 18). Yet this rejection of a future for themselves is balanced by Marie Ursule's other, complementary plan: on the morning of the suicide she sends her small daughter Bola away with Kamena, an escaped former slave, so that Bola may have a future, even if her mother does not. The first chapters narrate Marie Ursule's story, the next chapter turns to Bola and Kamena, the following chapters tell the stories of some of Bola's many descendants, most of whom are in the generation of her great-grandchildren, and whose stories date from the early to late twentieth century and are spread across the Caribbean, South and North America and Europe, before the final chapter returns to Bola to tell her story once again.

Marie Ursule's opening chapter introduces the contradictions and paradoxes of history, kinship, memory and temporality with which the rest of the novel will grapple. Marie Ursule wishes to escape history, on the one hand, because her own history is one of immense suffering and of a sense of powerlessness in the face of that suffering, but she also insists on the possibility of an anticolonial history which emerges from the dreams and memories of enslaved people like herself. The mass suicide is thus *already* history for Marie Ursule, even before it physically takes place: 'She had lived it already night after night when the Sans Peur Regiment met to dream it and to make it true' (*Moon* 15). The text maintains a sense of this alternative, subaltern history

---

11 Trouillot, *Silencing the Past*, p. 17.

alongside an acknowledgement of the event's likely erasure—as suicide and rebellion—from the colonial-historical record, as Marie Ursule's owner, de Lambert, knows he must insist on a different history, he must 'prov[e] that the rebellion was instigated from another estate, prov[e] liability' in order to 'get compensation' (*Moon* 23). Although Marie Ursule feels unfit for the modern, industrialized future she has seen prophetic visions of, those same visions indicate her connection to that future, underscoring her vital, if denied, place in it, as one of the many enslaved people whose physical labour literally and economically built the modern western world.

Her alienation from the world built by her corporeal labour is just one sign of the troubled relationship to the body brought about by its enslavement. According to Marie Ursule's understanding, the body is multiply enslaved: forced to work in the cocoa fields, restricted in movement, regularly flogged, sometimes mutilated or in chains, yet 'burning to live' (*Moon* 18), chained to life, even when it is a life of suffering. Before their suicide, which they understand as an attack upon both these forms of bondage, Marie Ursule and the other enslaved women have long resisted one further means of instrumentalizing and commodifying their bodies: they have refused to bear children. They understand that, in this context, reproduction means primarily the reproduction of wealth and capital for their owner and thus Marie Ursule 'had washed out many from between her legs [...] had vowed never to bring a child into the world, and so to impoverish de Lambert with barrenness as well as disobedience' (*Moon* 8).

Marie Ursule does eventually bear a child, but that child is seemingly independent from birth: it has 'all itself intact' and 'came as if already feeding itself', as though 'it was ready to survive on its own' (*Moon* 8). This independence does not signal the lack of a bond between mother and child, for they are devoted to each other, but it is an example of the ethos of passionate attachment combined with autonomy that is to be found among all the slaves. In preparing for and carrying out their suicide the adult rebel slaves generate similarly intimate but non-coercive bonds among themselves, as 'following was not what was needed for that journey, no one could take you or compel you' (*Moon* 32). This is a queer kinship which joins them together in death even more than in life. When they cut the poison into their veins they become blood brothers and sisters in death, thereby asserting autonomous yet collective control over their lives and bodies. This collective action is organized so that the slaves are both together and apart, sitting in a circle yet arranged so that they cannot see each other, 'so no one would see the other dying and lose courage' (*Moon* 17). Although it marks control of their own bodies, it is also a fight *against* those bodies, because 'they knew that the body was a terrible thing that wanted to live no matter what' (*Moon* 17). It is a kinship which refuses conjugality and genealogy and deprioritizes life and futurity, and yet also one which evokes aspects of normative colonial kinship discourse, especially in the trope of 'blood', which is gradually rewritten and resignified throughout the novel.

The conditions of kinship under enslavement mean that normative kinship is impossible—but these other, queered, forms of kinship are both possible and necessary. The novel thus offers an alternative both to July's claim, in *The Long Song*, of the failure and impossibility of all kinship among slaves (discussed in chapter 3), and to scholars who argue that slavery annihilated kinship among slaves. Orlando Patterson argues that the loss of genealogical knowledge and the erasure of legal relationships based upon genealogical bonds generated the state of 'social death' that he identifies as the paramount condition of the enslaved.[12] While Patterson focuses mostly on slavery's erasure of legal paternity and the resulting erosion of patriarchal authority, Hortense Spillers makes a similar argument about the destruction of kinship as part of her analysis of black women's violent degendering by enslavement and the subsequent experiences of African-American women. For Spillers, an analysis of the 'powerful ties of sympathy' or 'the support systems that African-Americans derived under conditions of captivity' is irrelevant; instead, her emphasis is on the loss of legal rights attached to kinship, replaced by the property rights of the slave owner so that under enslavement, 'kin, just as gender formation, has no decisive legal or social efficacy'.[13] Brand's novel offers a revaluation of this assessment of the relative importance of legal kinship and lived, performed kinship bonds; the text's depiction of slave kinship does not deny the destructive effects of slavery, not does it promise 'restored affiliations' in the form criticized by Saidiya Hartman; rather, the focus is upon the generation of new forms of kinship both as a result of slavery and through *resistance to* slavery.[14]

The figure of Kamena, an escaped former slave who returns on the morning of the mass suicide to take Bola away, demonstrates that the concept of descent, or of a vertical line of (patriarchal) kinship, can have little meaning in the context of enslavement, without naturalizing or mourning either paternity or patriarchy. Many readings of the novel describe Kamena simply as Bola's father, but the text explicitly guards against any such simple designation, instead offering varying and somewhat contradictory explanations of his relationship to Marie Ursule and Bola. On the one hand, the text states that 'Bola was his child too' (*Moon* 7), on the other:

> He was not Marie Ursule's man, not her brother and not her child's father, but they had lain in the same shack and breathed the same air of broken fields and broken hearts. And if something had been done between them, if

---

12 Patterson, *Slavery and Social Death*. Judith Butler argues that Patterson seems to mourn primarily the erosion of enslaved black men's 'natural' patriarchal authority, see Butler, *Antigone's Claim*. The determined childlessness of the women slaves in the novel also stands in contrast to Patterson's argument that slave motherhood was a 'life-affirming action [...] an act of defiance': see Deborah Gray White qtd in Patterson, *Rituals of Blood*, p. 33.
13 Spillers, 'Mama's Baby, Papa's Maybe', pp. 218–19.
14 Hartman, 'The Time of Slavery', p. 762.

their bodies had opened to each other like earth where too much has been planted and the soil gets weary and crumbles, he was still more her brother than her child's father. (*Moon* 34)

In this passage, the text suggests the impossibility or undesirability of a certain kind of kinship even as it affirms the existence of another kind. Kamena is 'not Marie Ursule's man, not her brother and not her child's father', but it is not immediately clear whether this indicates that such positions in kinship are impossible, legally or socially, or whether they are rejected as unfitting or undesirable. The sexual relationship between Marie Ursule and Kamena is placed under erasure, rewritten first as an uncertainty—'*if* something had been done between them'—and then recast as an aspect of the overwork, of both people and land, of plantation slavery—'like earth where too much has been planted'. The novel thus recalls Spillers's argument that slavery destroyed not only kinship but also sexuality: 'sexuality, as a term of implied relatedness, is dubiously appropriate, manageable, or accurate to *any* of the familial arrangements under a system of enslavement, from the master's family to the captive enclave. Under these circumstances, the customary aspects of sexuality, including "reproduction", "motherhood", "pleasure", and "desire", are all thrown in crisis'.[15] Yet at the same time, the text goes beyond Spillers's pronouncement to *also* affirm the existence of a lasting and intimate bond between Marie Ursule and Kamena generated by their shared experiences of enslavement and resistance. It suggests that this bond retains its force and meaning beyond the erasure of legal kinship, and that this bond, this form of kinship, is privileged by Kamena over any possible 'biological' link between himself and Bola; that is, it is privileged over lineage or genealogical descent. Later, during the years that Kamena and Bola live in Culebra Bay, he continues to understand his relation to Bola as a duty owed to Marie Ursule, rather than to Bola herself: 'He bided his time until she grew up so that he would finally have no more obligations to Marie Ursule, already gone her way' (*Moon* 55), thereby again affirming the importance of the bond of experience and resistance over that of genealogy. It is only in the final chapter of the novel, which returns to Bola and Kamena and re-narrates their escape from the plantation and arrival at Culebra Bay, that Kamena is referred to, once, as 'her father' (*Moon* 295). This ambivalence of kinship terms could be read as an indication of the impossibility of fatherhood in a legal sense and its difficulty in a social sense under slavery in the way discussed by Patterson and others. I suggest, however, that it be read more as an attempt, generated out of the collective of enslaved rebels, to go *beyond* the terms offered by normative, genealogical kinship and simultaneously an indication of the difficulty of doing so, of naming or describing kinship or intimate relations outside of normative institutions and practices. The text rejects the available terms and positions in kinship discourse, so that Kamena is 'not Marie Ursule's

---

15 Spillers, 'Mama's Baby, Papa's Maybe', p. 221.

man, not her brother', but has no other words to describe the bond between them—and this contorted relationship to normative kinship, simultaneously inescapable and impossible, desirable or necessary *and* limiting or unfitting, will continue through the novel and its generations.

For Marie Ursule and Kamena, kinship operates primarily horizontally rather than vertically—it is generated by shared dreams, labour and suffering and is not oriented towards a lineage, a future, or immortality through reproduction. Marie Ursule is not opposed to the future; she passionately hopes to give her daughter a chance to reach a future beyond slavery, although she foresees a future of hard labour and gendered violence in which her descendents 'emerge, sore and disturbed, in another century', but she sends Bola into that future 'with no hope of gratitude or remembrance' for herself (*Moon* 21–22). The future 'was not where Marie Ursule would arrive. Bola would go somehow' (*Moon* 47). This difference is shown in the contrast offered between Marie Ursule's diasporic family-to-come and the future descendants of her owner, Monsieur de Lambert: his 'blood would run the same through him to his generations' and he will be found 'in the faces of the photographs that would speak of a great family' (*Moon* 19). In contrast, 'what Marie Ursule is leaving she knows she cannot put into a face' (*Moon* 20). Marie Ursule's distant offspring will not have 'blood' to 'run the same' through their generations; they will not have the promise of essential identity guaranteed by physical similarity, although perhaps she will leave something 'in bones or gestures muscular with dispossession' (*Moon* 19–20). It is again the shared experiences of 'dispossession', suffering and exploitation that will tie Marie Ursule and future generations of her family together.

Bola, Marie Ursule's daughter, does not reject history as her mother does, but she lives for many years in a liminal relationship to it. Her position is underscored by the geography of her home in Culebra Bay, on the edge of the island where the land 'skitter[s] off into islets and rocks' (*Moon* 51). The second chapter of the novel, which recounts Bola's life, begins with the text of a letter from the Lieutenant-Governor of Trinidad, written in 1833 to announce the coming emancipation—but Bola never sees or reads or even hears of this historical document, for 'this grudgeful news does not arrive at Culebra Bay' (*Moon* 51). Marginal though she may be to this official, colonial history—and it to her—nevertheless she grows up surrounded and burdened by the past. Bola's mother once lived in Culebra Bay and two ghostly nuns, the former owners of Marie Ursule, haunt the site. Kamena is also ghostly: he can think only of finding or dreaming his way back to Terre Bouillante, a maroon camp in the mountains, and as he fades away, 'starved with remembering', she feels burdened by the stories and directions he asks her to 'hold' for him (*Moon* 60).

These burdens lead Bola to mistrust stories and instead follow her lusts and her hunger for sensory experiences. These lusts and cravings are momentary, soon forgotten, and Bola seems marked by this forgetting even in, or especially in, matters of kinship: she 'always looked down at her swollen belly in surprise [...] forgetting it was her third child, it was her fourth child, it was her sixth' (*Moon* 67–68). Some critics have seen in Bola's behaviour and particularly her mothering the cause of much suffering in the novel: Erica Johnson describes Bola as a 'mother of forgetting', that is, 'a figure of colonized consciousness who cannot pass on to her children their own histories, or, by extension, a communal, ethnic, or national history'.[16] This reading not only elides the forms of memory practised by Bola and the evidence in the text of future generations with specific knowledge of their forebears (various characters refer to their knowledge of Bola, Kamena and Marie Ursule); it risks blaming subjects like Bola, her sexuality and her mothering, for the ongoing effects of slavery—Johnson argues that by 'refus[ing] to testify' to family history Bola 'bequeath[s] to them the phantom', that is, the trauma, 'whose source lies in her own parents' psychic lives', and she constructs a nationalist and heteronormative model of kinship.[17] For Johnson, kinship means genealogical knowledge, and the purpose of that knowledge is to create national consciousness.

Bola is characterized by cycles of infatuation and forgetting, but she too insists on the power of embodied, sensory memory. She tells her children, 'no matter what it seems, and even after that someone will remember you. And even after that it could be just the whiff or thought of things you loved' (*Moon* 297–98). For Bola, forgetting and remembering are not counterposed, but intrinsically bound together. In the case of her forgotten pregnancies and children, Bola's "forgetting" is not an act of erasing objects of memory from the historical or family record, or her personal memory, but rather it inscribes a mode of relationality, an understanding of kinship, similar to that practised by her mother, and a mode of subjectivity of her own. Bola's temporarily forgets her pregnancies and 'the fathers soon vanished or were forgotten too' (*Moon* 68). (Interestingly, these vanishing men are not accused of perpetuating intergenerational trauma by the novel's critics, perhaps because it would too obviously recall the racist stereotype of absent black fathers.) Bola has a 'self-centredness' and a 'lust' for sensory experiences that puts her at odds with conventional norms—which are also nationalist norms—of femininity and motherhood. Jacqui Alexander writes that

> women's sexual agency, our sexual and our erotic autonomy have always been troublesome for the state. They post a challenge to the ideological anchor of an originary nuclear family, a source of legitimation for the state, which perpetuates the fiction that the family is the cornerstone of society.[18]

---

16 Johnson, 'Unforgetting Trauma'. Johnson takes the term 'mother of forgetting' from Rody, *The Daughter's Return*.
17 Johnson, 'Unforgetting Trauma'.
18 M. Jacqui Alexander, 'Erotic Autonomy as a Politics of Decolonization: An Anatomy of Feminist and State Practice in the Bahamas Tourist Economy', in M. Jacqui Alexander and Chandra Talpade Mohanty (eds.), *Feminist Genealogies, Colonial Legacies, Democratic Futures* (New York: Routledge, 1997), p. 64.

Bola has no interest in forming her children in her own image, or in making herself immortal through future generations: whether or not her children take after her, 'it was nothing to her', and she too, like Marie Ursule before her, has no 'thought of gratitude or remembrance' (*Moon* 68). As this echo of Bola's own mother suggests, like Marie Ursule, Bola both cares for her children and simultaneously leaves them to go their 'own way' (*Moon* 69) and '[grow] by themselves without her assistance' (*Moon* 71). Yet this evidently does not preclude her from passing on both the knowledge of prior generations and with it a certain shared ethic and experience. Decades later, Eula, Bola's great-granddaughter, writes in a letter to her mother, 'I remembered what you said about Marie Ursule with her iron ring, limping through forests' (*Moon* 236), and 'we all loved it when you said that [...] Marie Ursule loved us and sent us to the future because she could not hold us, and in turn we could not hope to hold our own lives together and that was her art and ours' (*Moon* 253). Furthermore, the novel suggests that knowledge about the lives of ancestral relatives and their psychic bequests cannot be easily separated in the way Johnson implies. Later in the novel, Adrian stands in Amsterdam, late at night, some time in the 1980s: 'the street looked to him like blood gone vermilion from air' (*Moon* 179). The scene not only impressionistically recalls the morning of Marie Ursule's mass suicide, when the 'air resembled blood gone bad' as the morning was turning 'vermilion, the colour of old blood' (*Moon* 5), it also shows that Adrian knows about his distant relatives: 'Here he was like Kamena trying to find a destination. [...] He wanted something harder. Cocaine. To hit his head like a sucrier crying at night. Lift him off this square' (*Moon* 180). Adrian's wish to be lifted off the square echoes and re-enacts the actions of Marie Ursule; he searches for drugs to lift him out of this world, just as Marie Ursule aimed to 'take everyone to the heavens' (*Moon* 296) with her poison; it also recalls Kamena's long-ago search for the maroon camp high in the mountains, guided by the sound of a sucrier bird whistling in the night (*Moon* 27–30).

While there may be ways in which a theory of queer diasporic trauma can be derived from the novel, as discussed below, existing scholarship on trauma in Brand's text tends to problematically identify genealogy as a key element of either or both the original traumatic injury or the process by which the psychic wounds of trauma are passed on.[19] These readings naturalize assumptions—such as that kinship requires, and does not exceed, genealogy, and that collective histories must build upon (normative, genealogical) family histories—which are actively questioned by the novel, and the way in which the novel challenges notions of kinship limited to genealogy are not recognized by these readings, which instead subsume the text's imagining of alternative forms of kinship into their narrative of the traumatic loss of

---

19 Johnson, 'Unforgetting Trauma'; Moynagh, 'The Melancholic Structure of Memory'.

genealogical knowledge. The project of questioning of what history is, what its role in identity and subjectivity is, and how it is intertwined with various understandings of kinship, of which genealogy is only one, is central to *At the Full and Change of the Moon*; it is therefore crucial that the relationship of these terms is not set or assumed in advance.

Bola has many children whom the text references in various ways: the stories of some are told in detail, others are referred to only briefly. Some are not mentioned by the narrative at all—or so it seems, if we accept the authority of the family tree printed at the front of the book after the table of contents. This chart casts doubt on 'blood' and biology even as it appears to shore up the centrality of the genealogical; it has been interpreted as a reminder of the genealogical relations of the characters and a help for the reader, others note the lack of 'necessary' father figures.[20] But there are reasons to doubt whether the chart is correct and trustworthy—there are discrepancies between it and the narrative—and whether the relations mapped out by it are genealogical at all. According to the dates on the chart, Bola's first child is born when Bola is twenty years old, the last when she is sixty. Most of the children who feature in the story are born when Bola is in her mid-forties or older. It is therefore not only biological paternity which is obscured by the chart—Bola's biological motherhood is put into some question even as the chart affirms her place as the mother of a vast diaspora. The narrative's descriptions of Bola's children further complicate the chart's status, for the narrative suggests that some of children who are given descriptions rather than proper names in the chart, such as 'the one unrecalled', are not or not only singular persons, but also typologies of colonial and postcolonial subjects. One child is listed in the chart as 'the one who ran to the Rupununi b. 1872'. Is this, or is it not, the same child described in the narrative:

> The one who was born just when the rain falls [...], that one left at fifteen with a man from the Guaripiche who sold her to a waggonload of loggers [...]. She would live from ever and ever, rematerializing along roads where there is forest waiting. She will hike to towns, bringing necessary rain and floods. (*Moon* 70–71)[21]

This child's story offers an individual tale of exploitation, as well as a typology of trans-Caribbean labour migration, moving from Trinidad to the South American

---

20 Moynagh, 'The Melancholic Structure of Memory'; Grandison, 'Bridging the Past and the Future'; Lucy Evans, 'Tidal Poetics in Dionne Brand's *At the Full and Change of the Moon*', *Caribbean Quarterly* 55.3 (2009), p. 6.
21 The correlation of the chart entry with this description in the narrative is questionable, for while the Rupununi and the Guaripiche (also written Guarapiche) are both regions on the South American mainland somewhat close to Trinidad, they are still some 1,000 km apart. Similarly, one could argue that *running away* (to the Rupununi) and *being sold* to loggers are hardly the same, further suggesting that the child listed in the chart and the child described in the narrative are not the same.

mainland for work in the logging industry, and a particularly gendered iteration of such labour migration, evoking a seemingly inevitable partnership of sex work and the forestry industry. Finally, this daughter, who is also a multi-generational collective of women, leaves the realm of human altogether, gaining goddess-like powers to bring 'rain and floods'. As the description enters the domain of the supernatural it reveals as impossible the fantasy of perfect rational categorization promised by the chart, suggesting that human relationships exceed such categories, yet the presence of the chart and its position at the front of the book also suggest the ongoing importance of such structures and categories despite their inadequacy. The puzzles which remain—about the nature of the relationships, the fate of the children, even the existence of some of the children as individual persons—compliment the ambivalence of numerous other descriptions of relationality in the text, emphasizing that these relations are not contained by the terms available to describe them, and that the 'truth' of origins and history cannot be known not, or not only, because it has been lost, but because it is continually remade, retold in the present.

Bola's children, who are real and metaphorical at once, spread across and around the Atlantic. Some of Bola's children do not leave of their own volition, but are given away, often according to a logic of association: 'she gave the serious-eyed one to the serious-eyed man because it must have been his. [...] And she gave the boy who liked golden things [...] to the man from Venezuela whose skin was golden' (*Moon* 69–70). In another case, 'the one who cried incessantly she made in the dry season and milked his tears for water' (*Moon* 71), the presumed temporal logic of a lineage is undone by the reversal effected when the child's ceaseless crying is invoked as the reason for his conception and birth. David Eng suggests that queer diaspora is a means of 'reorganizing national and transnational communities based not on origin, filiation, and genetics but on destination, affiliation, and the assumption of a common set of social practices or political commitments'.[22] The lateral logic of association which organizes parts of Bola's diasporic family—as, for example, when she gives the boy who 'liked golden things' to the man with 'golden' skin—seems to echo Eng's call for a diaspora of affiliation, but overall the diaspora of the novel does not entirely escape the normative language of 'origin, filiation, and genetics' which Eng rejects. Instead, the novel simultaneously deploys *and* undermines the normative force of that language, demonstrating both its ongoing currency *and* its inadequacy to describe postcolonial, diasporic subjectivity.

Bola's being in the world, including her mothering, models Gayatri Gopinath's suggestion that a queer diaspora founded on queer female subjects both overturns the patrilineal, Oedipal logic which usually underlies theorizations of diaspora and challenges 'the logic that situates the terms "queer" and "diaspora" as dependent on the originality of "heterosexuality" and

22 Eng, 'Transnational Adoption and Queer Diasporas', p. 4.

"nation".[23] In Alexander's terms, Bola's 'erotic autonomy brings with it the potential of undoing the nation entirely, a possible chance of irresponsible citizenship or no citizenship at all'.[24] It is not that the presumed temporal order of diaspora and nation are reversed, in the way that Brian Keith Axel argues that all diasporas retrospectively create the homeland or place of origin.[25] Rather, with rare exceptions, the novel's characters are uninterested in origins, valuing instead indirect, non-linear modes of relation. They exemplify Eng's claim that queer diaspora 'declines the normative impulse to recuperate lost origins, to recapture the mother or motherland, and to valorize dominant notions of social belonging and racial exclusion that the nation-state would seek to naturalize and legitimate through the inherited logics of kinship, blood, and identity', with the important exception that those 'logics of kinship, blood, and identity' are not erased in the novel, but reworked; they retain some importance whilst also being succeeded.[26]

Both the story of Bola and the stories to come of her descendants also make clear that, even in the presence of heterosexual relations, *heteronormativity* is impossible for black subjects in the context of colonialism and (post)slavery. Bola and the later generations of Bola's queer family are non-heteronormative less because of their choice of sexual partners or practices (although these, too, are sometimes queer) than because they are 'outside the rational time of capital, nation, and family'.[27] Meg Wesling suggests that 'configurations of family and kinship are rendered particularly queer in the context of diaspora', but Brand's novel offers a reminder that black Atlantic diasporas are displaced from normative sexuality and kinship not only by diaspora, but the history of enslavement as well.[28] Cathy Cohen has argued that the overlap thus generated between the queered 'deviance' of racialized or diasporic kinship and discourses of queer, 'deviant' sexuality is both a technique of discipline and oppression *and* a potential resource for radical alliance politics.[29] Yet in Brand's novel, the queer kinship of diaspora is not necessarily liberatory, and alliance politics are nowhere to be seen; nonetheless, rather, the radical potential of queer kinship is to be found in its challenge to history and narration itself.

The twentieth-century generations of the novel, Bola's grand-children and great-grandchildren, whose stories are told in the remaining chapters, have inherited and enormously magnified the ambivalence suggested in the early

23 Gopinath, *Impossible Desires*, pp. 5, 13.
24 Alexander, 'Erotic Autonomy as a Politics of Decolonization', p. 64.
25 Axel, 'The Context of Diaspora'; Axel, 'The Diasporic Imaginary'.
26 Eng, *The Feeling of Kinship*, pp. 13–14.
27 Roderick A. Ferguson in Dinshaw et al., 'Theorizing Queer Temporalities', p. 180.
28 Wesling, 'Neocolonialism, Queer Kinship, and Diaspora', p. 649.
29 Cohen, 'Punks, Bulldaggers, and Welfare Queens'.

chapters towards both genealogy and kinship, which they both yearn for and reject, alongside an ambivalence towards becoming part of recorded and legitimate history, which they similarly regard with both longing and suspicion. This 'inheritance', however, is not a relic of the past that is passed on intact, whether consciously or unconsciously; rather, it is created and experienced anew in specific historical circumstances as the characters become caught in the cross-currents of conflicting understandings of kinship and the conflicting effects of colonial, postcolonial and anticolonial kinship discourses. In the postslavery era these contradictions generate a deep-seated ambivalence to state-regulated, institutionalized kinship forms that claim to mitigate black diasporic shame, govern bodies and sexualities, and create disciplined subjects. That is, the novel demonstrates a deep suspicion of colonial and neoimperial kinship discourses which demand normative, heteropatriarchal kinship as a key condition and proof of liberal subjecthood and deny the validity of other forms of intimacy, even as black subjects are actively excluded from such normative institutions.

The story of Samuel Sones, Bola's grandson, makes clear the impossibility of black liberal subjecthood within colonial regimes. As a young man who volunteers to fight for the 'mother country, Great Britain' (*Moon* 76) in World War I, Sones appears to epitomize the model of a young man leaving the home and the private sphere to sacrifice himself for the state: the process identified by Judith Butler as the Hegelian subordination of kinship to the state, and the process identified by Hegel as that which creates citizenship.[30] However, as a colonized, black subject, Sones's experience instead confirms him as a non-citizen, a non-actor in history; his service neither creates a tie between him and 'the state'—in part because, in the context of British colonial rule of Trinidad, it is not clear what citizenship would mean—nor does it construct him as a subject worthy of state recognition. During his wartime service, Sones discovers that he has no acknowledged or respected place in either the colony or the metropole or, indeed, the entire western world. He is one of the disavowed, rather than one of the remembered, of modern history; he feels himself to be invisible in any archive. Even when he is released from prison after his dishonourable discharge, 'they let him out as if they had forgotten him' (*Moon* 84). For decades, he punishes himself for his foolish dreams of self-advancement, his belief that 'a man could rise' (*Moon* 79) *and* for his failure to achieve those dreams. Significantly, Sones's loss of faith in history, progress and the

---

30 Butler, *Antigone's Claim*. Hegel writes: 'Sacrifice on behalf of the individuality of the state is the substantial tie between the state and all its members and so is a universal duty', see G. W. F. Hegel, *Hegel's Philosophy of Right*, trans. T. M. Knox (Oxford: Clarendon Press, 1942), § 325. Furthermore, in war, 'the brave youth [...] now has his day and his worth is openly acknowledged', see G. W. F. Hegel, *Phenomenology of Spirit*, trans. A. V. Miller (Oxford: Oxford University Press, 1977), § 475.

mother country also causes him to lose any interest in either genealogical futurity or close bonds of any kind. Only if he had *not* gone to war might he have been 'a young man who could have stayed home and married a girl and made many children' (*Moon* 97), thus undoing the presumed connection between heterosexual kinship and reproduction and state citizenship, that is, undoing the logic of heteronormative history which Butler identifies in Hegel.[31] For Sones, both history and family have become like the pulp in the tamarind tree's seed pods, which looks tempting, 'like some brown jam but was sour' (*Moon* 74). He reflects on the tamarind tree, on whether it was brought from Africa 'by his great-great-grandmother, as a seed in the pocket of her coarse dress' (*Moon* 73), or perhaps from India, 'in his grandfather's cheek or in his broken toes' (*Moon* 74). Sones understands himself to be a diasporic subject, he identifies himself with the tree, and he has some knowledge of the origins of the 'seeds' of his diasporic community, but like the spindly branches of the tamarind tree, his knowledge of his family history provides little comfort.

A generation later in the USA, the impossible desire for a place in recorded history still exists, but the circumstances of life for a black man without legal papers are very different. Priest leaves Trinidad determined to get rich as a dealer, con-man, badjohn, but despite his bravado his is a disavowed and marginal existence. He claims to be in 'the belly of the game', in 'the heart of the world' (*Moon* 173), but his ability to shape-shift—to use different passports, pass as a man or a woman, regularly escape from immigration detention, and always use different names—is not only a result of his charm and cunning but also a sign that he is infinitely exchangeable, only a unit of cheap black labour or a crime statistic. Not only is he not an individual of worth, he is not even an individual. His friend Icepick claims to have been imprisoned in Attica during the riots there, in an attempt to write himself into recorded history and the history of black resistance to US state racism, but they both know it was only 'some prison' (*Moon* 166), as anonymous and exchangeable as the men themselves, not Attica, not during the riots, and not worth recording. Priest's violence might be read as another permutation of historical trauma, but Denise da Silva suggests that such a pathologization of violence, particularly diasporic black male violence, may function only to return authorized violence to white subjects. She suggests that instead we might understand 'violence as a referent of other desires, other figurations of existence, or any other and all possible modes of being human in the world'.[32] Priest's violence might therefore be read as another way of indexing a striving to be otherwise in the world which many of the novel's character's exhibit; a striving for something which they themselves cannot fully imagine or describe, but which they nonetheless yearn for.

31 Butler, *Antigone's Claim*.
32 Denise Ferreira da Silva, 'To Be Announced: Radical Praxis or Knowing (at) the Limits of Justice', *Social Text* 31.1 (2013), p. 53.

Priest both rejects and abuses kinship, claiming to feel no connection to anyone, but more than willing to exploit any remaining bond of loyalty or love that others may feel towards him; this is in large part a result of his status as a disavowed, anonymous subject barely capable of the mutual recognition of kinship. Priest meets Adrian in a detention centre for illegal immigrants in Florida; Adrian is much younger than Priest, but their faces are eerily similar. Priest sees in Adrian's face a sign that the other man is his 'blood' (*Moon* 197). Priest's evocation of *blood*, with its history as a key trope of discourses of race, colonialism and slavery, and of the *face*, move both of these into the space of the camp, apparently reclaiming them for those without papers and without land from the privileged descendants of Monsieur de Lambert.[33] The camp necessarily queers these tropes as well: Priest claims blood but cannot trace a bloodline, suggesting that he and Adrian are connected by something other than the lines of a genealogical chart. Priest sees in Adrian a chance of 'repeating himself' (*Moon* 195), of getting another chance, 'another play' (*Moon* 168), making Adrian at once a repetition of Priest, his son, and a clone: a product of queer autogeneration and diasporic dispersal. While this is a non-heteronormative variation of the tropes of 'extendability'[34] and futurity common to kinship discourses, it is not necessarily liberatory. In the space of the camp—meaning not only the detention centre as the twentieth-century incarnation of the plantation, but for poor, black, diasporic subjects like Priest and Adrian, anywhere in the western world—alternative kinship forms may be equally oppressive.[35] Queer as it may be, Priest's claim upon Adrian is exploitative and abusive, as Priest uses it to forcibly incorporate Adrian into his drug-running business. Adrian is wary of the discourse of 'blood', yet he gets caught in its net. He understands that what Priest calls 'blood' is something much broader and other than a 'biological' relation; he suggests that it is instead the space of the camp which ties them together: 'a place like all places like this, as far back as any blood between Adrian and Priest would go' (*Moon* 197). This place, and the kinship it signifies, 'was both the place Kamena wanted to find and the place he was running from all mixed up in one catastrophe' (*Moon* 197), and Priest and Adrian run from it and towards it as well.

Priest's sister Eula, living in Toronto in the 1980s, also struggles with this same attraction to and repulsion from kinship ties. In a letter to her dead mother she expresses a desire for a normative genealogy and a sense of home:

---

33 I use 'camp' here in the sense of Giorgio Agamben, *Homo Sacer: Sovereign Power and Bare Life*, trans. Daniel Heller-Roazen (Stanford: Stanford University Press, 1998).
34 Freeman, 'Queer Belongings', p. 297.
35 Jared Sexton argues that Giorgio Agamben is mistaken to date 'the advent of the paradigm of the camp' to the European interwar years of the twentieth century—rather, it is Atlantic slavery which instituted the camp. See Jared Sexton, 'People-of-Color-Blindness: Notes on the Afterlife of Slavery', *Social Text* 28.3 (2020), p. 40.

> I would like one single line of ancestry, Mama. One line from you to me and farther back, but a line that I can trace. [...] A line that I can reach for in my brain when I feel off kilter. Something to pull me back. I want a village and a seashore and a rock out in the ocean and the certainty that when the moon is in full the sea will rise. (*Moon* 246–47)

Often read by critics as a simple desire for that which she supposedly lacks—an unbroken family line, and the unitary personhood and place in history that it promises—Eula's professed longing for the simplicity and security represented by a 'line' of genealogical kinship is complicated and contradictory on several levels. First, it is contradicted by Eula's own life and migration choices: she has never returned to Trinidad since moving to Toronto; she has cut off all contact with her sisters who also live there; she writes this letter to her mother only after her mother's death. Her own 'biological' daughter lives in Trinidad, unaware of Eula's existence (she understands Eula's mother, her genealogical grandmother, to be her mother), thereby erasing the 'line' between Eula and the child. The yearning for a geographical home expressed in these lines is jarring, because the landscape Eula longs for *is* the landscape of Culebra Bay, the home of her great-grandmother and at one time her great-great-grandmother, and Eula knows it—she has an old drawing of the bay made by Bola. Yet she sends back the drawing with her letter, saying she has no use for it. She simultaneously yearns for family history and an ancestral home and rejects them, just as she claims to want a genealogical line and acts herself to break it—all these desires are deeply ambivalent, both painful and soothing, inescapable and inadequate, demonstrating the complexity of the losses and longings of her diasporic subjectivity. Her desire for a line of ancestry echoes her love of maps, whose 'definite lines brought order', whose 'steadiness steadied' her (*Moon* 231). Yet her use of random maps to help her find her way also demonstrates how '*misdirections* become the way for diasporic Africans—always painfully, always partially'.[36] Although Eula seeks lines of ancestry as a comfort, she rejects kinship in practice: not only has she cut off contact with her birth family, but she 'didn't want anyone bothering me or holding me up' (*Moon* 232–33), and instead seeks 'people who didn't want me at their bedsides or when they hurt themselves, others who would not ask and not expect' (*Moon* 239).

Eula's story makes clear that her fraught relationship to kinship is caused at least as much by contemporary kinship discourses, which premise the recognition of personhood on a certain family form, as it might be a result of her family history and the psychic inheritance it entails. First Eula ends her relationship with her sister because of Sese's attempts to enforce a particular model of migrant, black, female subjectivity through a disciplining of Eula's behaviour, clothes, work, friendships and sexuality.

---

36 Tinsley, 'Black Atlantic, Queer Atlantic', p. 208, emphasis added.

Later, she experiences her lover's expectations of family life as a form of violence: she feels 'choked' and 'want[s] to run' (*Moon* 248). When she becomes pregnant, the gendered expectations attached to motherhood cause her to reject the role entirely. She prefers connections of an abstract and impersonal kind, such as the pleasure she gets from sorting letters in the post office and seeing the many places they come from. The pleasure she gains from handling the letters recalls her mother, who 'loved letters from abroad' (*Moon* 255), even as the difference between Eula and her mother—her mother read the letters from her emigrant children, and always believed the unflaggingly happy stories contained therein, Eula only sorts the letters and does not read them—suggests Eula's mistrust of promises of textual transparency or truth (thus putting into further doubt the truth claims of her own letter to her mother). Using the letters, she creates a map of connections: 'I put a small red dot [on a map] at every town in the world that I remember sorting that day' (*Moon* 231). Despite her doubts about communicative or textual truth, this labour makes apparent Eula's ongoing attachment to intimate communication, however partial, as she diligently records the places from which unknown people have written to unknown others. It also demonstrates her investment in movement and displacement themselves, as well as to all who have reason to write such letters; it generates connections to all those with non-local bonds, to a global diaspora of transnational migrants and travellers.

The effect of contemporary gender norms and migration and labour patterns upon the characters' attitudes to kinship are made clear by another young woman of Eula's generation, Maya. She moves from Curaçao to Amsterdam to leave behind the memory of her father and his violence—a violence enabled by the officially sanctioned patriarchy of institutional kinship: when her father hits her, as he does regularly, she feels 'the heavy dull ring on [his] marriage finger' (*Moon* 218) against her face. But in Amsterdam she discovers that such violent, gendered regimes of institutionalized kinship and domesticity are difficult to escape, not least because of her dependence on various forms of emotional labour. She refuses the quasi-domestic work of a trainee nurse in a hospital for the elderly, choosing instead to earn her living as a sex worker. Thus she hopes to live in the moment, as if 'this moment were all she must live' (*Moon* 207), and to 'drift' (*Moon* 215) through life. To *drift* signifies not so much Glissantian 'errantry' as a spectral existence; to Maya the word 'suggest[s] streams of her appearing and dissipating in air' (*Moon* 215), and this contrasts sharply with the mute fleshiness she attributes to domestic life, which she imagines as a form of feminized labour in which married women work at 'decorating the abattoir where they were soon slaughtered' (*Moon* 212).[37] But she cannot escape domesticity, because she is required to simulate it even in her window in

---

37 Glissant, *Poetics of Relation*.

the red-light district. As a black woman, she is further expected to provide exoticism and cosmopolitanism to her white clients, for whom she is a 'way of knowing the world like a sophisticate, a man who crossed boundaries and therefore a man who was dangerous' (*Moon* 211); her racialized, displayed body is way for these men to escape the limitations of the body, to achieve the elitist, cosmopolitan, 'gendered privilege of knowing no bodies', or in Donna Haraway's formulation, 'a conquering gaze from nowhere'.[38] For Maya, however, such a disembodied, drifting, borderless existence proves ever more elusive. After she marries a client to escape from her pimp, she finds herself again held still: trapped in front of the television, anchored to domesticity and materiality by a husband and child. Like Eula, Maya has tried to escape her family stories, but her even more precarious socio-economic position leaves her drowning in a flood of them.

A comparison to Maya's story which makes the socio-economic component of Maya's fate clear is that of Cordelia Rojas, a generation older, who is perhaps the only identifiably *happy* figure in the novel. She too initially accepts marriage as the price of material survival and accepts the associated strictures of sexual and kinship normativity for many years; at the age of fifty, however, she abandons all social proprieties, ostentatiously takes two lovers, a man and a woman, and cannot be swayed from pursuing her desires by the complaints of her husband, adult children or other community members. As a mature woman she chooses 'the enjoyment of her body clear and free' (*Moon* 121) over the more conventional hopes she had had as a young woman, when 'she imagined one day a piano in her living room with a photograph atop it of her children and her husband standing and her seated in the centre' (*Moon* 109). She thereby rejects the standard of white colonial kinship, choosing no longer to emulate the slave owner de Lambert, in chapter one, whose family feature in 'photographs on the mantelpiece' (*Moon* 19) while Marie Ursule's kinship goes unrecorded. While Freeman has suggested that 'not only queer belongings but mainstream families themselves come into being through visual technologies', Cordelia is no longer interested in recognition or validation.[39] The luminous happiness of Cordelia's story is a striking exception to most chapters of the novel, but her socio-economic situation is also an exceptional one: she lives during a time of rare prosperity and full employment in Trinidad due to the burgeoning oil industry, and it is her material well-being after a lifetime of work that enables her comparative freedom.

The novel thus inhabits normative and, in part, colonial discourses of kinship and genealogy to reveal both their ongoing valency *and* their

---

38 Bruce Robbins, 'Comparative Cosmopolitanisms', in Pheng Cheah and Bruce Robbins (eds.), *Cosmopolitics: Thinking and Feeling beyond the Nation* (Minneapolis: University of Minnesota Press, 1998), p. 248; Donna Haraway qtd in Robbins, 'Comparative Cosmopolitanisms', p. 248.
39 Freeman, 'Queer Belongings', p. 307.

inadequacy for the racialized, gendered, postcolonial, diasporic subjects of the novel. The novel is haunted not so much by the loss of genealogical knowledge as such, but by the dual spectre of cultural unintelligibility and patriarchal oppression which it entails in the present. As long as genealogical kinship is demanded by various colonial and postcolonial discourses and institutions as a condition of recognition as a full human subject, then this 'loss' is doubly bitter for black diasporic subjects: the erasure of genealogical ties by slavery and colonialism makes impossible that which is then demanded as a condition of recognition, as one condition of being what Judith Butler terms a 'grievable life'.[40] At the same time, as long as material survival, citizenship rights and transnational migration options continue to be based upon normative, patriarchal kinship forms, black diasporic subjects must continue to subject themselves to the violence which that normativity entails as a part of their survival strategies. The twentieth-century characters of Brand's novel struggle for and against both normative and non-normative kinship forms; they twist within the straitjacket of kinship discourse; their many contradictions demonstrate their position in this bind of kinship: they simultaneously yearn for it and run from it, they recognize it as unsatisfactory or damaging and long for it as well.

In a similar way, they both utilize and resignify the metaphor of 'blood'. For the family of de Lambert, the owner of Marie Ursule, 'blood' is first a liability or mark of quality: Monsieur de Lambert himself is 'mercifully removed from any black blood' (*Moon* 13). Blood is also a code for the promise of continuity, of future wealth and power for the de Lambert family: 'his blood would run the same through him to his generations' (*Moon* 19). Elements of these colonial metaphors re-emerge at times, such as when a description of Cordelia as having 'a waywardness that had been passed down and passed down by blood and was responsible for the child Cordelia threw away' (*Moon* 100) suggests that her 'blood' carries the taint of moral degeneracy. When Cordelia moves from Venezuela to Trinidad after procuring an abortion, the text notes that 'she had arrived at the small country of her blood' (*Moon* 120–21), suggesting an essentialized connection to the island due to her genealogical link to Bola—yet this explanation is undermined by the uncertainty of Bola's 'biological' or 'blood' relation to her children. Nonetheless, the text also describes Bola's legacy to her children in terms of blood: 'If the language describing their life was her lusory idiom, it was not because she gave it but because she gave it by blood without thought of gratitude or remembrance' (*Moon* 68). Something is passed on by blood, unconsciously or unwittingly, but it is no longer coded as a form of pollution—black blood or moral waywardness—but a mode of relation to the world, a playful relation that undermines the seriousness attributed to blood in colonial discourse.

40 Butler, *Precarious Life*.

The beginnings of a resignification of blood can be discerned here, whereby blood begins to connote not an essential, inescapable dimension of a person, nor a guaranteed lineage, but is a sign of connection or shared experience, a medium of transmission and perhaps also of transformation. Priest's claim on Adrian, 'I sure you is my blood', is rewritten by Adrian to mean their shared experience of the camp and before that, the plantation, which goes 'as far back as any blood […] would go' (*Moon* 197). At the very beginning of the novel, on the morning of the mass suicide, when 'the air resembled blood gone bad' (*Moon* 5), blood is the sign of the significance of the morning, a morning out of the ordinary, a 'morning of doing something that was not directed or ordered from outside' (*Moon* 15) and thereby overturning the frozen temporality of the plantation, where 'every turning stood still' (*Moon* 9). On 'a morning turning from ochre to white with the smell of frozen blood' (*Moon* 17), the slaves cut the poison into their veins, mixing the poison into their blood and mingling their blood together on the blade of the knife. As they cut the poison into their flesh, 'the woorara tar was a river flowing through their hands. A river they were going to, to wash themselves of this life and Mon Chagrin and all the other places they had been' (*Moon* 16). Their blood becomes a medium of bondage *and* release, freeing them from slavery and suffering and binding them together, a sign of their shared experience, shared resistance, and the means of their transformation.

The transformative power of blood is not only personal, but may have historiographical ramifications. After the suicide of the others, Marie Ursule is slowly tortured to death by her owner: 'Her grey dress was clotted with blood. The threads were stiff and rewoven in the bleeding of her body' (*Moon* 22). Her flowing and clotting blood alters the fabric of her dress, both adding to and interrupting the 'signifying practices' of textiles in the New World;[41] in the same way, blood and bleeding—and the suffering it often signals (if rarely quite as brutally as in the case of Marie Ursule)—has the capacity to alter and reweave the fabric of history in the novel, although not necessarily in a way controlled or directed by wilful or autonomous actors, just as Marie Ursule does not and cannot know what will become of her future generations. For Kamena in the maroon camp, 'entering Terre Bouillante was like entering his own blood. Tangled in the rope and in the trees, he gave up any control, his body becoming porous and falling apart like rotted meat' (*Moon* 30). Rather than signally inevitability or control over history, as 'blood' does for de Lambert, for Kamena it signals becoming-by-undoing as he gives up control and his body becomes 'porous'. Generations later, Maya experiences her menstrual bleeding as a pleasure in power withheld or redirected: 'she felt euphoric at the warm feel of her blood gushing uncontrollably as if a breath was let out, as if rightly she could give birth to the world and wouldn't […]. Not even the window could

---

41 Danielle C. Skeehan, 'Caribbean Women, Creole Fashioning, and the Fabric of Black Atlantic Writing', *The Eighteenth Century* 56.1 (2015), pp. 105–23.

contain her when she was bleeding' (*Moon* 221), and this transformative power contained in her body and her history are balanced against the socioeconomic factors which would keep her trapped in place.

In the last chapters of the novel, both the burdens of the past and the desire for other futures are emphasized, in two chapters that fit (appropriately enough) somewhat uncomfortably with one another. In the penultimate fragment, Eula's 'biological' daughter, also named Bola, refuses to accept the death of her mother (that is, the woman she considers her mother, who is also Eula's mother), and instead convinces her ghost to return home from the cemetery so that they may live together again. Living with her ghostly mother, eventually Bola too 'turn[s] to a ghost' so that she is 'there and not there' (*Moon* 278). Some critics identify this young Bola as a paradigmatic melancholic who refuses to mourn the loss of her mother, and whose 'withdrawal from the world speaks to the burden of the "rupture in history" that is the Middle Passage'.[42] In Moynagh's reading it is not the death of Bola's mother directly that drives Bola to isolate herself; rather, that death is a symbol of 'the loss of an origin, the loss of genealogical knowledge attributable to the experience of diaspora'.[43] According to this logic, Bola is driven mad by a lack of genealogical knowledge and the non-normative kinship forms which characterize her family history. Yet considering the violence and oppression which normative, heteropatriarchal kinship has been shown to cause in the novel, particularly for women like Eula, Maya and Cordelia, there is good cause to read the second Bola's story differently.

In recent years several thinkers have offered queer of colour oriented reworkings of Freud's concepts, seeking to depathologize melancholia and to understand it in diasporic and postcolonial contexts. Rather than understanding melancholia as a refusal to grieve and let go which leads to a withdrawing from the world, José Esteban Muñoz, David Eng and Shinhee Han all argue that it can instead be understood as a tactic of political struggle or simply an everyday migrant experience which keeps the dead—whether a person or a lost object, like the diasporic homeland—active in the present.[44] Building on this work and following Edward Said, Neville Hoad suggests that African cosmopolitanism 'may bear some relation to a depathologized melancholia that seeks to refigure identity and sociality' by recognizing

---

42 Moynagh, 'The Melancholic Structure of Memory', p. 66; see also Johnson, 'Unforgetting Trauma'.
43 Moynagh, 'The Melancholic Structure of Memory', p. 66.
44 José Esteban Muñoz, *Disidentifications: Queers of Color and the Performance of Politics* (Minneapolis: University of Minnesota Press, 1999); David L. Eng and Shinhee Han, 'A Dialogue on Racial Melancholia', *Psychoanalytic Dialogues* 10.4 (2000), pp. 667–700; David L. Eng, 'Melancholia/ Postcoloniality: Loss in *The Floating Life*', *Qui Parle* 11.2 (1999), pp. 137–50.

that 'the self/other relations are structured not only in antagonistic reaction formation, but that the self is indebted to the other in more proximate and intimate ways'.[45] In a similar vein, Johnson understands Bola's life-with-ghosts as one which 'provides hospitality for the ghosts [...] sustaining their presence in the world'.[46] But while young Bola's kinship with her ghostly mother might be seen as another form of disavowed, diasporic kinship that cannot be recognized within colonial modernity—including by her sisters, whom young Bola describes as 'unfaithful' (*Moon* 269) to their dead mother—it is questionable whether young Bola's life is to be understood as a model of how to live, any more than it is a warning against the supposed pathologies of non-genealogical kinship. Rather, the text suggests that this too is unsatisfactory—the wounds of neither slavery nor the racist present can be salved by young Bola's melancholia or her alternative writing of a history in which the past is kept alive.

Rather than remaining trapped in melancholia, the novel gestures at finding new ways of being and moving in a black Atlantic context. This movement beyond given frameworks of kinship and history is imagined by Marie Ursule at the beginning of the novel, when she envisions how her future diasporic family would not stay enclosed 'in photographs on the mantelpiece [...] in the old house', but instead would 'spill all over floors and glass cases and the verandas and the streets in the new world coming' (*Moon* 19–20). This is a vision of an uncertain future which does not deny the suffering it may entail, but which, in imagining lives which will spill—like spilled blood and flood tides—out of the frame of racist colonial modernity, offers radical and yet unknown possibilities. In this way, the novel seeks new ways of responding not only to the traumas of history but also the contemporary trauma of historicity. Trouillot argues that we must constantly renegotiate historicity to understand how the present moment shapes and punctures the representation of the past and the inevitable gaps in each story.[47] The 'rupture in history' identified by Moynagh (by which she means the destruction of kinship and loss of genealogical knowledge) is not contained in the past, nor is it present only as a traumatic phantom.[48] Rather, the historical cut which produces the characters of the novel as outside history is continually recreated and filtered through contemporary kinship discourses (including those of some critics) and their relation to the economic exploitation, imperial aggression, and the racialized

---

45　Neville Hoad, *African Intimacies: Race, Homosexuality, and Globalization* (Minneapolis: University of Minnesota Press, 2007), p. 116.
46　Johnson, 'Unforgetting Trauma'.
47　Trouillot, *Silencing the Past*.
48　Moynagh, 'The Melancholic Structure of Memory', p. 66. 'Rupture in history' is a quotation from Dionne Brand, *A Map to the Door of No Return: Notes to Belonging* (Toronto: Doubleday Canada, 2001), p. 5. However, I argue that the term—including Brand's use of the term—should be interpreted very differently to Moynagh.

Dionne Brand's At the Full and Change of the Moon

gender and sexual norms of a particular historical moment and location. Another history writing is necessary, but it is not enough.

Brand's novel does not provide a happy ending; it indulges in neither 'nostalgic [nor] promissory forms of happiness'.[49] It refuses to idealize any past, nor does it promise that the future will definitely be happy. But it offers a sense that it is sometimes possible, although difficult, to move differently through the world, to respond to the past differently, and relate to one another differently—it offers *happier futures, perhaps*.[50] The story of the second, young Bola is not the final chapter of the novel. The final chapter returns to the first Bola to remind us of her remarkable practices of relationality: to her children, with her insistence that 'no one is anyone's' (*Moon* 298), to the sea and to the whales—it thereby suggests the limits of communication, writing and historiography, and gestures at connections nonetheless.[51] In Brand's novel, the sea is not history nor a graveyard; rather its flowing tides and currents, which both dissolve and connect dispersed people and lands at once, offer a means of fluid and flexible attachment—perhaps not a submarine *unity*, but a submarine potential for connection.[52]

The shattering and dissolving which will create Dionne Brand's unknown futures stand in clear contrast to July's vision of the future in Andrea Levy's novel, which hopes only to rise to the top of the colonial hierarchy. In Levy's text, voices other than those of July and Thomas remain in the margins: there, they may show the limits of July's narrative, but they do not write history themselves. In Jennifer Terry's terms, this is 'deviance as a taxonomic mode', in which alternative but marginalized voices function to construct a narrative such as July's as 'normal' and desirable.[53] In Brand's text, in contrast, such 'other' voices are the only voices of the novel; the text offers instead 'deviance as a counterdiscursive mode'.[54] Brand's characters—lost, wayward or drifting—pose more of a challenge to the narrative conventions of both historical fiction and conventional historiography than July and Thomas, the wilful, self-possessed subjects of a national narrative. The disjointed lives narrated in Brand's novel refuse the normative temporality of national, modern heteronormativity, just as the fragmentary and looping structure of the novel offers an inchoate and at times incoherent history. Thus July's

---

49 Sara Ahmed, 'Happy Futures, Perhaps', in E. L. McCallum and Mikko Tuhkanen (eds.), *Queer Times, Queer Becomings* (Albany: State University of New York Press, 2011), p. 160.
50 Ahmed, 'Happy Futures, Perhaps'.
51 Jonathan Steinwand, 'What the Whales Would Tell Us: Cetacean Communication in Novels by Witi Ihimaera, Linda Hogan, Zakes Mda, and Amitav Ghosh', in Elizabeth DeLoughrey and George B. Handley (eds.), *Postcolonial Ecologies: Literatures of the Environment* (Oxford: Oxford University Press, 2011), pp. 182–99.
52 'The unity is sub-marine', from Edward Kemau Brathwaite, is one of the epigraphs in Glissant, *Poetics of Relation*.
53 Terry, 'Theorizing Deviant Historiography', p. 300.
54 Terry, 'Theorizing Deviant Historiography', p. 300.

efforts to upset colonial historiography by inhabiting it and rewriting it from within are set against Brand's queer anti-history: a story which drifts at times on the tide, and which does not know where it will lead or end, and which thereby offers a story of the enduring afterlife of slavery and colonialism, but which also, despite its bleakness, contains moments of and strategies for anticolonial resistance, especially in its rewriting of diasporic kinship. While July pursues normative kinship as a means to enter and write history, Brand's characters insist on some way of becoming otherwise, on others ways of being, connecting and remembering.

Part III

Queer diasporic relationality

CHAPTER FIVE

Queer creolization in Patrick Chamoiseau's *Texaco*

Texaco offers an engagement with many of the themes to be found in Levy's *The Long Song* and Brand's *At the Full and Change of the Moon*, including questions of post- or decolonial historiography and the place of narration and storytelling amidst the weight of colonial history, although its somewhat different reworking of these debates is influenced by its setting on Martinique, a department of France rather than an independent postcolonial nation-state, like the Jamaica which Levy's novel looks forward to. While Levy's novel imagines the bourgeois heterosexual family as the fundament of the postcolonial nation, and Brand's novel gestures towards, but does not explicitly imagine alternative forms of diasporic and postcolonial community, in Chamoiseau's text the tussle with historiography—its 'ability to unravel their History into our thousand stories'—is centrally connected to its project of imagining a form of creolized community as an alternative to the ongoing racism and neocolonialism of its troubled relationship to France.[1] This creolized community and subjectivity, I suggest, rests upon a partial and ambivalent, yet crucial sidestepping of the logics of biological kinship and genealogical lineage, in order to subvert Martinique's oft invoked ties to the 'so-good mother France' (101) ['la si bonne mère France'].[2]

The novel can be understood as a fictional exploration of many ideas from the work of Édouard Glissant, particularly as expressed in his *Poetics of Relation*. The debt to Glissant is made very clear: Glissant provides one

---

1 Patrick Chamoiseau, *Texaco*, trans. Rose-Myrian Réjouis and Val Vinokurov (New York: Vintage International, 1998), p. 54. All further English quotations are taken from this edition and page numbers are given in the text as *Tex*.
2 Patrick Chamoiseau, *Texaco* (Paris: Gallimard Folio, 1992), p. 133. All further French quotations are taken from this edition and page numbers are given in the text.

of the epigraphs of the novel and the epigraph of its epilogue, the opening timeline is adapted from Glissant's *Caribbean Discourse*, and Glissant's writing is invoked by one of the characters as a model for an open and transformational poetics that would enable, rather than immobilize, becoming. Glissant's concepts—of marronage, for example, and Caribbean historiography—are referenced more or less explicitly throughout the text. I wish to focus on another Glissantian influence in *Texaco*—one that is explored and partly problematized in the novel—that has received no attention in readings of Chamoiseau's novel and, more surprisingly, very little attention in Glissant scholarship: Glissant's theorization of black Atlantic—that is, postslavery—kinship and its relationship to diaspora and creolization. I argue that kinship in the novel is shown to be necessarily displaced from colonial ideals of genealogy, or 'filiation' in Glissant's terms, and that this can be understood as a form of queered community and culture, in that it undoes the assumption that culture and cultural reproduction is built upon and guaranteed by genealogy, filiation, or heteronormativity. In *Poetics of Relation*, Glissant suggests that such a displacement is inevitably the case in the Caribbean due to its history, and that it represents the avant garde of a world in which filiation is being gradually swept aside—but the novel suggests that recognizing and accepting this displacement, rather than longing for filiation, is a more difficult and ambivalent process for colonized and postcolonial subjects than Glissant accounts for, and that filiation continues to operate as a technology of power in European colonialist discourses.

Despite Glissant's close attention to the two kinds of relationality he names 'filiation' and 'Relation', this aspect of his thought has only rarely been explored for its implications for kinship. Instead, his theory of Relation is often read as pertaining to relations between cultures or between a subject and the world than as a means of theorizing relationality, including intimate kinship, between subjects, or, at most, as having consequences for identity rather than kinship.[3] Michael Dash notes that for Glissant, both in *Caribbean Discourse* (*Le discours antillais*) and in his novel *Le quatrième siècle*, 'the longing for pure origins and a clear line of descent is an impossible dream', and that Caribbean history means that linearity is inevitably and irretrievably lost; a similar reading is occasionally offered of Glissant's novels, but only rarely of his philosophical works.[4]

---

3 See for example Nick Nesbitt, *Caribbean Critique: Antillean Critical Theory from Toussaint to Glissant* (Liverpool: Liverpool University Press, 2013). Britton mentions the critique of filiation in passing but quickly moves on to identity: see Celia M. Britton, *Edouard Glissant and Postcolonial Theory: Strategies of Language and Resistance* (Charlottesville: University of Virginia Press, 1999).

4 J. Michael Dash, *Edouard Glissant* (Cambridge: Cambridge University Press, 1995), p. 76. There is more discussion of family in *Le quatrième siècle* along similar lines on pp. 72–90. For a similar reading of the novel *La Case du commandeur*, see Richard D. E. Burton, 'Comment Peut-on Etre Martiniquais?: The Recent Work of Edouard Glissant', *Modern Language Review* 79.2 (1984), pp. 301–12.

More recently, Valérie Loichot has argued that the concept of Relation is concretely linked to kinship in Glissant's later work, particularly *Faulkner, Mississippi*, and she reads Glissantian kinship as 'a complex, wounded, and inextricable interracial family whose black and white [descendants] are stuck in the same house'—a definition carried over in Loichot's own work on the narrative creation and maintenance of 'post-plantation' kinship.[5]

This reduction of Glissant's theory of kinship to a troubled domestic scene is perhaps too hasty. Without it, the similarities of Glissant's work to current work on queer diaspora, for example, become clear, offering another way to bring Francophone and Anglophone Caribbean theorizing, as well as literature, into dialogue with one another. The commonalities between different Caribbeans, and between Caribbean and other black Atlantic experiences and philosophies can thus be brought to the fore.[6] In *Poetics of Relation*, Glissant offers a theory of kinship which suggests that a *discourse* of kinship, which he terms 'filiation', has long been central to European understandings of time and history, has underpinned major forms of European literature and has been adopted and used as a technique of imperialist aggression. Filiation is a claim to community or national belonging on the basis of genealogical legitimacy, that is, on the ability to trace one's genealogy backwards in time to the supposed origin of a community. By generating a 'fixed linearity of time, always toward a projection, a project' it inaugurates a form of historiography and justifies imperialist expansion and conquest: 'Territorial conquest and scientific discovery (the terms are interchangeable) were reputed to have equal worth. The absolute of ancient filiation and conquering linearity, the project of knowledge and arrowlike nomadism, each used the other in its growth'.[7] Thus, with imperialist conquest the ideal of filiation also spread to Europe's colonies. Glissant's theory of kinship and colonialism is thus far similar to the work of Povinelli and Rifkin, as well as to that of Johannes Fabian.[8] While all of those scholars engage more thoroughly with the history of anthropological kinship studies than Glissant (who only forays very briefly into the territory of traditional kinship studies with his comments on 'matriarchal' societies),[9] the broad thrust of the argument is similar: European cultures lay great value on genealogy, and this value was exported to Europe's colonies as a norm and measure of supposed civilization, alongside a linked concept of strictly linear time and historical progress.

5 Valérie Loichot, 'We Are All Related: Edouard Glissant meets Octavia Butler', *Small Axe* 13.3 (2009), p. 38; Loichot, *Orphan Narratives*.
6 The difficulties that have sometimes been encountered in this cross-Caribbean and trans-Atlantic project are discussed in Kathleen Gyssels, 'The "barque ouverte" (Glissant) or *The Black Atlantic* (Gilroy): Erasure and Errantry', in Bénédicte Ledent and Pilar Cuder-Domínguez (eds.), *New Perspectives on the Black Atlantic: Definitions, Readings, Practices, Dialogues* (Bern: Peter Lang, 2012), pp. 59–82.
7 Glissant, *Poetics of Relation*, pp. 47, 56.
8 Povinelli, *The Empire of Love*; Rifkin, *When Did Indians Become Straight?*; Fabian, *Time and the Other*.
9 Glissant, *Poetics of Relation*, p. 60.

Glissant's key difference from these other scholars lies in his claim that colonial discourses of kinship and filiation are bound to fail in colonized lands. While he acknowledges the 'forms of domination perpetuated by present-day heirs of the discoverers and of their intentions to restore filiation "elsewhere"—by imposing familial or cultural models and ways of life or settings for this', that is, the violent imposition of kinship norms upon enslaved, transported and colonized peoples and cultures, he suggests that this project has no chance of success: 'taking root, henceforth, will be of a different nature. It is in relation. Filiation cannot be replanted elsewhere; its myth is not infinitely disclosable; and Oedipus cannot be exported—into the expanse of extension'.[10] Thus, for Glissant, the emergence of alternative understandings and practices of kinship in the black Atlantic, in the wake of the slave ships, is an inevitability rather than attributable to resistance by colonized peoples, as Rifkin suggests. Nonetheless, these positions remain in many ways compatible, as while Glissant claims that filiation was bound to come undone in the colonies, he also suggests that the specific alternatives which developed were very much connected to the practices of resistance and survival of the enslaved. He suggests that 'the Plantation is one of the focal points for the development of present-day modes of Relation' where 'forms of humanity stubbornly persisted' despite the dehumanization, domination and oppression of slavery.[11]

Glissant does not mean that 'forms of humanity' or of relationality persisted *unchanged*, however; the Plantation did not preserve African modes of kinship and personhood. Rather, his claim that on the plantation 'the tendencies of our modernity begin to be detectable' because there, the logic of filiation and legitimacy 'comes undone' as entirely new cultures emerge which cannot call upon filiation due to their violent separation from their African past.[12] The plantation also marked the emergence of a culture of slavery in which Europeans themselves changed the meaning of filiation, legitimacy and paternity on the basis of race: as Spillers and Patterson argue, black—but also often white—paternity became meaningless in the context of slavery, just as kinship bonds between enslaved persons were unrecognized by slave codes and colonial laws. Glissant extends this insight to argue that white slave owners thereby contributed to the emptying out of the meaning and power of filiation and legitimacy.

This legacy has created the cultural and social forms that Glissant refers to as 'expanse [l'éntendue]'.[13] This is understood to mean not only family forms which Glissant argues are typical for the Caribbean, including 'generations are caught up within an extended family in which our root stocks have diffused' and an 'extended family style' characterized by the 'pileup of patronyms, of

10 Glissant, *Poetics of Relation*, pp. 60–61, see also p. 56.
11 Glissant, *Poetics of Relation*, p. 65.
12 Glissant, *Poetics of Relation*, pp. 65, 61.
13 Glissant, *Poetics of Relation*, p. 53.

mixings of blood whether forced or not, of double lineages (black and white)', but more generally in a 'relation to the other' that threatens the colonial order by insisting on democratic forms of political legitimacy and social organization.[14] Glissant refers to this as a 'force of opacity' in which disparate elements '[join] one another (without conjoining, that is, without merging) in the expanse of Relation'.[15] Another name for this process is creolization, which Glissant defines as 'not merely an encounter' and not merely *métissage*, but 'a new and original dimension allowing each person to be there and elsewhere, rooted and open':

> If we posit *métissage* as, generally speaking, the meeting and synthesis of two differences, creolization seems to be a limitless *métissage*, its elements diffracted and its consequences unforeseeable. Creolization diffracts, whereas certain forms of *métissage* can concentrate one more time.[16]

Thus, métissage works in a way analogous to a concept of (hetero)sexual reproduction, in which two, and only two, different substances produce a synthesis of themselves—this, Schneider suggests, is the dominant imaginary of kinship as sexual reproduction in Euro-American cultures—while creolization is more chaotic, open, transformational and queer.[17]

The queer potential of Glissant's thought has not gone unnoticed among scholars in queer studies, but his work has not yet been drawn upon in recent work on queer kinship or queer diaspora.[18] Glissant's insistence on the queerness of black Atlantic cultures—violently wrenched away from any claims to filiation, and having developed a 'vivid genius' not dependent on roots, origins or linearity, but on a 'transversality' and 'inexhaustible tangle', is nonetheless eminently suitable for thinking about the queerness of diasporic kinship, community and relationality.[19] While Glissant distances his work from the concept of 'creoleness' (*créolité*), preferring 'creolization', a similar queered kinship can also be discerned in the etymology of *créolité*, even if this potential was not explored—indeed, it seems actively denied—in Bernabé, Chamoiseau

14 Glissant, *Poetics of Relation*, pp. 72, 58, 53.
15 Glissant, *Poetics of Relation*, p. 62.
16 Glissant, *Poetics of Relation*, p. 34.
17 Schneider, *A Critique of the Study of Kinship*.
18 See for example Zach Blas, 'Opacities: An Introduction', *Camera Obscura* 31.2 (2016), pp. 149–53; Mikko Tuhkanen, 'Queer Hybridity', in Chrysanthi Nigianni and Merl Storr (eds.), *Deleuze and Queer Theory* (Edinburgh: Edinburgh University Press, 2009), pp. 92–114; Rinaldo Walcott, 'Queer Returns: Human Rights, the Anglo-Caribbean and Diaspora Politics', *Caribbean Review of Gender Studies* 3 (2009), pp. 1–19. In particular, Walcott's insistence on the queer potential of a Glissantian poetics offers an interesting counter-claim to analyses which identify an ongoing masculinism in Glissant. Cf. Max Hantel, 'Toward a Sexual Difference Theory of Creolization', in John E. Drabinski and Marisa Parham (eds.), *Theorizing Glissant: Sites and Citations* (London: Rowman & Littlefield International, 2015), pp. 85–102.
19 Glissant, *Poetics of Relation*, pp. 72, 58.

and Confiant's manifesto.[20] Thomas Stephens suggests that the term is derived from 'criar', meaning to raise, nourish, create, and 'cria', meaning a baby, infant or person without family; it was initially used to mean a child born away from its homeland, that is, a child of European parents born in the colonies.[21] Whether applied to European exiles, as in the original uses of the term, or to diasporic cultures, as in both Glissant and the *Éloge*, to be creole means to be displaced from Euro-colonial norms of kinship, filiation and lineage, and thereby nation. While both 'In Praise of Creoleness' and the debates it has inspired have little to say on kinship, *Texaco* takes up the troubled history and transformative potential of black diasporic kinship—its implication in the violence of slavery, the enslaved's resistance, and its role in creating a new culture (which is not, however, a new national culture).[22] This concern with challenging colonial models of and discourses of kinship, acknowledging alternative forms of relationality as a key product of black Atlantic culture and colonial resistance, and finding ways to imagine intersubjective bonds that are 'queered' in their distance from national, metropolitan heteronormativity and the norms of nation, community, subjectivity which emerge from it indicates potential moments of exchange and shared affinities between *Texaco* and both contemporary anglophone Caribbean or black Atlantic writing and other Francophone Caribbean writing such as that of Maryse Condé, the significant differences between them (as well as Maryse Condé's long-standing critique of Chamoiseau's language) notwithstanding.[23]

---

20 Glissant, *Poetics of Relation*, p. 89; Jean Bernabé, Patrick Chamoiseau, Raphaël Confiant, 'In Praise of Creoleness' [*Éloge de la créolité*], trans. Mohamed B. Taleb, *Callaloo* 13.4 (1990), pp. 886–909. For example, Bernabé et al. advocate 'descending in ourselves, but without the Other' (p. 898).

21 Thomas M. Stephens, 'Creole, Créole, Criollo, Crioulo: The Shadings of a Term', *The SECOL Review* 7.3 (1983), pp. 28–39.

22 An overview of these debates is offered in Wendy Knepper, *Patrick Chamoiseau: A Critical Introduction* (Jackson: University Press of Mississippi, 2012), pp. 95–101; they are further contextualized in David Scott, 'Islands of *Créolité*?', *Small Axe* 13.3 (2009), pp. vii–x. An important response to the *Éloge* is A. James Arnold, 'The Gendering of Créolité', in Maryse Condé and Madeleine Cottenet-Hage (eds.), *Penser la créolité* (Paris: Kartala, 1995), pp. 21–40; along with the other essays in the volume.

23 On kinship in Condé's novel *Desirada*, see Celia Britton, *The Sense of Community in French Caribbean Fiction* (Liverpool: Liverpool University Press, 2008), pp. 131–50. On kinship in *Crossing the Mangrove*, see Christopher Ian Foster, 'The Queer Politics of Crossing in Maryse Condé's *Crossing the Mangrove*', *Small Axe* 18.1 (2014), pp. 114–24. For Condé's critiques of Chamoiseau, see for example Eva Sansavior, 'Playing the Field/Performing "the Personal" in Maryse Condé's Interviews', in Patrick Crowley and Jane Hiddleston (eds.), *Postcolonial Poetics: Genre and Form* (Liverpool: Liverpool University Press, 2011), pp. 71–88; Emily S. Apter and Maryse Condé, 'Crossover Texts/Creole Tongues: A Conversation with Maryse Condé', *Public Culture* 13.1 (2001), pp. 89–96.

Patrick Chamoiseau's Texaco

The novel is centrally concerned with 'City', that is, about how to live as a black person in Martinique. In a footnote to the epilogue, the novel's narrator, the 'Word Scratcher', explains the meaning of City: 'The Creole language does not say *la ville* ["the city"], but rather, *l'En-ville* ["the In-city"]'—although the literal translation 'the In-city' is given in this footnote, throughout the rest of the novel the English translators render *l'En-ville* as 'City', a proper noun, a practice I follow in this chapter—'City thus designates, not a clearly defined urban geography, but essentially a content and therefore a kind of enterprise. And here that enterprise was about living' (*Tex* 386). The novel narrates approximately 150 years of that enterprise, the 'rush toward City' (*Tex* 34), the struggle to find ways to live for black Martinicans. They struggle against slavery, then against the legacy of slavery and the historical rupture of the Middle Passage, then against colonial exploitation and racism, and they struggle to define their selves, culture and way of being in the world and on the island of Martinique. This struggle is also about developing new forms of relationality, community, and commonality that challenge and renew the meaning and place of kinship in this society.

It its opening pages *Texaco* indicates the way in which this diasporic relationality emerges from Caribbean history and from colonial, heteronormative historiography: a timeline on the first pages combines events of Martinican, Caribbean, French and world history with fictional events from the novel. The timeline gestures both at family history in a traditional sense and begins to exceed it:

> [...] 1502 Christopher Columbus arrives in Martinique
> 1635 France definitively takes possession of Martinique and erects a fort, around which the city of Saint-Pierre will be built.
> 1667 Construction of Fort-Royal, which will bring about a second city: Fort-de-France. *Our great squatter districts will cluster around it. At this point the site of the future Texaco Quarter is but thickets and mangrove.* [...]
> 18— *Probable time of birth of Esternome Laborieux, the papa of Texaco's founder-to-be; he is a slave on a plantation near the city of Saint-Pierre.* [...]
> 19— *Probable time of Marie-Sophie Laborieux's birth; it is she who will found Texaco.* [...]
> 1945 Aimé Césaire is elected mayor of Fort-de-France.
> 1946 *March 19*: Law establishing Martinique as a French province (département).
> 1950 *Marie-Sophie Laborieux's first settlement on the future site of Texaco, and her first police expulsion.* [...] (*Tex* 3–5)

This timeline partially repeats and expands the one offered by Glissant in *Caribbean Discourse*: it too lists key dates such a '1502 Discovery of Martinique by Columbus', '1848 Abolition of slavery', '1946 Departmentalisation'.[24] Glissant argues, however, that 'once this chronological table has been set up and completed the whole history of Martinique remains to be unravelled. The whole Caribbean history of Martinique remains to be discovered'.[25] *Texaco*'s timeline is equally unfinished: the events added in—from Marie-Sophie's family history, the key events of Texaco's founding, additional events of Martinique's history like Césaire's election—do not achieve the task of 'unravelling', let alone completing, history, but rather suggest, as Loichot has argued in regard to Glissant, that 'no chronology can clarify the reading of an opaque Caribbean history—either familial or Martinican [...]. [A]ny ancestor could be chosen, but each could be completed, contradicted by another figure. As there is no one origin in Martinique, there is no one ancestor'.[26] *Texaco*'s opening timeline suggests the necessity for personal and familial histories to become part of Martinican historiography, but without the promise that such histories might complete or correct the historical record. Furthermore, the familial entries in the timeline reveal similarly little about this family history; to paraphrase Glissant, once this chronological table has been set up and completed the whole history of *this family, these people* remains to be unravelled.

That genealogy is not history, therefore—at least, not a history that does justice to this Caribbean location—might be inferred from these opening pages. Towards the end of the novel, however, an ongoing faith in the promise of genealogy is ascribed to the békés (the white Martinicans); among them, 'a very clear genealogy, without any dubious holes, exacted the highest respect from all, more than the rustle of money in a register, *respect*' (*Tex* 363). The knowledge of 'how to marry and marry off one's children' is deemed 'the only way of climbing up the strata of the caste' (*Tex* 363). This obsession with genealogy is also an obsession with race: the béké insists that 'the blackman was their brother but never their brother-in-law and God help whoever broke that rule', and the burden of upholding this fantasy of racial purity falls exclusively on women: 'it was tenable for a male béké to have blackids out of wedlock, but was an impossible crime for a béké woman to give away her belly' (*Tex* 363).

This is the field of tension which persists throughout the novel: the knowledge that (family) chronology explains nothing, that is, that Caribbean culture and history cannot be explained by tracing origins or lineages, and the ongoing pressure of the colonial imaginary of filiation and nation. In *Texaco*, the discourse of filiation, and its importance to ideas of race and racial superiority, has not vanished—the fall of filiation in a globalized world of Relation heralded by Glissant has not entirely come to pass here. For the black Martinican characters of the novel, this fantasy of filiation takes

---

24 Édouard Glissant, *Caribbean Discourse: Selected Essays*, trans. J. Michael Dash (Charlottesville: University Press of Virginia, 1989), p. 13.
25 Glissant, *Caribbean Discourse*, p. 13.
26 Loichot, *Orphan Narratives*, p. 46.

the form of an attachment to France—often called 'mother-France' or the 'Mother-Fatherland'—even as it is clear that this claim, which is an attempt to substitute cultural affiliation for the claim of filiation, or genealogical origin, will not and cannot provide black Martinicans with cultural practices, forms of intimacy or an understanding of their own history suitable to their place and the world they live in.

Marie-Sophie insists that 'to understand Texaco and our fathers' rush toward City, we'll have to go far, deep down my own family tree [loin dans la lignée de ma propre famille], for what I know of collective memory is only what I know of my own. Besides, memory is only faithful when it tells the history of my old flesh' (*Tex* 34 [48]). However this 'family tree', or the 'line' of her family, is neither straight, nor is it dictated by 'blood or law', biology or state recognition. On the plantation where Marie-Sophie's father, Esternome, is born, pregnancy and birth—or rather the lack of pregnancies and births—have become matters of political resistance, poison and magic, beyond the laws of 'biology' and beyond the economic imperatives of the white slave owners: 'The men of strength would say *No children born in chains* [*Pas d'enfants d'esclavage*], and the women would only open withered wombs to the suns of life' (*Tex* 35 [49]). Like the Trinidadian plantation in *At the Full and Change of the Moon*, pregnancy and childbirth are prevented—just as plagues, floods and animal deaths are called up—in order the obstruct the 'unjust prosperity' (*Tex* 35) of the slave owners. The novel also echoes Glissant in *Le discours antillais*: '"Manjé tè, pa fè yiche pou lesclavaj" [eat dirt, don't make children for slavery], as the enslaved women murmured or cried out'.[27] Unlike in both Brand and Glissant's accounts, however, in *Texaco* these are not acts which assert the enslaved women's control over their own bodies and fertility, but are attributed to the actions of a few 'men of strength'. This privileging of male power over women's bodies, is soon turned around, however—although this too is an ambivalent act. The father of Esternome is reported to be one of those 'men of strength', and the 'the news of this pregnancy was a misfortune for the man [...]. Bitter as a lump of salt, he almost insulted her by shouting, *No children born in chains!* [...] He wanted to make her swallow some foul tea' (*Tex* 41). His attempts to end the pregnancy are foiled by the pregnant woman, whose joy at the pregnancy, troublingly, is shared by her owner, who 'danced with joy around her belly' (*Tex* 41).

This uneasy coalition between the enslaved pregnant woman and her owner is echoed in the confused attachments of the child, Esternome, who grows up with the ambivalent intimacies common to fictional house slaves: he regards the 'cane blacks' with disdain, regarding the field slaves as 'outside humanity' (*Tex* 44). He schemes to receive favours from the owners or their children and to complete relatively pleasant tasks for them; eventually, he

---

27 Glissant, *Le discours antillais*, quoted and translated by Loichot, 'We are all related', p. 46. This section of *Le discours antillais* was not included in the English translation *Caribbean Discourse*.

kills a maroon who has attacked the béké (the slave owner) and wins his own freedom in return. In the early days of his emancipation, however, he can imagine no other life than the one he knows on the plantation: he cannot make contact with any maroons, everywhere outside the plantation is filled with hostile and suspicious white people, and thus 'he dared neither leave nor really stay. Strange baggage, the plantation had become for him a kind of haven' (*Tex* 49). For Esternome, gaining his nominal freedom is easier than breaking out of the colonial episteme, its norms of 'humanity', its way of life. If the plantation marks the start of modernity, as Glissant (among others) suggests, and the start of Relation and 'expanse' rather than filiation, then it also marks the start of a torturous desire for filiation, and for France, that will accompany the emergence of a distinct Caribbean culture and form of relationality throughout the novel.

The falseness of the promise of France is always clear, but this does not prevent Esternome, Marie-Sophie and other black Martinicans from continuing to idealize mother-France. After the abolition of slavery, the newly freed flood into Saint-Pierre, 'shaking laurels or little flags of the so-good mother France' (*Tex* 101). During World War I, many sign up to defend 'Sweet France, crib of our liberty, that so-generous land of the universal' or because they 'found in the Army the chance of becoming French' (*Tex* 190). They *hoped to find*, that is—for the fate of the returned soldiers has already been described: they return 'without a penny for pension, and without strength for odd jobs' (*Tex* 190). When Esternome tries to volunteer, 'the servicemen wanted nothing to do with me. A dog of a warrant officer chased me away. I think I heard him curse, something about blackmen unworthy of carrying a gun or of raising their filthy selves under the flag' (*Tex* 192). Later again, after World War II, as debates rage in Martinique over autonomy or assimilation, Marie-Sophie's employer Monsieur Alcibiade defends colonialism as a bringer of civilization and 'definitive progress' (*Tex* 245) and continues to use an idiom of kinship to describe the colonial relationship:

> when the colony becomes an autonomous State under the control of the Mother-Fatherland [la Mère-Patrie], the latter sees her child leave her, more and more ungrateful [...]. Assimilation is, however, just the opposite! The Mother-Fatherland and her children are developing themselves together [...]. The Mother and her children will, from now on, walk in step, in full equality. (*Tex* 247–48 [317])

Marie-Sophie describes this as 'a debate I would hear all my life, nonstop, again and again' (*Tex* 248). The grotesqueness of this belief in France is again evident at De Gaulle's visit to Martinique in 1964: 'An old man carried his World War I shoes as a token of his love (he had lost four of his toes in them). Another one, hauled there in a wheelbarrow, came to remind him of his legs given to the Motherland and tell De Gaulle he was ready for his next call' (*Tex* 329). The relationship to the 'Mother-Fatherland' has become a double-bind for black Martinicans: it does not fulfil its promise, but it is seemingly the only cultural ancestor or origin that they can call upon in asserting their humanity—as long as the possibility of cultural legitimacy not based on origins has not yet emerged.

While mother-France is problematized and idealized at once, it is clear that there can be no mother-Africa. Esternome's father is said to have revealed to his mother 'the pleasure of the memory of an impossible land which is, he whispered, Africa' (*Tex* 40). Africa may exist as an eroticized fantasy, 'the pleasure of [a] memory', but the enormous majority of the population has no conscious connection to the continent (although knowledge and cultural practices, including snippets of various languages, the magic of the Mentoh, and Esternome's lover Ninon's immense farming know-how may in fact be cultural inheritances from Africa). When Ninon's mother, simply called 'the African', dies, Esternome muses that she passed on nothing about 'that enormous country about which none knew squat'; instead, she 'had only evoked a cargohold, as if she had been born in it, as if her memories stopped throbbing there' (*Tex* 118). Thus, rather than 'mother Africa, matrix Africa, the black civilization' offered by Negritude (and criticized in the créolité manifesto), the novel instead invokes Glissant's 'open boat', in which he suggests the experience of the Middle Passage was one of being born again, isolated from the past: 'the belly of this boat dissolves you, precipitates you into a nonworld from which you cry out. This boat is a womb, a womb abyss'.[28]

What forms of culture, community and relationality emerge from the belly of the slave ship? Even as the characters of *Texaco* yearn for mother-France, they simultaneously enact and create understandings of history, ancestry, community and narrative that are multiple and rhizomatic, rather than singular and arboreal, and which value bricolage over separation. This is modelled in the opening pages of the novel which depict the arrival of the 'Christ' (the Urban Planner) in Texaco: 'Iréné, the shark catcher, saw him first. Then Sonore, the câpresse, hair whitened by something other than age, saw him come. But only when Marie-Clémence, whose tongue, it is true, is televised news, appeared was everyone brought up to speed' (*Tex* 10). The arrival of the Urban Planner, and what it might mean for the Texaco community, is then narrated three times, once by each of these characters—although those narratives do more to introduce the characters themselves, rather than the Urban Planner, recounting their own histories and arrival in Texaco. This multiplicity is found in the narrative form of the novel as well: it offers a complex polyphony with the major part of the text written by a narrator variously named the 'Word Scratcher', 'Oiseau de Cham' or 'Chamoiseau', who ventriloquizes the voice and perspective of Marie-Sophie—or, sometimes, her father Esternome. This main text is interspersed with short excepts from several other texts: Marie-Sophie's notebooks, in which she wrote down her own life experiences and her memories of her father's stories (often, again, ventriloquizing the voice

---

28 Bernabé et al., 'In Praise of Creoleness', p. 888; Glissant, *Poetics of Relation*, p. 6.

of Esternome), notes from the Urban Planner, whose arrival in Texaco initiates the narrative, to the Word Scratcher, detailing the Planner's understanding and experience of the Texaco community, and letters from the Word Scratcher back to his 'Source', Marie-Sophie.

Multiple and non-linear origins also characterize the narrative as the story moves to the nineteenth century to tell the story of Esternome. Several events finally prompt him to leave the plantation of his birth: upon the death of an enslaved prisoner in the plantation's fearsome dungeon, whom his mother identifies as Esternome's father, Esternome decides to leave, but still does not. Then, another man, identified as a Mentoh, 'breathed into his heart the desire to leave' (*Tex* 54). This Mentoh is described as an ancestor of Marie-Sophie and the Texaco community: their encounter 'established the Mentoh at the beginning of our nettlesome conquest of the country' (*Tex* 54). He instructs Esternome 'to take with the utmost urgency what the békés had not yet taken: the hills, the Southern drylands, the misty heights, the depths and the ravines, and then besiege those places that they created' (*Tex* 54): the instruction to conquer City which will become the leitmotif of Esternome and Marie-Sophie's lives and of the novel. Even then, it takes a meeting with yet another man before Esternome actually leaves: Théodorus, a 'white master carpenter' to whom Esternome becomes unofficially apprenticed and in whose company he begins 'the descent into City' (*Tex* 58). All three men are fathers or ancestors of the Texaco community and the 'rush toward City'—the non-genealogical relatives perhaps more so than the man identified as Esternome's biological father.

As he begins that descent, away from the hills, from the life and logic of the plantation towards some as yet unknown culture and community, in an attempt to follow the Mentoh's demand for anticolonial action—to take the land and besiege the towns of the white colonists—we are reminded of another form of descent: a quotation from one of Marie-Sophie's notebooks records a 'fantastic reading by Théodorus [...] to underscore the wonders of the age':

> 'Descendants of mixed blood able to prove at least one hundred years and a day of freedom, whose great-grand-father, a legitimate son of a black father and mother or of colored people freeborn or affranchi, has taken for legitimate wife a woman who was at minimum a free mulatto, and whose grandfather has wed in freedom a mistive, and whose father has wed a quadroon, will be—because of the excellence of the blood—said to be themselves white'. (*Tex* 58)

This reminder of the importance of 'blood' and genealogy to colonial rule contains both a promise of racial ascendency via descent, if one accepts the racial logic of colonial discourse, and implicitly the suggestion that Esternome's 'descent' into City must not ascribe to this law, but must find other forms of connection and kinship than those offered by French colonial law, if it is to become the 'libertyland' (*Tex* 58) of which Esternome dreams.

It is immediately clear upon his arrival that the space, life and erotics of City potentially work against such clear categorizations: City is 'leaking', 'slippery' (*Tex* 61) and 'vibrating' (*Tex* 74). In the 'bric-à-brac' of the City's architecture and culture Esternome 'could see a kind of power. He understood that here the misery of the great plantations ended' (*Tex* 75). Yet Esternome's first stay in City is a failure, in part because the misery of the plantations has not yet ended for most—for the majority of Martinique's black population, still enslaved, 'City was a Big Hutch' (*Tex* 80), just a larger version of the plantation owner's house—in part because, despite the potential he senses, he and all others have not yet escaped from the logic of genealogy and paternity offered by French colonial law. His first lover there tells him she will be with him 'only until I meet my mulatto or my white man' (*Tex* 64), echoing the promise of a white lover in post-emancipation Jamaica in *The Long Song*. Esternome himself sees the city as fertile ground in a patriarchal sense: unlike the plantations, which were 'hostile to any seed other than the Béké's', City 'was open to the winds of the world [...] She offered herself [Elle s'offrait] to anyone who tried to dream life rather than live it' (*Tex* 66–67 [90]). (The translators' decision to describe City as 'she' rather than 'it' in this passage emphasizes this vision of City as an inviting woman.) He suggests that everyone 'dreamt of whitening themselves'; the black free men, like Esternome, 'lived as if they had [...] descendants to humanize with a ray of whiteness. That didn't stop them, all the same, in the depths of their being, from hating that white skin' (*Tex* 70). Alongside this dream of whiteness, and thus humanity, via genealogical descent, kinship with mother-France is also used to claim humanity in Saint-Pierre. The mulatto class 'were all forever coming back from a wonderful stay in the sweet land of France where the slave creature was becoming human again' (*Tex* 67); once returned, 'against the béké ferocity, they erected France's generous eternity, Oh goodly mother lost in the horizon and filling our hearts' (*Tex* 70). The racism and obstruction from the whites on Martinique, who wish to stop the mulattoes obtaining political or economic power, causes the mulattoes to fantasize a mother-France who would (but somehow does not) protect them from mistreatment by the békés. This invocation of kinship is not only metaphorical: it is very much anchored in claims for rights and recognition for the mulattoes, and thus is an attempt to mobilize a claim of filiation, of origins and lineage, supported by appropriate practice—the mulattoes 'gathered in studious pomp to read the newspapers, comment upon them, write lines in pretty-pretty French (*Tex* 70)—against colonial power, albeit only for the benefit of the mulattoes, not the rest of the colonized and enslaved population.

Downcast by his apparent failure to make headway in City, and as abolition approaches, Esternome becomes convinced that freedom will not come 'from the great traditions of France', as some claim, but 'from the land slaves, from the conquest of that land' (*Tex* 82). After trying to establish a life in City 'without finding the right door', he wondered 'if that door truly existed for him, or for Ninon, or for others of his kind' (*Tex* 119). The news that abolition does not mean the redistribution of property and farmland, as many former slaves believed, further strengthens his conviction: Esternome and Ninon head for the hills to try 'marooning' (*Tex* 120). The property laws they hope to escape and the dream of achieving whiteness by genealogical lineage are not entirely absent there; nonetheless, for a time they become part of a utopian community of solidarity where 'helping each other was the law' (*Tex* 131). It is here that the novel begins to reclaim and rewrite an idiom of kinship—not mother-France, and not lineage, origin or aspiring to whiteness, but working together and in connection with the land: 'one's brother to the right of your garden, one's sister to the left' (*Tex* 131). Reflecting on her father's stories of this community, Marie-Sophie concludes that 'without understanding it I knew this: our Texaco was budding in all that' (*Tex* 123). That this kinship is decidedly not genealogy is emphasized by Esternome's mistaken belief that he might be able to keep Ninon in the Hills—when she, like many others tired of subsistence farming and the vagaries of nature, is lured to return to work in the new factories by the promise of industrial modernity—with a child: 'he thought [...] that a child would busy her enough to pluck out her desire of flying off to the factory' (*Tex* 140). But genealogy cannot provide the roots Esternome hopes for after all; Ninon runs off with an itinerant musician, and Esternome retreats into a 'thousand-year stupor' until, many years later, the eruption of Mount Pelée forces him to leave the hills that have long since ceased to be the community of solidarity they once were.

After he moves to Fort-de-France he does have a child—the novel's protagonist Marie-Sophie—but again, this pregnancy and birth is ruled more by the forces of magic that controlled reproduction on the plantation than by laws of biology. Among a multitude of miracles, including biological ones, Esternome meets first Adrienne, who 'had a twin sister, maybe not as old as she' (*Tex* 169), and that sister is Idoménée—a woman bearing the name of a Cretan warrior.[29] Her surprise pregnancy, when both she and Esternome are already very old, is less a confirmation of genealogy than the inauguration of a communal kinship: 'the baby was the Quarter's. I had, before I was even born, a load of papas and just as many mamas' (*Tex* 188). Likewise, when Idoménée asks Esternome to tell her 'his name, age, origin, family', this does not result in a recourse to or claim of a single origin; rather, he 'began to tell the tale' (*Tex* 169)—that is, everything recounted so far, all of which does less to assert an origin or family lineage than to twist normative concepts of identity and kinship: his surname, Laborieux, given to him by a city clerk after emancipation, his age uncertain, his 'origin' and his family all of the opaque twists and turns which the previous pages have narrated.

Many aspects of Marie-Sophie's life in Fort-de-France after the death of both her parents mirror her father's experiences on the plantation and during his first stay in City, suggesting that despite the obvious changes over the

---

29 Idoménée is the French rendering of Idomeneus, a Cretan warrior in the *Iliad*.

past seventy years, some of the tensions particular to diasporic relationality continue. Her work as a housemaid or nanny means that she usually lives with her employers—a mode of intimate and ambiguous contact that recalls the plantation house, added to by the almost constant threat of sexual assault. After she is raped by an employer, she determines 'to never let anyone order me around, to decide all by myself what was good for me and what had to be done' (*Tex* 254), but she too, like Esternome before her, finds it difficult to choose between ambivalent attachments: 'that hatred fastened me to him with the strength of mahoe rope. *What a foul poison hatred is!* ... It has no limits, it mixes everything up ...' (*Tex* 258). She too gets to know a mulatto culture which idealizes France—and through which she acquires literacy. Her elderly teacher is described as 'a castrated being [un être castré]' due to 'all that [French] learning' (*Tex* 216 [277]), but by teaching Marie-Sophie to read and write he becomes another of the queer progenitors of her text. Her lover Basile is little more than an emergency stopgap, with his useful ability to procure food during the wartime hunger years. In this period Marie-Sophie decides not to have children—and this, too, could be read as an echo of the resistance via sterility of the plantation.[30] Rather than a sign that the relations of the plantation simply live on, however, it demonstrates the way in which practices recur and yet are *not* a continuation, as they acquire new meanings. Marie-Sophie does not aim to impoverish a slave owner with her abortions, but preserve her own ability to seek a good life amidst the myriad challenges of City: her decision comes from 'a sort of repulsion, fright, refusal, which came both from the war and from my scorn for Basile, my fear of facing City with a child on my shoulder' (*Tex* 239). Despite Marie-Sophie's sense that the enterprise of City is one best faced alone, with neither sexual or emotional intimacy nor the responsibility for a child, nonetheless the community bonds created when her neighbour teachers her different methods to end a pregnancy recall the ethos of solidarity of the utopian community of the hills and prefigure the role Marie-Sophie will later take in the Quarters.

At the same time as Marie-Sophie's early life is being recounted, however, the text foreshadows the coming community via excerpts from notes from the Urban Planner. He describes Texaco as a queer child (triply engendered or fathered) of Fort-de-France, the plantations and the community of the hills: 'The town, Fort-de-France, reproduces itself and spreads out here in a novel way. [...] We have to understand that this Creole town has been dreamt—I mean engendered [engendré]—by its plantations, our plantations, by every Big Hutch of our hills' (*Tex* 115–16 [152]). In another note, he describes his understanding of Texaco as formed by a particular kind of rootedness: 'here people bring very old roots, not deep and rigid, but diffuse, profuse, spread over time with the lightness of speech' (*Tex* 170).

---

30 Véronique Maisier, 'Patrick Chamoiseau's Novel *Texaco* and the Picaresque Genre', *Dalhousie French Studies* 57 (2001), pp. 128–36.

Marie-Sophie experiences a community like this, and the process by which shallow roots might be widely spread, for the first time in Morne Abélard, the Quarter (shanty town) of Fort-de-France where she lives with Nelta. Everyone in the Quarter cares for Marie-Sophie, teetering on the edge of madness after her rape and imprisonment by an employer. She 'received nets of tenderness, cast seines full of dreams in which hands were held together' (*Tex* 263). She learns to see the Quarters 'as an ecosystem, made up of equilibriums and interactions' (*Tex* 257), and this demands, as well, a new relation to property: the huts are surrounded by 'private trees accessible to everyone' (*Tex* 266). The realization that she is now infertile is a blow, a 'barely imaginable horror' (*Tex* 270), but her wish for a child finds a replacement in her renewed determination to found a community: 'It was then that there rose in me the Marie-Sophie Laborieux who [...] was going to fight against City with a warrior's rage' (*Tex* 271). Marie-Sophie throws herself into the job of community building, becoming a beacon of support to all, fulfilling the duties of neighbour–kin—including managing childbirth, disease and death—although not in a particularly motherly way:

> I tended to take care of others, not with pity, but to tell them how to outrun distress. I added a spoonful of oil to anyone's dry flour. Whoever had a sick child stopped by my hutch and I was the one who led the descent to the poorhouse or toward some old doctor, who'd do most anything for some fish. I organized the collections, the wakes and gathering, ran the errands whenever trouble came. (*Tex* 273)

Sensing that Nelta will leave to fulfil his dream of travel, Marie-Sophie knows that dyadic attachment only to her lover is not the form of kinship that suits this life: her fear of Nelta's desertion 'brought me to the others, because I felt my fate tied to theirs' (*Tex* 273).

If that form of kinship does not guarantee personhood, however, Marie-Sophie still hopes that property might:

> In City, to be is first and foremost to possess a roof. And I, though born there, felt like I was floating about like a country bumpkin. And then, it was to refute Nelta, to grab the country while he fled it, to take roots while he envied the clouds, to build while he dreamt. (*Tex* 275)

But after a disastrous fire in the Quarter of Morne Abélard, Marie-Sophie builds herself a new hut on the slopes near the sea behind the Texaco gasoline tanks, and she is soon joined by others to 'take root in the soil' (*Tex* 300). There, although Marie-Sophie claims 'we reinvented everything: laws, urban codes, neighborhood relations, settlement and construction rules' (*Tex* 317), in fact all of the elements that have swirled through the different forms of community and sociality in the novel reappear and are rewritten.

This remixing, the novel suggests, is in fact the mode of relationality of City: 'The plantation used to keep us apart. The hills planted us in rooted driftings. City get going ties moors blends and blends again at full speed

[L'En-ville met en marche noue amarre malaxe et remalaxe à toute vitesse]' (*Tex* 293 [375]). Papa Totone, another of the novel's mysterious 'men of strength', suggests that living in City is not a question of war, conquest or property, but one of knowledge: 'City is not to be taken. It's to be known' (*Tex* 293). He exhorts Marie-Sophie to 'maroon' in City as the enslaved once marooned from the plantations; now, rather than the womb of the slave ships birthing a new culture and people, he suggests that the same must happen in the industrial modernity of City: 'the gasoline offers you its cradle' (*Tex* 294). When the Texaco settlers are harassed by the city government they insist on a differentiation between the police and local government, on the one hand, and their still idealized dream of France on the other: their oppressors are 'not at all our beloved France, just some damn whites!' (*Tex* 314). But while the language of mother-France does not completely disappear, increasingly the community understands itself more in terms of other sites of militant resistance to French colonialism: Texaco is compared to 'Algiers' fellaghas' and 'mean chinese in Vietnam's forests' (*Tex* 306). Alongside this, the dream of private property is laid to rest: 'No private land, no collective land, we weren't the landowners [...]. In our mind, the soil under the houses remained strangely free, *definitely free*' (*Tex* 318–19, emphasis in original).

The rewriting of kinship, first seen in the community of the hills, continues here: kinship is formed by resistance against the béké who owns the land and wishes to evict the settlers, and against the 'seyaress' (CRS), the riot police he elists to help him. When some choose to leave Texaco for other houses after yet another mass assault and destruction, Marie-Sophie writes, 'My brothers and sisters [Mes compères et commères] were housed in Trénelle as announced. [...] I often think of them [...] turned blood siblings [frères de sang] under the first fury of the seyaress' (*Tex* 308–09 [395]). Here, the French offers the transformation from 'compères et commères' to blood siblings, more complex than that from 'brothers and sisters'. *Compères* are friends, partners, comrades who become kin, an intensification of a positively connoted connection, while *commères* are gossipy women turned sisters—a transformation not only from a negative to a positive connotation, but also from a term which implies anti-solidarity to one which implies strong bonds of mutual support. If creolization is always linked to anticolonial resistance, as Françoise Vergès suggests it should be, then this is a creolized kinship indeed.[31]

This transformation hints at one aspect of the gendering of the Texaco community: there, women form the first line of defence—'At first the men would stand aside, and only us ladies would face the police' (*Tex* 307), and this fight for their community is underscored by the sexist insults Marie-Sophie hears from the béké owner, including 'Whore', 'Gutterbitch',

---

31 Françoise Vergès, 'Creolization and Resistance', in Encarnación Gutiérrez Rodríguez and Shirley Anne Tate (eds.), *Creolizing Europe: Legacies and Transformations* (Liverpool: Liverpool University Press, 2015), pp. 38–56.

'Cunt-ever-smelling', 'Madwoman', and 'Harlot' (*Tex* 309). Marie-Sophie believes that the women must fight for Texaco, because 'with their lines of children they weren't so mobile on the good Lord's earth', while the men 'treaded light on this earth [...] they would forever entertain a temporary contract with this earth' (*Tex* 336). Thus the novel does not exclude women from a role in creating and transmitting creole culture, as some have identified in the créolité manifesto, but accords them a specifically feminine role in that process.[32] This, in turn, draws upon stereotypes of women as more grounded and attached to place, particularly because of their children, and of men as more likely to roam or 'drift', however these stereotypes are at least partially undermined by Marie-Sophie, the founder of the community of Texaco, who does not have children of her own but is fiercely attached to the community. The stereotype of men as drifters—seen, for example, in Marie-Sophie's lover Arcadius, whom she tries to 'anchor' (*Tex* 357) in Texaco with sexual pleasure or perhaps a miracle child—becomes less dichotomous when it is redefined not as the opposite of the rootedness of the women, but as enabling that form of community in a different way:

> The drifter's destiny is to carry us, all together, toward worlds buried in us. He assumed what we were looking for and allowed us to look for it, without our having to suffer. The drifter, he was our desire for freedom in the flesh, our way of living worlds in ourselves, our City maroon. (359)

Nonetheless, in Texaco it seems that the performance or doing of community and kinship is not enough to bring those bonds into lasting effect. Despite the worth it offers its inhabitants—not only the practicalities of housing, but the help and support they offer each other, and the sense of belonging together as siblings in struggle—the community is fragile. It is not only subject to regular destruction by the police, it lacks recognition by outsiders, who see only 'tangled miseries' (*Tex* 320) there, and it also lacks a sense of its own worth. Marie-Sophie hopes to stabilize the community and win it recognition by writing down its stories—although she *also* fears that this will stabilize it too much. Although she feels that writing will secure the community, she also experiences as it as a form of death though immobilization: writing in French distances her from Esternome and his stories in Creole; writing about herself in the present feels like 'petrifying the tatters of my flesh' (*Tex* 322). She is fearful that immobilizing the history of Texaco in writing will halt its becoming, just as she fears that herself will become fixed, although 'I felt the person I was now (pledged to what I was going to be) still elaborating' (*Tex* 322). She seeks and imagines a form of writing that would not immobilize, which would remain 'a living thing, moving in a circle [...] ceaselessly irrigating with life the things written before' (*Tex* 322).

---

32 Arnold, 'The Gendering of Créolité'. Arnold argues that Marie-Sophie's prominent role in *Texaco* in fact *supports* the thesis that créolité is conceived in masculine terms as she is described in a 'defeminized' way (p. 38).

She seeks a form of writing which would enable cultural transmission *and* transformation, a reproduction that would also be a renewal, stability and becoming, rootedness and drifting.

A letter from the Word Scratcher to Marie-Sophie suggests Édouard Glissant's books as a model of the writing she seeks—but of course the writing of the novel itself is also a model, as well as a dramatization of the dangers she perceives. The Word Scratcher's editing of this novel is evident, noting deliberate omissions or the editorial process as the narrative progresses, and in the epilogue he describes in more detail the process of listening to, recording, and editing Marie-Sophie's stories. On the one hand, this means subduing and at least partly immobilizing Marie-Sophie's narration: from her original sentences, which 'whirled at a delirious pace' and her ordering of her experiences, 'never [...] in a linear fashion', and her own sense that 'the writing of stories with so little nobility was a waste of time', the Word Scratcher notes dates and numbers lines to order the stories, and it is he alone, he claims, who perceives their 'literary' and 'aesthetic' qualities (*Tex* 388). It was Marie-Sophie's wish, he writes, that he '"fix up" her speech into good French' (*Tex* 388). This all suggests that, despite the novel's rejection of 'History' in favour of 'stories', those stories nonetheless need an expert, educated and masculine hand to make them fit for publication. On the other hand, however, elements of the text suggest that the editorial process has not worked entirely this way. Both the Word Scratcher and the Urban Planner repeatedly attest to Marie-Sophie's influence on them. The Urban Planner claims that she 'taught me to see' (*Tex* 257) the city in a particular way, that she 'gave me new eyes' (*Tex* 165). The Word Scratcher's words, which were never in 'good', that is, standard French to begin with, change further as the narration progresses, their spelling changing to adapt to Creole pronunciation, for example: thus 'Jean-Raphaël' becomes and remains 'An-Afarel' (*Tex* 74), 'mulattoes' [mulâtres] becomes and remains 'milatoes' [milâtes] (*Tex* 77 [103]). The relationship between the Word Scratcher and his Source, Marie-Sophie, is therefore one that destabilizes the text, opening it to the whirl of Relation which Texaco embodies, as it clings to the cliff-face, open to the ocean and the other islands of the Caribbean. The creolization of the text, the queer child of multiple parents and unable and unwilling to locate an origin, mirrors the creolized kinship that enables the enterprise of living as a black diasporan in City.

CHAPTER SIX

Writing self and kin: diasporic mourning in Jackie Kay's *Trumpet*

Jackie Kay's *Trumpet*, set after the death of its central character, is most of all a novel about grief and mourning and the conditions under which these can take place, and it is thereby a novel about diasporic kinship. It also returns to several themes already prominent in Kay's poetry, particularly adoption, the definition of family, and the im/possibility of being black and Scottish.[1] Through its depiction of mourning—at times mourning interrupted or denied—it explores intimate connections and kinship bonds to both the living and the dead. The novel makes clear that kinship is performatively constituted in part through mourning, but also that both kinship and subjectivity are reshaped by mourning, the reverberations of which alter past, present and future relationships. The novel's multiple, enmeshed story lines make visible both the web of kinship, friendship and other connections in which the characters live, as well as the conditions—bureaucratic, state institutional, and medial—which shape and limit those bonds. It is through mourning and its reshaping of kinship and subjectivity that the differences and differentiations of race, gender, sexuality, nation, and citizenship become visible, and the interplay of voices in the novel enables a complex picture of the intersection of these differences in contemporary Britain—a space and society showed to be shaped by diasporic experiences, identities and aesthetics.[2] Through an analysis of the work of mourning it becomes clear

---

1 Kay's best known work on these themes is *The Adoption Papers* (Tarset: Bloodaxe Books, 1991), but she also treats them in her memoir *Red Dust Road* (London: Picador, 2010).
2 H. Adlai Murdoch makes a similar argument about the 'the ways in which migrant Caribbean diasporas inscribe critical paradoxes of migrancy and citizenship in contemporary Europe' using the example of France. See H. Adlai Murdoch, 'Continental Creolization: French Exclusion through a Glissantian Prism', in

how institutional, state-recognized kinship and national heteronormativity, on the one hand, and diasporic forms of kinship, intimacy and history, on the other, intersect and influence each other in contemporary Britain.

Based loosely on the life story of a white American jazz musician named Billie Tipton, *Trumpet* consists of a collection of stories centred around a black Scottish trumpet player, Joss Moody. Set in the period immediately following Joss's death, the novel is narrated by or through a host of characters. Many chapters come from Joss's closest kin—primarily his wife Millie and son Colman, as well as one chapter from his bandmate and friend Big Red. These are mostly narrated in the first-person and jump between recollections of earlier events and reflections on the current situation. These chapters are interspersed with several short chapters narrated in the third-person and focalized through characters with a less personal, sometimes institutional relationship to Joss: the doctor who attends Joss's death and writes the medical certificate, the registrar who registers the death, the director of the funeral parlour. Finally, a number of chapters are narrated by Sophie Stones, a tabloid journalist who is eager to capitalize on the minor scandal which has erupted after Joss's death.

The news story is that, after his death, and to the surprise of everyone except his wife, Joss's body is discovered to have an unexpected form: he does not have a penis; he does have breasts and a vagina. He is retrospectively deemed by some to have been female and/or a woman—although this categorization is rarely easily made, nor does it prove stable. This 'scandal' of gender is the starting point for the novel's reflections on love, mourning, kinship, belonging, race and cultural inheritance; it partly structures the conditions in which these reflections take place, but gender is not the chief concern of the novel nor of its main characters, Millie and Colman. It *is* the main concern of the journalist Sophie Stones—but the novel's representation of Stones as not only unethical and greedy, but also as a somewhat stupid and contemptible tabloid hack indicates that her obsession with Joss's gender is misplaced. It is a great irony, therefore, that the fascination with the 'truth' of the 'scandal' and of Joss's identity that closely mirrors the tabloid exploitation represented by Stones is also to be found in much of the critical work on the novel, which tends to insist upon a distinction between (social) gender and (bodily, material, biological) sex—both in the case of Joss and the case of Tipton—and to fall back upon a rigidly dualistic categorization of bodies, even though precisely these tendencies are identified by the novel as problematic.[3]

Encarnación Gutiérrez Rodríguez and Shirley Anne Tate (eds.), *Creolizing Europe: Legacies and Transformations* (Liverpool: Liverpool University Press, 2015), p. 58.

3 Linda Anderson, 'Autobiographical Travesties: the Nostalgic Self in Queer Writing', in David Alderson and Linda Anderson (eds.), *Territories of Desire in Queer Culture: Refiguring Contemporary Boundaries* (Manchester: Manchester University Press, 2000), pp. 68–81; Jeannette King, '"A Woman's a Man, For a' That": Jackie Kay's *Trumpet*', *Scottish Studies Review* 2.1 (2001), pp. 101–08; Mark Stein, 'Life Border

In fact, the very difficulties encountered by these critical engagements with the novel in their attempt to define Joss's sex and gender demonstrate the key work of the text with regard to gender: as Tracy Hargreaves argues, 'what falls into crisis in Kay's narrative is not just an understanding of masculinity and femininity, but "category itself"'.[4]

In the immediate aftermath of Joss's death, both Millie and Colman, his white wife and black son, struggle to adjust and to grapple with their loss. Both report a similar sense of self-alienation as a result of Joss's death: Colman feels that 'he [Joss] has made us all unreal'; later, Millie feels that 'reality has stopped'.[5] Both experience a sense of suspended animation in the weeks immediately following Joss's death, as they struggle to mourn Joss and to accept the transformative effects that mourning will have on themselves and their pasts and futures. Their mourning of Joss is interrupted or made difficult by several factors: the media attention generated by his death (particularly for Millie), the gender crisis (particularly for Colman), and their shared unwillingness to undergo the subjective transformation that mourning demands. That is, their mourning is complicated by the difficult juxtaposition of two elements of contemporary politics and mourning identified by Judith Butler: the need to '[submit] to a transformation [...], the full result of which one cannot know in advance' on the one hand, and the desire for 'bodily integrity and self-determination', on the other.[6] For a time, the conflicting tension between these two makes it impossible for Millie and Colman to mourn Joss. In this way the novel reflects on the conditions which determine which lives can be mourned, and under which circumstances; it traces the outlines of a 'grievable life' in contemporary diasporic Britain.[7] These conditions include the necessity of recognition to mourning and kinship and the mutual imbrication and transformation of the past, present and future caused by mourning, which demands a

---

Writing', in Tobias Döring (ed.), *A History of Postcolonial Literature in 12½ Books* (Trier: WVT, 2007), pp. 169–80; Alice Walker, 'As You Wear: Cross-dressing and Identity Politics in Jackie Kay's *Trumpet*', *Journal of International Women's Studies* 8.2 (2007), pp. 35–43. A small number of essays are more openly transphobic, declaring for example that Joss and Millie are 'lesbians in denial', that 'Joss was not a man—[...] his masculinity was no more than a costume', and that 'Joss is a construction rather than a reality' (Ceri Davies, '"The Truth is a Thorny Issue": Lesbian Denial in Jackie Kay's *Trumpet*', *Journal of International Women's Studies* 7.3 (2006), pp. 6, 11). For a rare exception see Mandy Koolen, 'Masculine Trans-formations in Jackie Kay's *Trumpet*', *Atlantis* 35.1 (2010), pp. 71–80.
4 Tracy Hargreaves, "The Power of the Ordinary Subversive in Jackie Kay's *Trumpet*," *Feminist Review* 74 (2003), p. 4.
5 Jackie Kay, *Trumpet* (London: Picador, 1998), pp. 1, 60, 155. Further references to the novel are given in the text as *Tr*.
6 Butler, *Precarious Life*, pp. 21, 25.
7 Butler, *Precarious Life*, p. 20.

willingness to let go of the notion of both a stable, autonomous self and linear time. In *Trumpet*, mourning not only performs kinship, both making it visible and performatively constructing and affirming kinship bonds; the novel also makes clear that death and mourning are part of an active process which may reshape the life which preceded it and the lives of the living surrounding the deceased, reshaping history and futurity along the way. This sentiment is directly articulated by numerous characters including Millie, the doctor and the funeral director, and the novel as a whole performs this process: not only is Joss's life literally rewritten multiple times, but so are Millie and Colman's lives, their identities, their bonds to others, the history of the British jazz scene, British migration history and more.

The work of mourning is another key way in which the relationship of the diasporic past to the present is understood and potentially reworked in contemporary black Atlantic literature. The management of dying and performance of the rites of mourning is often considered a vital responsibility and key act of kinship, and loss and mourning can also be understood as central structuring forces of diaspora. These acts maintain the memory of the losses entailed in diasporic dispersal, generate a relationship between the past and the present, and create connections and community between subjects, thereby performatively generating diaspora—a queer diaspora reproduced through mourning, rather than sexual reproduction and genealogy. In the context of postslavery and the black diasporas of the Americas, Saidiya Hartman argues that mourning functions both to remember the past and contextualize and historicize present injustices:

> Mourning, as a public expression of one's grief, insists that the past is not yet over; this compulsion to grieve also indicates that liberal remedy has yet to be a solution to racist domination and inequality. [...] In that it enables the aggrieved to recount the history that engendered the degradation of slavery and the injurious constitution of blackness, mourning can be considered a practice of countermemory that attends to that which has been negated and repressed.[8]

What is needed, Hartman insists, is a 'disentangle[ment of] mourning from overcoming the past', that is, a means of mourning in which the past retains its ability to affect the present, but also retains its alterity; a non-teleological mourning in which the 'outcome' of mourning is not fixed nor determined in advance.[9] In *Antigone's Claim*, Judith Butler reads Sophocles's play, a story of forbidden mourning, to consider how legitimate life, love and mourning are connected through kinship which is recognized by the state and/or other regimes of legitimacy. Butler argues that such legitimacy is a necessary condition of being human, so that 'those relations that are denied legitimacy, or that demand new terms of legitimation, are neither dead nor alive, figuring

---

8 Hartman, 'The Time of Slavery', p. 771.
9 Hartman, 'The Time of Slavery', p. 771.

the nonhuman at the border of the human'.[10] In Butler's formulation, mourning is a key sign of kinship, and one's ability to mourn deceased kin, and to have one's mourning recognized by others, is a sign of the legitimacy both of the kinship bond and the subjects who mourn and are mourned. In the case of forbidden or unrecognized mourning, such as that of Antigone for her brother, or that of the queer relationships with which Butler is primarily concerned, publicly mourning such lives means demanding recognition for the dead as 'grievable lives' and recognition for the mourners as their loved ones and their kin. The public identification and recognition of these mourners may expose previously invisible kinship networks, including bonds which exceed the dyadic couple or vertical parent-child bonds. Butler is primarily concerned with, and her work has mostly been read in the context of, the intimate bonds of queer sexual minorities, but the analysis of queer diaspora developed in this book—including the claim that all intimacy and kinship in diaspora is queered by its displacement from national heteronormativity—suggests the applicability of Butler's analysis to diasporic mourning and kinship in general. In *Trumpet*, kinship and mourning are queered, but this queering is less a result of the queerness of the subjects involved, and more a result of their diasporic context and the practices of relationality thereby generated; it is to be found in the text's openness, its non-teleological histories, its permeable and becoming understanding of subjectivity, and its practices of mourning—all of which contribute to its queering of kinship and to the generation of queer diasporic bonds.

Mourning is a public activity, suggests Butler, in multiple ways: it requires and demands public recognition, she suggests in *Antigone's Claim*, and it may offer a way to create new political communities based on an acknowledgement of our 'fundamental dependency and ethical responsibility' on and for others, as she explores in *Precarious Life*.[11] For Millie, the media harassment she experiences after Joss's death, with journalists and photographers surrounding her house at all times, soon becomes an experience of acute *mis*recognition, made even worse after her receipt of a series of letters from a journalist, Sophie Stones, who wishes to write a 'tell-all' biography of Joss. Millie fears public misrecognition and mislabelling, of both herself and Joss: 'No doubt they will call me a lesbian. They will find words to put on me. Words that don't fit me. Words that don't fit Joss' (*Tr* 154). Millie's experience of misrecognition hampers her mourning of Joss; she feels alienated from her own grief and too distracted to reflect and remember. Perhaps most critically, she feels that her status as a grieving widow is not acknowledged. Without adequate recognition as a grieving subject, Millie feels unable to mourn Joss, and, in turn, recognition of her mourning of Joss is necessary to confirm Joss's life as one worthy of grief and mourning. In response, Millie attempts—for

---

10 Butler, *Antigone's Claim*, p. 79.
11 Butler, *Antigone's Claim*; Butler, *Precarious Life*, p. 22.

a time—to establish herself as a subject worthy of public recognition as a grieving widow, and Joss as a subject worthy of mourning by constructing their relationship as 'ordinary' (*Tr* 205), that is, as bourgeois, heteronormative and national as possible.

To this end, Millie's chapters increasingly turn from her memories of Joss and their life together to become appeals to an imaginary public, as she seeks to portray herself and Joss as figures worthy of respect, citizenship, and grief. She first claims the status of a widow, writing repeatedly: 'My husband died. I am now a widow' (*Tr* 205). The repetition of the phrase, three times in a row, emphasizes Millie's increasing sense of desperation, but it also reveals the dependence of the performative aspect of the spoken phrase on the recognition it seeks to evoke: it will become true in a meaningful way only once it is recognized as such by others. This turn to a legally and socially recognized kinship status to anchor her claim for recognition and to guarantee Joss recognition as a grievable life suggests first the key role of kinship in the categorization of grievable and ungrievable lives: if 'kinship is the precondition of the human', Butler suggests, then only those subjects with recognized or recognizable kinship ties qualify as grievable and grieving.[12] Secondly, just as kinship may be a condition of mourning, mourning also confirms and performs kinship: Millie needs her mourning of Joss to be recognized in order to affirm and make real the intimate relationship which preceded it. Her claim of widowhood is also a claim of conventionality; she is just one of 'many women [who] have become widows' (*Tr* 205). In the passage immediately following this, Millie imagines speaking to her friends or another public audience to answer their anger or their questions, and to restore the ruptured communication she senses between them: 'My friends don't know how to talk to me or write to me any more. They are embarrassed, confused, shocked. Perhaps angry. [...] Perhaps they want to know how I "managed" it' (*Tr* 205–06). In response to this imagined demand to explain herself, Millie offers an appeal to her imagined audience; a public defence which reinforces her claim of conventionality, ordinariness and sexual normativity, and which situates her within a particularly capitalist discourse of work performed and rewards earned:

> I managed to love my husband from the moment I clapped eyes on him till the moment he died. I managed to desire him all of our married life. I managed to respect and love his music. I managed to always like the way he ate his food. I managed to be faithful, to never be interested in another man. I managed to be loyal, to keep our private life private where it belonged. To not tell a single soul including my own son about our private life. I managed all that. I know I am capable of loving to the full capacity, of not being frightened of loving too much, of giving myself up and over. I know that I loved being the wife of Joss Moody. (*Tr* 206)

---

12 Butler, *Antigone's Claim*, p. 82.

The repeated use of 'I managed' in this passage generates multiple and perhaps contradictory interpretations: on the one hand, it evokes a middle-class respectability and work ethic, demanding respect for hard work and a job well done; on the other, it paints life as a managed or choreographed performance and portrays love as an active doing, a kind of work, rather than uncontrollable or 'natural' emotion. The passage taps into a series of normative expectations about what kind of love relationships should be recognized and worthy of respect: those that are monogamous, all consuming, long-term or lifelong, and which take place in private. Millie seeks to portray herself as a good wife: one who conforms to traditional gender roles and is full of respect for her husband and his work, in order to gain the recognition as a grieving widow that she desires. In this passage and the one discussed above, in which Millie repeatedly asserts her status as a widow, it becomes clear that in *Trumpet*, a story of liminal legitimacy and humanity, it is not only sex and gender which determine a subject's access to national heteronormativity, but these in interaction with race and class as well. Imagining accusations of gender deviance and perversion, Millie counters these not only with the assertion of gender and sexual conformity, but also with white bourgeois norms of hard work and privacy. Despite Millie's repeated claims of her own heterosexuality, her situation is nonetheless comparable to that described by Suzanne Lenon, who argues that, for subjects seeking to attain (homo)normativity the 'domestic/familial subject position is not sufficient for the attainment of respectability garnered through ordinariness; rather its pursuit also requires an investment in and alignment with white racial normativity', including its norms of privacy and property.[13] In order to claim for herself the status of a mourner and a widow and for Joss the status of a grievable life, she tries to insert them both into white national (hetero)normativity.

This connection between sexual or gender normativity and whiteness also contributes to an understanding of the curious tension in the novel between its very apparent queerness and Millie's insistence on the conventionality, even heterosexuality, of her relationship with Joss. The vital desire to be considered a living, lovable, grievable subject and a subject worthy and capable of kinship—and to thus enjoy the rights and benefits awarded to such subjects—is rendered precarious for Joss and Millie due to both race and gender, and an understanding of how these create and inflect each other is critical. Most analyses of race in the novel do not consider gender, with the important exception of the work of Matt Richardson.[14] Richardson reads the text as, most

---

13 Suzanne Lenon, '"Why Is Our Love an Issue?": Same-Sex Marriage and the Racial Politics of the Ordinary', *Social Identities* 17.3 (2011), p. 357. See also David Theo Goldberg, *The Racial State* (Malden: Blackwell, 2002); Jasbir K. Puar, *Terrorist Assemblages: Homonationalism in Queer Times* (Durham, NC: Duke University Press, 2007).
14 Peter Clandfield, '"What Is in My Blood?": Contemporary Black Scottishness and the Work of Jackie Kay', in Teresa Hubel and Neil Brooks (eds.), *Literature and Racial*

of all, a reflection on 'the fragility of black manhood': not only for Joss, but also, indeed particularly, for his (cis-gender) son Colman, and he identifies this gender crisis not as specific to Joss's body or gender identity, but as part of the afterlife of slavery, traceable back to the violent degendering caused by slavery and forced transportation, as discussed by Hortense Spillers.[15] Richardson suggests that this 'undoing and reworking of black gender categories is a key facet of social death' as conceptualized by Orlando Patterson, and that this social death extends far beyond the end of slavery, so that black bodies (in this case particularly black men's bodies) are 'socially dead' or 'dead to the Scottish nation': they have never and still cannot achieve the status of the 'living', who have access to 'a full range of subjectivity and citizenship'.[16] For Richardson, the novel demonstrates that 'the normative [is] an untenable option, especially for racialized subjects'.[17] Richardson's insistence on the relevance of slavery to the text is revealing, because Atlantic slavery features in the novel only as a possible history—but not the family history that is finally told. (In the history Joss offers at the end of the novel, his father John Moore migrated to Scotland from Africa at the beginning of the twentieth century.) Yet it is also clear that even for black diasporic subjects with no family history of slavery, no 'direct' or genealogical link to enslaved Africans, the history of slavery impacts upon them, and they too are part of its afterlife.

Richardson adapts the term 'social death' from Patterson and applies it to racialized gender; however, Patterson's original use of the term is not concerned with *gender* but with *kinship*. For Patterson, the chief causes of 'social death' were the loss of genealogical knowledge and the erasure of legal relationships—specifically legal paternity—based upon genealogical bonds which resulted from the Middle Passage and the institutions of New World slavery.[18] Richardson thereby reorients Patterson's work away from its original focus on (the loss of) patriarchal masculine authority towards non-normative and anti-patriarchal ends, but he nonetheless skips a crucial aspect of the equation: it is not only non-normative gender which may cast diasporic black subjects into a state of social death, but also non-normative kinship.

As Richardson argues, racialized subjects, particularly black men, in the novel are always in danger of being termed non-human, ungrievable, and

---

Ambiguity (Amsterdam: Rodopi, 2002), pp. 1–25; Alan Rice, '"Heroes across the Sea": Black and White Fascination with African Americans in the Contemporary Black British Fiction of Caryl Phillips and Jackie Kay', in Heike Raphael-Hernandez (ed.), *Blackening Europe: The African American Presence* (New York: Routledge, 2004), pp. 217–31; Matt Richardson, '"My Father Didn't Have a Dick": Social Death and Jackie Kay's *Trumpet*', *GLQ: A Journal of Lesbian and Gay Studies* 18.2–3 (2012), pp. 361–79.

15 Richardson, 'My Father Didn't Have a Dick', p. 361; Spillers, 'Mama's Baby, Papa's Maybe'.
16 Richardson, 'My Father Didn't Have a Dick', pp. 361–62.
17 Richardson, 'My Father Didn't Have a Dick', p. 363.
18 Patterson, *Slavery and Social Death*.

unworthy of mourning. I suggest that the novel goes further than this, and shows that this even extends to their white, native-born kin, their mourners, who are in danger of trespassing the borders of legitimacy themselves when they attempt to mourn in public, as experienced by Millie. A similar dynamic of policing white femininity, in particular, is repeated at the end of the novel with the story of Joss's white mother, Edith Moore, attempting to mourn her black husband, John Moore, and the way in which her claim of kinship with him through mourning endangers her own respectability and recognition by others. Thus, the impossibility of Millie's claim to national British heteronormativity and thus 'normality' is made apparent by Joss's gender, but not caused entirely by it. Her claims of conventionality are therefore not necessarily, or not only, an attempt to deny the gender-non-normative aspects of their relationship, but to ward off the pernicious effects of racism.

Millie's use of the phrase 'I managed' in this passage also offers another reading—one which undermines the picture of bourgeois normativity which the passage also creates. Even as the passage emphasizes continuity and stability—in phrases such as 'from the moment I clapped eyes on him till the moment he died', 'all of our married life', 'always', 'never'—it also reveals Millie's own role in creating Joss. This identification of a process of creation and transformation undermines any sense generated by the passage of Joss's identity as stable and unchanging—or for that matter of Millie's identity as similarly stable—and it enables a reading of Millie, Joss and many others in the novel as engaged in a process of mutually imbricated becoming. Such an understanding of their relationship is clear early in the novel: Millie recalls that Joss claimed she had 'created him' (*Tr* 36); a track on his first album and the album itself is called 'Millie's Song' (*Tr* 34). In later chapters, when Millie seeks to defend herself against an (imagined) hostile public audience, she chooses instead to assert subjective stability. This suggests that public recognition of kinship and mourning requires a stable and autonomous subject—in the case of both mourner and mourned. Yet precisely this notion of the subject is undermined by grief and mourning, Butler suggests, in which it becomes apparent that we are 'not only constituted by our relations but also dispossessed by them', and the way in which, through mourning, it becomes apparent that deceased 'primary others', intimates or kin, 'haunt the way I am [...] periodically undone and open to becoming unbounded'.[19] The novel explores this tension, presenting a model of diasporic kinship and mourning that exists alongside, rather than replacing, state-recognized kinship and publicly acknowledged mourning. This diasporic kinship is not limited to diasporic subjects; it does not require a personal history of migration or racialization, but it is made more necessary by such a history of dispossession, displacement and (re)invention, and it is thus made accessible in the novel by diasporic aesthetic forms—particularly jazz.

---

19 Butler, *Precarious Life*, pp. 24, 28.

Thus two primary understandings of kinship operate in parallel and intertwined in *Trumpet*: the normative, state-recognized kinship which Millie tries to claim after Joss's death, and an alternative conception of kinship, mourning and subjectivity; one that is both queer and diasporic—and which resists any separation of those two terms. This alternative model of kinship rests upon either shared history or experience or shared creative responses to that history, and it is represented in particular by the queer bonds of the jazz community and Joss's understanding of black diaspora, both of which emphasize an unending process of becoming kin through subjective undoing, permeability and often indirect intimate bonds. Similarly, while in the chapter discussed above Millie temporarily denies the transformative power of love and mourning, emphasizing instead stability, the bulk of her narrative offers ample evidence of it. In contrast to the picture of conventionality which Millie at times seeks to portray, the relationship between Joss and Millie, represented primarily in the recollections narrated by Millie herself, but also supplemented by other narrative threads, is one of queerly inflected becoming—and not only, indeed not even primarily, because of Joss's non-gender-normative body. The relationship between Millie and Joss is a courtship full of queer moments long before Millie watches Joss undress for the first time. When they first meet, their hobbies are jive dancing and jazz. Millie remembers the dance halls: 'it seemed nobody would ever get old. Nobody would ever die' (*Tr* 14) and the feel of dancing: 'there is no tomorrow. There is just the minute, the second, the dip. The heat and the sweat. That feeling of being in your body' (*Tr* 15). If jive dancing suspends time, thereby refusing to participate in the scheme of age-appropriate behaviour which heteronormativity demands, and offers an eroticized experience of one's own body, then jazz—both the music and the culture of the scene—fosters diverse and multiple attachments and other queer forms of eroticism. As Millie really listens to jazz for the first time, the queer erotics of the jazz club reveal themselves to her; remembering the night, she writes of Joss, 'I feel as if I've lost him, that he belongs to the music and not to me' (*Tr* 17). This soon proves to be not a disconnection, but a reconfiguration as an indirect connection, routed through others and through the music. The norms of dyadic heteronormativity are further undermined by the behaviour of the audience, which Millie first observes and then becomes part of: in the smoky, dark, erotically charged club, 'people shout out, little words of intense pleasure—"Yeah!"', their faces are 'rapt, euphoric, dedicated' (*Tr* 17). Millie describes the feeling of going 'inside the music' (*Tr* 18) as an experience of entering into communion with both the music and the crowd, as well as with Joss *via* the music. It is an experience of both ecstatic and permeable subjectivity, of subjective dissolution and the creation of a strong yet indirect bond between Millie and Joss—and it is immediately after this evening that Joss reveals his body to Millie for the first time.

Eve Kosofky Sedgwick conceives of a model of 'permeable intersubjectivity' or 'interpenetrated psyches' as a way to reconceive of self and other in dynamic interrelation.[20] Sedgwick seeks to imagine and make possible kinship based on 'a completely different principle of affiliation' than blood or law: 'people who come or stay together because they love each other—can give each other pleasure—have real needs from each other'.[21] Secondly, she is explicitly concerned with trans-mortem relationality, with the relationship to a deceased other, and with developing an ethics of intersubjectivity which extends beyond an individual lifespan. Kay's novel suggests that this line of thinking can and should be extended to understanding how not only queer 'post-Proustian' love might create such bonds, but how diasporic experiences of intimacy, kinship and mourning also create permeable subjects, 'riven and open to movements within and through' them, and that diasporic intimacy might only involve 'an expansive network of relations that precede and exceed the self without a definable limit'.[22]

The queer bonds of diasporic cultural production conjured in these passages—between band members, between musicians and listeners, and across the Atlantic and across chronological time, as the jazz community reinvents and reimagines bonds to jazz musicians and audiences of the past— are reflected in the multiple narrative strands of the text and in the textuality of several of those strands. The rotating narrators and focalizers echo the performance aesthetic of jazz itself, with multiple characters offering a short 'solo' chapter, and the novel as a whole, as Lars Eckstein notes, offering a 'collective improvisation' on the theme of Joss Moody.[23] Mark Stein suggests that jazz offers Joss the 'necessary cultural authority' to write his own story— at least during his lifetime—but that this authority is lost upon his death, leading to the question of 'who controls his memory'.[24] Yet jazz aesthetics also pervade Millie's chapters after Joss's death in another way, and in a way which undermines any authority which would seek to legitimate a single memory: her personal, intimate and very specific memories of Joss are often interwoven with, and intersected by, snippets of song text. She recalls her wedding:

> I smile at him dancing with pretty Eileen Murray, raise my eyebrows, blow him a kiss over big Bill Brady's shoulder. *When I'm takin' sips from your tasty lips, seems the honey fairly drips, you're confection, goodness knows, honeysuckle rose.* (Tr 29)

The scene stages an indirect and non-dyadic connection between the couple— both are dancing with other wedding guests, who thereby become part of the

---

20 Sedgwick, *A Dialogue on Love*, p. 139; Tyler Bradway, '"Permeable We!": Affect and the Ethics of Intersubjectivity in Eve Sedgwick's *A Dialogue on Love*', *GLQ: A Journal of Lesbian and Gay Studies* 19.1 (2013), pp. 79–110.
21 Sedgwick, *A Dialogue on Love*, p. 130.
22 Sedgwick, *A Dialogue on Love*, p. 114; Bradway, 'Permeable We', p. 90.
23 Lars Eckstein, 'Performing Jazz, Defying Essence: Music as Metaphor of Being in Jackie Kay's *Trumpet*', *Zeitschrift für Anglistik und Amerikanistik* 54.1 (2006), p. 56.
24 Stein, 'Life Border Writing', p. 173.

bond between Millie and Joss. The integration of the song lyrics also offers a hint of gender ambiguity, given that these lyrics might be sung by male and female jazz singers, as in another scene recalled by Millie:

> He sings a Pearl Bailey song into my ear, changing the name to my own. *Oh, Millie had to go and lose it at the Astor/ She wouldn't take her mother's good advice.* We dance around the room, Joss kissing me and singing at the same time. *Had to go and lose at the Astor, at the Astor last night.* We make love on the living room floor. (*Tr* 36)

Here the song text interrupts but also complements Millie's memories, creating a tension between personal and collective memory and suggesting that both her memories and subjectivity are formed in part by collective diasporic cultural production. The interaction and overlap of Millie and Joss's love story, and the text of a love song, suggests first—as Millie has been claiming—that their relationship is a 'ordinary' one, that the love song speaks to them as much as to any other lovers. It also, however, undermines Millie's claims of privacy and of a nuclear family closed off from other bonds and connections; through the music, their partnership is opened up to innumerable others. This is also shown in the incorporation of passages from strangers into the narrative:

> Can we please let the dead rest in peace? Has this country forgotten how to do that?
> *Ann Gray, address provided*. (*Tr* 160)

This note is included in a chapter called 'Letters', comprising seven such short notes, seemingly letters to the editor of a newspaper, and clearly intended for a public audience. Some are from known characters—Joss's bandmate, Big Red McCall, or the journalist Sophie Stones—or plausible associates, such as 'John Anderson, Columbia Records' (*Tr* 160), but others are from people unlikely to have known Joss personally, but who feel affected by him and attached to him: 'Soloman Davis, Joss Moody fan' (*Tr* 159) or the 'Transvestites Anonymous Group (TAG)' (*Tr* 160). The chapter titled 'Obituaries' contains only a list of Joss's albums:

> 1958 *Millie's Song* (Centre)
> [...]
> 1994 *The Best of Joss Moody* (Columbia)
> Joss Moody, trumpet play, born 1927;
> died 27 July 1997. (*Tr* 208)

The names of these albums recall numerous scenes from the novel: '*Torr*' or '*Sunday Brunch*' (*Tr* 208), yet are, once again, public and intended for a wide audience, emphasizing that the intimate family life of Joss, Millie and Colman was never isolated or closed.

Millie's memories of Joss, herself and their life together offer numerous examples of similarly transformational and transgressive experiences that exceed and undermine national heteronormativity. Even before they meet, Millie remembers, 'I wanted a passion, somebody to speed up time with a fast ferocious love' (*Tr* 10), suggesting her partial resistance to the given timetable of a life under the 'straight' linear time of heteronormativity and capitalism, despite her simultaneously adhering to other aspects of it: 'I always wanted marriage, I remember. Marriage, children' (*Tr* 8). Upon meeting Joss she is motivated to break with the gender conventions of the time: 'I approach him and ask him out. It is 1955. Women don't do this sort of thing' (*Tr* 12). Although Millie generally minimizes the importance or role of race in her account, their interracial relationship in 1950s Scotland is itself a challenge to national heteronormativity. Remembering their first meeting, Millie describes Joss's skin as 'the colour of Highland toffee' (*Tr* 11). On the one hand, this description simultaneously exoticizes and domesticizes Joss and makes him into an object for her consumption; it could be read as evidence of Millie's unawareness of the social import of race, her naivety or denial. On the other hand, it can also be read as part of Millie's process of creating Joss (and being created by him in turn): her memory of Joss as 'the colour of Highland toffee' insists on recalling and retroactively constructing Joss as Scottish, on inserting him into Scottish history. It emphasizes the performative, rather than essential, nature of national and racial identity. When Millie and Joss meet for the first time, it is at the 'blood donor's hall in Glasgow' (*Tr* 11). As they share their blood with unknown, multiple others, they literally make their blood the lifeblood of the Scottish nation, and form a bond with each other that is radically open, circulating through a network of donors and patients. Theirs is a bond generated out of a different kind of shared blood than the 'pure blood' of racist nationalism or colonialism: a circulating, life-sustaining—and potentially infectious exchange.

Colman, the adopted black son of Millie and Joss, grapples throughout the novel with two losses: the loss of his father, and the apparent loss of his father as a man. He learns about his father's gender when he sees Joss's naked body in the funeral parlour, and he remains shocked by the sight for much of the novel. His memories, history, and self seemed to have dissolved beneath him: 'the life, the one I thought I knew I'd lived, changed. Now I don't know what I've lived' (*Tr* 46)—and this experience of self-alienation is attributed to the news of Joss's gender, rather than the destabilizing effect of his father's death and his own grief. He first tries to regain a sense of history and self by investigating his parents' legal kinship: he becomes 'obsessed' (*Tr* 49) with the question of how his parents achieved state-licensed legitimacy such as a marriage certificate or his own legal adoption; he hopes that official state documentation might provide a voice of authority to restore order and linearity to both his own memories and his sense of self, both of which are 'all jumbled up' (*Tr* 54). Yet parallel to these events, even as he sets out to search his parents' house for the relevant papers, in the hope that they might give him a sense of stability, his childhood memories reveal a history of repeated creative subjective formation and reshaping. He reflects upon his own adoption and renaming as a creative process which undermines any notion of a fixed or essential self: 'Before I became Colman Moody, I was William Dunsmore. If I'd stayed William Dunsmore all my life I'd have been a completely different man' (*Tr* 56). Yet he also recalls a long-standing desire for a sense of family history and continuity, a sense of identity based not on genealogy but knowledge of the past: he 'didn't give a toss about my real parents' (*Tr* 57) but desperately wanted to know the story of Joss's father: 'Tell me really, that's what I kept saying, tell me where your father was really from' (*Tr* 58).

As Colman's narrative continues, it becomes clear that his sudden sense of unreality and his precarious sense of self is not caused by the recent revelation of his father's gender status, but rather is a regular feature of Colman's experience as a black man in Britain, and this experience of racialization makes it especially difficult for Colman to open himself up to the vulnerability and undoing caused by and demanded by mourning. Richardson emphasizes the similarities between Joss and Colman: Joss is 'like any other black man, ambiguously gendered and caught in tangles of denial of his own femininity in order to claim manhood'; Colman is 'a black man who is ultimately in a feminized position in relationship to legitimate patriarchal white masculinity'.[25] Colman is finally forced to acknowledge that mourning his father also means mourning 'black gender coherence', revealing along the way that 'black genders are nonnormative and unstable'.[26] He too experiences constant misrecognition: as a criminal, a threat, as someone without rights or without a voice: 'Black guys like him. People always think they are going to be wrong or they've done something wrong or they're lying, or about to lie, or stealing or about to steal' (*Tr* 189). Thus it becomes clear that Colman's insecurities around his identity are prompted at least as much by his experienced as a racialized subject, an always at best precariously legitimate subject, as they are by the revelation of his father's gender. Colman hopes to (re)gain control of his own life and redefine himself by (re)writing his father's history. Yet the book project he embarks upon with the journalist Sophie Stones, which seeks to portray Joss as a pervert with sizeable penis envy, proves demeaning and dissatisfying, and it becomes clear that whilst rewriting the past is necessary and desirable, it must be done within a project of transformative, diasporic mourning, rather than within the terms of a heteronormative, capitalist historical revision which seeks to fix and exploit, rather than open up, the past and the future.

Historical revision in *Trumpet* takes various forms: the tabloid media's rewriting of Joss and Millie as 'big butch frauds' (*Tr* 170), the uncertain classification of Joss as 'female' by state and medical authorities after his death, and the multiple memories and rewritings of the characters who knew him (and some

---

25 Richardson, 'My Father Didn't Have a Dick', pp. 370, 362.
26 Richardson, 'My Father Didn't Have a Dick', p. 368.

who did not). It is this mixture of forms of rewriting which makes Colman and Millie's task of mourning difficult, and which demonstrates the complex interaction of forms of memory, history and mourning in this diasporic space. For a time, the medial, medical and state rewritings of their family history cause both Millie and Colman to seek reassurance in the promise of either a stable past (particularly for Millie) or a stable identity (particularly for Colman). For example, Millie writes: 'I don't know how to be myself any more. I don't even know if I am being genuine. [...] The only thing that feels authentic to me is my past' (*Tr* 36–37). She feels that the past is stable and comforting, unlike the tumultuous present she is experiencing, and her fear of subjective transformation is countered by the recourse to this supposedly fixed past. The novel suggests, however, that rewriting the past is a critical and inevitable task of mourning, and that through mourning subjectivity and kinship are reformed and both the past and the future, mutually enfolded, reshaped.

Three characters in the novel, each of whom is the focalizer of one chapter, chart one aspect of the attempt to rewrite Joss and his family's past: the doctor who attends the house after his death and writes out the medical certificate, the registrar who registers the death and writes the death certificate, and the funeral director charged with embalming the body and organizing the funeral. Each has extensive experience of death, and each of them describe death and dying as a slow, somewhat uncanny, and transformational experience—upon all involved. Yet in the case of Joss's gender, they are also confronted with the need—mandated by medical or state categories, or by their own expectations—to fix and define the meaning of Joss's body. This is precisely the sort of redefinition Millie fears, yet curiously, the chapters show that even this official, state, medical or public rewriting fails to create the definitive classification it seeks, and rather operates to further undermine such categories. As the doctor examines Joss, she rewrites the medical certificate multiple times. After 'filling in the obvious, prior to her own examination. [...] Sex: Male' (*Tr* 43), she undresses Joss, then 'she crossed "male" out and wrote "female" in her rather bad doctor's handwriting. She looked at the word "female" and thought it wasn't quite clear enough. She crossed that out, tutting to herself, and printed "female" in large childish letters' (*Tr* 44). Despite the clear categorization which the doctor intends to make, and believes it is possible to make, her rewriting of Joss's life via his death as 'female' instead demonstrates the *failure* of that categorization. First, the doctor's classification of Joss's body is not easily made, and the basis for such a classification seems to be in some doubt:

> When she first saw the breasts [...] she thought that they weren't real breasts at all. At least not women's breasts. She thought Mr Moody must be one of those men that had extra flab on top—male breasts. [...] It took her pulling down the pyjama bottoms for her to be quite certain. (*Tr* 43–44)

Secondly, her attempt to bring authority and clarity to bear on the medical certificate instead destabilizes gender categories, which are finally presented on the certificate under erasure: ~~male~~ ~~female~~ FEMALE, the authority of the last term further undermined by its 'childish letters'.

The chapter of the funeral director, Albert Holding, describes a process of categorizing Joss's gender both strikingly similar and strikingly different to that of the doctor.

> The first thing he noticed was that the man's legs were not hairy. Then Holding noticed that he had rather a lot of pubic hair. A bush. The absence of the penis did not strike him straight away. Perhaps because he was expecting it, he imagined it for a while. When he did notice after a few moments that there was no visible penis, he actually found himself rummaging in the pubic hair just to check that there wasn't a very, very small one hiding somewhere. [...]
>
> He began to take the pyjama shirt off. [...] Even though Holding was expecting them, he still gave out a gasp when he saw them. There they were, staring up at him in all innocence—the breasts. (*Tr* 108–09)

Holding's classification of Joss's body is slow and uncertain, just as it is for the doctor; it becomes increasingly unclear how this classification is to be made. While for the doctor, Joss's breasts were inconclusive but the lower half of his body confirmed him as 'female', for the funeral director it is the other way around: the lack of a penis is less meaningful or decisive than the presence of breasts. Even after Holding has classified Joss as a 'woman' (*Tr* 109), this categorization seems both unstable and threatening:

> If there was anything untoward in the death certificate, he would be duty bound to correct it with this very red pen. [...] He almost wished it would happen. If he could have the satisfaction of brutally and violently obliterating 'male' and inserting female in bold, unequivocal red, then at least he would have something to do. (*Tr* 112–13)

Holding takes comfort in imagining official, authoritative action, but, as the doctor's experience has already shown, even a red pen is unable to achieve the 'unequivocal' certainty he desires. The disjunction between the language of his imagined action—'brutally and violently obliterating'—and the bureaucratic banality of a death certificate demonstrates the enormous stakes of this question to Holding. In the end, the death certificate as prepared by the registrar offers a compromise: the name 'Joss Moody' (rather than his birth name Josephine) and the category 'female': once again, a categorization which only serves to undermine the category it invokes.

It is in this context of official and medial rewritings of Joss (and Millie) that Millie and Colman respond by seeking stability, but at the end of the novel, both Millie and Colman begin to accept that they themselves, Joss, and their shared past will be changed by Joss's death and their mourning of him. Millie reflects on her relationship to her own past in particular after leaving London to escape the media harassment and travelling to her cottage in Torr, a small village on the coast of Scotland that she has visited since childhood. Upon her arrival she feels that the place contains the past unchanged: it holds not only the 'the smell of the past' but the past itself: 'the past had lived on in those small airless rooms whilst we had been away living our life. The past had been here all the time, waiting' (*Tr* 7). She reflects on the subjective changes she has experienced over her lifetime: from her childhood as a 'fearless girl' to 'marriage, children' to 'Joss Moody's widow' (*Tr* 8). Gradually, she begins to realize that Joss's death and her mourning *have* changed Torr and the past: 'it is familiar the way a memory is familiar, and changed each time like a memory too' (*Tr* 92). Yet she still resists this transformation and fears that her life is losing its coherence:

> I don't know what feeling like myself is any more. Who is Millicent Moody? Joss Moody is dead. Joss Moody is not Joss Moody. Joss Moody was really somebody else. Am I somebody else too. But who else was Joss? Who was this somebody else? I don't understand it. Have I been a good mother, a good wife, or have I not been anything at all? Did I dream up my own life? (*Tr* 98)

Here, Millie shows her awareness that she cannot mourn if she does not open herself up to change, and accept that Joss may be retrospectively transformed too, yet she fears that becoming 'somebody else' means subjective destruction—the fear that she might not have been 'anything at all'.

Perhaps because he has less to lose, as someone who has experienced this risk of dehumanization and misrecognition all his life, it is Colman, rather than Millie, who first comes to accept and embrace a rewriting of the past in order to properly mourn, by engaging with Joss's past and family history. Colman travels from London to Glasgow with the journalist Sophie Stones; they intend to research Joss's family history for their planned book, and to make contact with Joss's mother, who, Stones has discovered, is still alive. Colman believes he is there to 'find out about his father's real life' (*Tr* 190)—that is, to restore order, linearity and clarity to the story. But he gradually comes to accept that both his father and 'reality' are more complex and more ambivalent than this during his visit to Joss's elderly mother, and especially after seeing a childhood photograph of Joss as a little girl, Josephine. The photograph, originally sought as valuable material for the book, has an unexpected effect: 'Now that he's seen the little girl, he can see something feminine in his memory of his father's face that must have been there all along' (*Tr* 241). He stares at the picture, 'waiting for something to happen. Some other image to appear behind the one that he is holding in his hand. Some transformation to occur to make sense of it all' (*Tr* 241–42). The transformation of the photograph that Colman expects and hopes for—in which, presumably, a more masculine picture would become visible—does not occur, yet his attitude towards his father's gender *is* transformed. When Colman thinks of the photograph, it is not this newly apparent femininity that he focuses on; rather, as he thinks of the photograph 'his father keeps coming back to him' (*Tr* 256). The sight of Joss as Josephine has *restored* his father to him, not taken him further away.

The photograph of Joss/Josephine as a child, more than 60 years old, is able to move through time, representing not only Joss's childhood (until then unknown to Colman), but equally his father as an adult, an old man, and his spectral ongoing presence. Rather than trying to fix or stabilize his father's identity, Colman now sees that Joss as a girl is able to recall and represent Joss as a man: a figure that combines ambivalence and changeability with stability. The photograph leads Colman to break off his agreement with the journalist, announcing, 'He'll always be daddy to me' (*Tr* 259).

After accepting that his father might be simultaneously an ambivalent and reliable figure, as well as man and girl at once, Colman finally opens the letter that his father left for him, which he has been too angry and confused to read until now. Colman's expectation at the time he discovered the letter—'it'll just be a list of excuses and reasons. I'm not interested' (*Tr* 65)—is shown to be mistaken, for the letter is not, or not explicitly, about Joss's gender at all. Instead, it contains the story of Joss's father, demonstrating the importance of this diasporic history to Joss's, Colman's and Millie's stories. It is a story Colman has long wished to hear, but even as the letter purports to finally tell a story of origins, it warns that fixed origins are an impossible fantasy. Joss writes, 'You wanted the story of my father, remember? I told you his story could be the story of any black man who came from Africa to Scotland. His story, I told you, was the diaspora. Every story runs into the same river and the same river runs into the sea' (*Tr* 271). Joss recounts the story of his father in the letter—his arrival in Scotland, his renaming as John Moore, his childhood and self-education as the servant of a wealthy Scottish family, his apprenticeship and then his death when Joss was eleven—but at the same time he warns, using the words of his father, that any story of the past is only one of many possible stories: 'The trouble with the past, my father said, is that you no longer know what you could be remembering' (*Tr* 273). His father, for example, 'couldn't remember what he wanted to remember', so that the country of his birth was lost to him, 'drowned at sea in the dead of a dark, dark night', and could never be recovered (*Tr* 273).

The letter and the story of Joss's father suggest that Joss's own story is not particularly unusual: it is not that his history is obscure, ambivalent and slippery because of his gender, but because *all* diasporic histories are that way. The metaphor of the sea functions in the letter in two apparently contradictory ways: first, as the repository of all that is lost, signifying the unrecoverability of an archive 'drowned at sea in the dead of a dark, dark night'. This recalls most significantly Derek Walcott's imagining of the sea as the 'grey vault' of History in which cultural knowledge, traditions and millions of people drowned during the violent creation of the modern African diaspora.[27] But there is also the sense of the sea as a connective medium,

---

27 Derek Walcott, 'The Sea is History', *Collected Poems 1948–1984* (New York: Farrar, Straus and Giroux, 1986), p. 364.

joining together diasporic peoples in particular, but by extension all who inhabit the diaspora space of contemporary Britain: 'every story runs into the same river and the same river runs into the sea', a metaphor of the sea as a medium of connection similar to that in Dionne Brand's *At the Full and Change of the Moon*.

Joss's letter offers an addendum, and perhaps corrective, to his own view of kinship, offered earlier in the novel. Colman recounts his father's attitude:

> My father always told me he and I were related the way it mattered. He felt that way too about the guys in his bands, that they were all part of some big family. Some of them were white, some black. He said they didn't belong anywhere but to each other. He said you make up your own bloodline, Colman. Make it up and trace it back. Design your own family tree—what's the matter with you? Haven't you got an imagination? (*Tr* 58)

In the letter, while it is clear that Joss still believes kinship to be created and performed, rather than essential or genealogical, he also acknowledges the importance of a shared history of loss, displacement and racialization for black diasporic subjects like himself, his father, and his son Colman. Yet the novel suggests that it is not only this line of black men who are important to understanding diasporic kinship and subjectivity: it is Colman's visit to Joss's white Scottish grandmother, Edith Moore, which initiates Colman's reconciliation with his memory of his father and his rethinking of the meaning and value of kinship and mourning.

At the end of the letter Joss passes the baton to Colman, inviting him to become the next storyteller and to assume responsibility for Joss's story:

> It is quite simple: all of this is my past, this is the sum of my parts; you are my future. I will be your son now in a strange way. You will be my father telling or not telling my story. [...] You will understand or you won't. You will keep me or lose me. You will hate me or love me. You will change me or hold me dear. You will do either or both for years. (*Tr* 277)

Colman's original plan of rewriting as revenge—'I'll tell his whole story. I'll be his Judas' (*Tr* 62)—is here recast as a rewriting which performatively enacts kinship and mourning. The proverb 'the child is father of the man' is rewritten and resignified here not as connoting linear continuity and a lack of change, as in Wordsworth's 'My heart leaps up', and more in the way suggested by Wole Soyinka, as 'a proverb of human continuity which is not uni-directional', with relational categories, 'child' and 'father', which are not 'closed or chronological'.[28] Joss casts history, kinship and memory as matters

---

28 Wole Soyinka, *Myth, Literature and the African World* (Cambridge: Cambridge University Press, 1990), p. 10. That Soyinka identifies this as a Yoruba worldview (but not exclusively Yoruba or African) suggests that Joss's African heritage is not entirely irrelevant or forgotten, but that it cannot provide an 'origin' in the way Colman wants.

of storytelling, and storytelling as a force which can create a home, a history and a family—a queer diasporic family—for diasporic subjects. This sense of connection, exceeding not only nuclear families but also national or racial affiliations, is captured in the text's rewriting of the metaphor of blood and its embrace of diasporic aesthetic forms.

The image of shared blood first evoked in the blood donors' clinic where Millie and Joss meet is taken up again later in the context of the jazz scene and the bonds which jazz generates between musicians, and/or between musicians and their audience. A short chapter, apparently focalized through Joss himself, both reworks the metaphor of blood and demonstrates the particular aesthetic qualities of jazz relevant to the notion of subjective becoming explored in the text. The chapter describes the experience of playing the trumpet as one of subjective excavation and transformation, even sensory permeability; Joss witnesses his own birth and death and 'he can taste himself transforming' (*Tr* 133). This transformation is, of course, partly a question of gender: 'from girl to young woman to young man to old man to old woman' (*Tr* 133). But it is also one of dissolving subjective autonomy into permeable jazz subjectivity, which in Joss's case is not limited only to those, like Millie or Big Red, with whom he has close relationships, but may include 'people [...] met or unmet, loved or unloved' (*Tr* 134). The 'trip' of making music, of 'running changes', is one of undoing: he loses bodily control, 'his left leg is uncontrollable', he loses his outward appearance: 'it all falls off – bandages, braces, cufflinks, watches, hair grease, suits, buttons, ties', until 'all of his self collapses' (*Tr* 134–35). This experience of undoing, of 'explod[ing]' the self and then 'piecing himself together' again is not done in isolation, neither is it accompanied only by the music; rather, it requires and involves the crowd who listens to him play, and this connection between audience and Joss is described as a matter of *blood*. Blood is evoked multiple times: 'It is all in the blood', 'There is music in his blood', 'They want more blood', 'The blood dreaming' (*Tr* 131–34). Finally: 'The music is his blood' (*Tr* 135). Thus the chapter moves from an understanding of blood as *containing* or *carrying* that essence or instinct which enables Joss to play music—an understanding which reverberates with racist notions of the 'natural' affinities of 'black blood'—to offer multiple alternative notions of blood which challenge and rework such racism: blood is what the audience wants from Joss, an image whose violence is mediated by Joss's own need for audience participation; blood is a thinking or dreaming force (undoing a mind–body binary which would assign blood to the unthinking body); finally blood *is* music, or rather, the music *is* blood: in this last image, is it the music circulating between the players and audience that defines (or undefines) the body. Jazz does not 'transcend gender totally', it is not 'gender free', but it does work to undo or destabilize assumptions about the integrity and identity of the body upon which gender ideologies often rest.[29] Eckstein argues that jazz

---

29 King, 'A Woman's a Man, For a' That', pp. 106–07.

functions in the text as 'a metaphor of being and identity formation' which 'radically values performance and self-creation over essence and determinism', but I would suggest that this self-creation is not only individual, but collective, interactive, or in Sedgwick's terms, interpenetrating.[30]

This description of the aesthetics of jazz has much in common with the radical black aesthetics identified by Fred Moten. When Joss 'hangs on to the high C and then he lets go. Screams' (136), the scream of his trumpet might be read as an example of the screams that echo through black music—echoes, Moten suggests, of the suffering of transport and slavery, and which enable black musical forms to '[perform] historical placement as a long transfer, a transcendental fade'.[31] This long, stretched out temporality brings the past into the present as echo, inspiration and imitation; Colman remembers that 'music was the one way of keeping the past alive, his father said' (190). Moten insists upon 'the anoriginality of black performances',[32] just as Colman reflects that 'all jazz men are fantasies of themselves, reinventing all the Counts and Dukes and Armstrongs, imitating them' (190); this anoriginality, this reiteration and reinvention, can also be understood as a temporal force which enfolds the present into the past and the past into the present. This positing of reinvention as a feature of jazz or diasporic aesthetics makes clear that the rewriting and subjective openness to which Millie and Colman must open themselves in the novel is not only a matter of death and mourning, but of diasporic life as well.

This reworking of the meaning of blood and the meaning of jazz is continued a few pages later in the chapter focalized through Joss's former drummer, Big Red McCall. His recollections chart a move from the queerly intimate bond of the two men to a more expansive group: 'McCall loved nothing better than a wee jam with Moody. A wee practice. Just the two of them' (146–47). This bond between 'just the two of them' then expands to draw in others via shared blood: 'Big Red McCall and Joss Moody together had people reeling and begging for more. The claps they got! They weren't normal appreciation. They were fucking desperate. Jazz was their fix. Jazz was in their veins' (147). This final image recalls not only the historical associations of the jazz scene with heroin use, but suggests once again a reworking of the metaphor of blood as a sign of connection, belonging and a form of kinship, with the connections between the musicians themselves and their audiences generated by together imbibing, sharing, circulating and transfusing a powerful substance, one which may dissolve the autonomous self. Thus, despite the sexism of the jazz community of the time, noted in the novel, it is simultaneously suggested that the modes of being and kinds of bonds created and imagined by the aesthetics and practices of a diasporic musical form like jazz might destabilize gender—not erasing or transcending

---

30 Eckstein, 'Performing Jazz, Defying Essence', p. 51; Sedgwick, *A Dialogue on Love*.
31 Moten, *In the Break*, p. 22.
32 Moten, *In the Break*, p. 23.

it, but showing the limits of notions of gender which try to define and delimit permeable, ecstatic bodies and subjects, just as the overlap and interaction of narration and song texts and the use of multiple narrative forms and song lyrics blurs the clear contours of each of the novel's stories, which remain separate yet are interdependent and interrelated.

The final, very short chapter of the novel, entitled 'Shares', indicates the potential and the necessity of this rewriting of subjectivity and history, a mutually imbricated rewriting to create an enfolded past and future. Joss's suggestion in his letter to Colman—'you will be my father telling or not telling my story' (*Tr* 277)—demonstrates the way in which kinship and mourning are central to this process: *how* we remember the dead (re)writes and creates the past, and mourning shapes not only the past through this rewriting, but also the future, because those who mourn are changed going into the future. In this way the novel also somewhat alters or corrects Joss's belief, recalled by Colman: 'There's more future in the past than there is in the future, he said' (*Tr* 190). According to the temporal logic created by kinship and mourning in the novel, there is both future in the past—the creative potential offered by black diasporic cultural forms, and the forms of relationality developed in diaspora—and much past to be found in the future—in the way the memory of mourned kin and lost others (trans)forms those in the present and influences their reshaping of present and future diaspora spaces. The final chapter of the novel gestures towards a reconciliation between Millie and Colman on the harbour front in Torr, but it is narrated in the form of an everyman story, suggesting both the applicability of the story to others, but also that the figures in the chapter, the woman and man, are no longer exactly the same Millie and Colman from earlier in the novel. The chapter in full:

> The woman walked down the hill and into the harbour. The bus had already arrived. She walked quicker. Just as she turned the bend, where the fishing boats pondered on the water, she saw him. He was walking towards her. He moved so like his father. A bird startled her by flying close to her head. It seemed the bird had come right out of her. She watched it soar right up into the sky, its wings dipping, faltering and rising again, heard it calling and scatting in the wind. (*Tr* 278)

This reconciliation takes place by the sea, the medium of both connection and separation, remembering and forgetting, a force which forms *and* undoes the outlines of subjects, just as the waves batter against the Scottish coast. The sea is a transnational and transtemporal vector: it connects the lost, forgotten African country from which Joss's father came to the Scottish port in which he arrived, just as it connects the past and present by offering a sense of ever changing stability: 'I have grown old with this sea in my life' (*Tr* 267), thinks Millie; Colman sees in the sea 'the same old fishing harbour where he spent many many hours as a boy' (*Tr* 270).

In this final chapter, the sea once again brings Millie and Colman back together, to a reconciliation that is open and connected to others—it takes place at the harbour front—yet also removed from the public, medial context which exerted great influence on both characters for much of the novel. Thus in *Trumpet* it is not public mourning which proves most important and vital in the end—at least, not the public of the scandal-obsessed, profit-driven media. Butler writes that in *Antigone*, forbidden *public* mourning may inaugurate political change: 'If kinship is the precondition of the human, then Antigone is the occasion for a new field of the human, achieved through political catachresis, the one that happens when the less than human speaks as human, when gender is displaced, and kinship founders on its own founding laws'.[33] Yet Colman's mourning of his father begins in the privacy of his—recently discovered—grandmother's home; the beginning of a relationship to her is also the beginning of his mourning. It is never narrated, and thus remains hidden, shielded even from the reader. It is hinted, but remains unclear, that Colman may have revealed Joss's death to Joss's mother; in this way, even the question of whether mourning is taking place—whether Joss's mother knows that he has died—is not made public. For Millie, she is relieved once the media storm has passed—'I have become yesterday's news' (*Tr* 267)—and no longer wishes to correct the public misrecognition of herself or Joss.

Trumpet thus suggests that the two modes of kinship present in the text: state-recognized, static, governed by genealogy or legal recognition, or mobile, performative, and created by shared experience and shared aesthetic creation, and their associated modes of mourning—the publicly enacted and recognized grief that stabilizes subjectivity, and some other, more transformative mourning—are not necessarily opposed to each other, but rather necessarily coexist in the context of late twentieth-century Britain. Just as state recognition of kinship may be crucial, and public recognition of grief desirable, particularly for a subject like Joss, his partner Millie, or their son Colman—in the well-known words of Gayatri Spivak, it is something they 'cannot not want'—the novel equally suggests that other notions of kinship and subjectivity are also vital to diasporic survival and flourishing.[34] In addition, while the novel demonstrates the continuing impact of state kinship norms, particularly on marginalized subjects, it equally suggests that other, queerly diasporic, notions of kinship have shaped contemporary Britain in numerous but largely unrecognized ways, and will continue to do so. The queer moment of dancing cherished by Millie for the eternal present it offers, seemingly isolated from the need to become part of history—or the fear of being forgotten—or insulated from the (re)writing of the past and the legacy left to the future, is transformed into a queer-*because*-diasporic history and present moment in which those pasts and futures are enfolded, constantly reshaped by the kinship and mourning which create them, and which create

33 Butler, *Antigone's Claim*, p. 82.
34 Gayatri Chakravorty Spivak, 'Bonding in Difference', in Alfred Arteaga (ed.), *An Other Tongue: Nation and Ethnicity in the Linguistic Borderlands* (Durham, NC: Duke University Press, 1994), p. 285.

subjectivity and diasporic relationality. In Jackie Kay's novel, the received narrative of liberalism, including liberal kinship and citizenship, is undermined by a story which exposes a diasporic Britain, riven through with racism, but even more undone—and thereby joined together again—by the jiving, screaming, syncopated bonds of its diasporic subjects, which offer rhythms for writing both sociality and subjectivity anew.

Conclusion: Diasporic futures?

The novels considered here were all written around the turn of the twenty-first century, in an age of increasingly rapid globalization, technologization and changes to established legal and institutional kinship forms in the Caribbean, European and North American locations in which they are set and were written. Migration and diasporic displacement are becoming common experiences, for ever more people, alongside global flows of capital, and global changes—to the Earth and its climate, to our interaction with technology, or to lived and legally recognized kinship—have motivated new theorizations of what it means to be human, and to be a subject, today. Amidst these efforts to find new ways to describe and imagine life in the global present, postcolonial and anticolonial scholarship and politics are not necessarily considered adequate resources—even when explicitly concerned with migration and diaspora and the resulting forms of subjectivity and community.[1] The novels considered here, however, prompt a different view of the current moment: they suggest a longer history of non-linear, non-unitary subjectivities and complex modes of interrelationality, restricted neither to the (white) western world nor the present; and not necessarily engendered only by the newest technological developments. They show that a focus on kinship enables both the historical and current ideological pressures on personhood and the limits

---

1 One example of this is Rosi Braidotti, *Transpositions: On Nomadic Ethics* (Cambridge: Polity Press, 2006). In this work, Braidotti argues that postcolonial theory is too tied to humanist traditions to enable the theorization of a posthumanist, post-liberal and non-unitary subject, although she suggests that postcolonial theory can act as a complement to posthumanism. In more recent work, however, Braidotti appears to rethink this position, newly positioning postcolonial thought as central to posthumanist scholarship. See her 'Critical Posthuman Knowledges,' *South Atlantic Quarterly* 116.1 (2017), pp. 83–96.

and meanings of humanity to come into view, particularly (but not only) in the diasporic contexts that are becoming more widespread amidst global migration flows and the multiple forms of displacement caused by climate change. By writing and rewriting diasporic kinship, they offer a vital reminder that current debates around posthumanism are necessary not only due to recent technological developments, but rather emerge from a longer history of black diasporic, indigenous, post- and anticolonial critiques of liberal humanism and modernity.[2]

Kinship is central to subjectivity, these texts suggest, but it is neither bound to normative forms nor unburdened by history, neither fixed nor entirely free. It can be, and has been, deployed as a political tool of colonial oppression and exploitation, and as form of resistance by the colonized and enslaved. It may limit and constrain subjectivity and codify legitimate personhood, and it may be the means to transformative becomings that promise other ways of being in the world, of relating to history and to each other. Understanding the pressures and the possibilities of diasporic kinship reveals much about the ongoing effects of colonialism in multiple modernities, but also imagines possibilities for cultures and subjects to come.

These novels take up Gilroy's challenge to rethink 'selfhood and individuation […] from the slaves' standpoint', and they demonstrate that such an imagining need not rely on colonial genealogy, even if it cannot fully escape it, and that it can thereby offer alternative perspectives on relationality and subjectivity in the past and present.[3] Although the texts were published in the decades on either side of the turn of the twenty-first century, mostly by writers now living in the postindustrial societies of western Europe and North America, they nevertheless insist on a return to the slave-worked sugar and cocoa plantations of the nineteenth-century Caribbean or the colonies of the early twentieth century, as well as to the numerous diaspora spaces around the Atlantic of the late twentieth century, in order to consider the current moment. In doing so, they emphasize not only the ongoing importance of this history to the present moment—a reminder that challenges to kinship and personhood today are not only generated by advances in genetic testing or engineering, or rather, that the origins of genetic engineering should be located earlier and elsewhere than contemporary Euro-America, such as on

---

2 Posthumanist scholarship has regularly been accused of ignoring the contributions of scholars of colour and non-western, particularly indigenous perspectives. See for example Zakiyyah Iman Jackson, 'Animal: New Directions in the Theorization of Race and Posthumanism,' *Feminist Studies* 39.3 (2013), pp. 669–85; Tiffany Lethabo King, 'Humans Involved: Lurking in the Lines of Posthumanist Flight,' *Critical Ethnic Studies* 3.1 (2017), pp. 162–85; Julie Livingston and Jasbir K. Puar, 'Interspecies,' *Social Text* 29.1 (2011), pp. 1–14; Zoe Todd, 'An Indigenous Feminist's Take On The Ontological Turn: "Ontology" Is Just Another Word For Colonialism,' *Journal of Historical Sociology* 29.1 (2016), pp. 4–22.

3 Gilroy, *The Black Atlantic*, p. 56.

the plantations and in the slave quarters of the New World. They also offer a conception of subjectivity, becoming and ethical relationality that has much in common with recent work in posthumanist scholarship, except that its origins, too, lie in the experiences of enslavement, colonization, resistance to oppression and cultural creation in Atlantic diasporas over the past five hundred years. The subjects which emerges from these histories and from these centuries of kinship destroyed and made anew are less attached to liberal humanism and its attendant modes of being and writing, such as teleologies of progress, or a linear history that can also be traced along the lineage of a genealogical chart.

Similarly, the understanding of diasporic community and cultural reproduction offered in these texts emphasizes queered modes of connecting and creating, rather than a group defined by 'blood' or descent, or cultural continuity guaranteed by heteropatriarchy. The postcolonial diasporas in these texts are born of suffering and oppression, as well as of resistance, reconnection and recreation. The vision of subjectivity, relationality and community they offer goes beyond their specific context, and might be understood as an example of diasporic discourses of 'non-Western, or not-only-Western, models for cosmopolitan life [...] for a fraught coexistence'.[4] These novels rework the possibilities of a 'cosmopolitan life' through their rewriting of diaspora, their reflections on the experiences and meanings of transnational movement and migration, non-national belonging and unbelonging, and diasporic intimacy. They do not shrink from the horrors of slave and colonial histories nor the oppressions and sufferings of contemporary black Atlantic diasporas in their depiction of diasporic being, becoming, and connecting, but neither do they reproduce the tendency of national narratives to make diasporic figures tragic and thus cautionary examples.[5]

In Patrick Chamoiseau's *Texaco*, echoing Glissant's *Poetics of Relation*, the ways of writing, living and relating which the novel seeks are intimately connected to the Caribbean landscape, yet open to the sea and to connections, in the same ways its poetics aims to 'open onto unpredictable and unheard of things'.[6] The reference to environmental destruction and neocolonial resource extraction in the closing pages of Pauline Melville's *The Ventriloquist's Tale* makes clear that the questions of indigenous cultural survival which the text explores are not separate nor separable from the question of broader human survival motivated by the environmental and climate crisis of the late twentieth century. At the same time, the novel also makes clear that environmental concerns cannot be separated from the text's rewriting of and challenge to anthropological–colonial discourse and its knowledges.

4 Clifford, *Routes*, p. 277.
5 Gunew, 'Resident Aliens', p. 30.
6 Glissant, *Poetics of Relation*, p. 82.

This interrogation of anthropology, including its historical support of racism and enabling of indigenous oppression, is a necessary part of developing a posthuman subjectivity, for, as Karen Barad suggest, thinking about the posthuman means above all understanding 'the materializing effects of particular ways of drawing boundaries between "humans" and "nonhumans"', that is, engaging with the delimitations and categorizations of anthropology.[7] Yet claims that such a rethinking is demanded by present or recent anthropological developments are challenged by *The Ventriloquist's Tale*, which suggests instead that the late nineteenth-century and early twentieth-century foundations of anthropology have been shaky from the start.[8] Both Melville's novel and Jamaica Kincaid's *The Autobiography of My Mother* imply that a 'rethinking' is required not as a result of technological advances, but both long overdue and long underway as a condition and strategy of anticolonial struggle. Furthermore, Melville's novel refuses the labelling of recent scientific and technological developments and of posthuman thinking as exclusively western, and it thinks through the implications of some scientific developments, particularly quantum mechanics, for both writing and the western knowledge production that would claim them as its own. The appropriation of indigenous identity and experience enacted by Xuela in *The Autobiography of My Mother*, and the way it functions to reify, rather than subvert western ethnography and its knowledges—especially around indigeneity—makes clear that the even post- or anticolonial rewritings of anthropology may nevertheless function to support some of its tenants, such as its long-standing racial thinking, or its temporalization of difference which confines indigenous people, in particular, to the past, offering a warning to any similar project.

The reflections on historiography and the meaning of the past in chapters three and four demonstrate both the demands and costs of linear historiography and teleology and the possibility of another relationship to history and the past. Rather than faithfully pursuing and adhering to linear historical time, these novels showcase a clear awareness in postcolonial, diasporic literature of both the continued influence of linear historicism and the limitations of this form of temporality and historiography. Andrea Levy's *The Long Song* makes clear what is to be gained, but also lost, particularly but not only for diasporic peoples in conforming to and accepting linear time and its

---

7 Karen Barad, 'Nature's Queer Performativity', *Kvinder, køn og forskning* [*Women, Gender and Research*] 1–2 (2012), p. 31.
8 Claims that a rethinking of the human is mandated by recent developments can be found, for example, in Braidotti, who writes of 'the present anthropological mutation' (*Transpositions*, p. 270); Thomas Strong argues that 'new arrangements and new technologies [...] demand a retheorization of culture and indeed of "the human", much as they demand a rethinking of "nature"'. See his 'Kinship Between Judith Butler and Anthropology? A Review Essay', *Ethnos: Journal of Anthropology* 67.3 (2002), p. 407.

associated modes of being and kinship, while Dionne Brand's *At the Full and Change of the Moon* both longs for and imagines drifting, tidal, non-teleological modes of subjectivity and history—even as it, too, acknowledges the forces that limit diasporic, racialized subjects access to the 'time of becoming'.[9] This is taken up in a different way in *Texaco*, in which a Glissantian understanding of a rhizomatic subjectivity—which Glissant asserts is the coming subjectivity of the globalized world, not confined to a parochial past—is predicated on both writing history and understanding kinship without recourse to filiation and origins.[10]

Finally, the becomings of loss, mourning, and queered diasporic subjectivity explored in Jackie Kay's *Trumpet* offer black diasporic perspectives on liberal citizenship, recognition and alternative forms of subjectivity. These modes of subjectivity: permeable, interpenetrated, at times posthuman, reflect Chela Sandoval's recognition of black, diasporic, *decolonial* love 'as a hermeneutics of social change', and as both engine and result of the 'differential consciousness' developed by anticolonial theorists and activists.[11] Both the ongoing importance of state and social recognition and the possibility of other modes of relationality and subjectivity are thematized as Millie, a white British woman, gradually abandons her attachment to liberal recognition in favour of a non-teleological becoming that allows her to mourn Joss and to thereby maintain her kinship with him and with others in a manner befitting their diasporic—and therefore queer—love. The past, present and future become enfolded into another in both Kay's and Brand's texts, and the queer textualities of *Trumpet*, alongside the search for an open writing of becoming in *Texaco*, offer evidence of both the breadth and impact of diasporic forms of non-linear writing.

These texts offer visions and histories of diaspora which rework diaspora relationality, communality, and subjectivity to both queer and decolonize diaspora. If a key aspect of diaspora is that it is always shared with others, these representations of diasporic experience rework this group identity into a form of post-individual relationality, offering a 'non-unitary vision of the subject' from a different perspective.[12] Yet they also demonstrate the risks or limits attendant on such a strategy of becoming and social change; exposing the past and present forces, including historical illegibility, socioeconomic constraints, legal migration regimes, complex discursive interactions over cultural traditions and change, or domestic and state violence, which might hamper such a project. These limits, too, are crucial to consider, so that a project of queer diasporic subjectivity does not replicate the 'denial of coevalness' that would fix racialized, particularly black and indigenous, populations in the past, and install white Euro-American subjects not only

9 Braidotti, *Transpositions*, p. 154.
10 Glissant, *Poetics of Relation*.
11 Sandoval, *Methodology of the Oppressed*, esp. pp. 138–57.
12 Braidotti, *Transpositions*, p. 9.

as the only makers of history, but as the only makers of the future.[13] Eliding the history of anticolonial challenges to anthropology, and posing such challenges as produced only by (implicitly white, western) technological developments, risks perpetuating 'the barring of nonwhite subjects from the category of the human as it is performed in the modern west'.[14] Neglecting to consider the history of slavery and forced transportation ignores a history in which it is precisely 'race' and the 'Nigger', as Sylvia Wynter insists, which come to define lack and the Other to the human (or what Wynter calls 'Man').[15] Through these novels' engagement with and rewriting of kinship, they are able to bring together reflections on the colonial history of kinship discourses, the forms of intimate resistance—and resistance via intimate connections—to colonialism, and the reverberations of both on forms of intimacy, family, and diaspora today. By rethinking and rewriting anthropology, historiography, and the meaning of loss and mourning, and in reworking key metaphors of both colonial and kinship discourses, such as 'blood', they challenge assumptions common to much of diaspora studies and colonial discourses about the meaning and enaction of forms of relationality to culture and subjectivity. They also offer a counterweight to claims that we live in a 'geno-centric' age, that is, one in which our genetic make-up is thought to define and determine us, by demonstrating the wealth of ways in which kinship has been and continues to be defined, experienced and lived in ways other than the presumed Euro-American norm of 'biological' or 'biogenetic' bonds.[16] In these novels, belonging in diaspora is de-essentialized and removed from genealogical bonds or claims of 'blood', and the participation in diaspora space is emphasized over a fixed or pre-determined claim to a group identity—even as the force of discourses of 'blood' and 'biology' is acknowledged, not disavowed. 'Home' is rarely a place—if so, often one that the subjects of these novels wish to leave behind—and more a mode of relating to others and the world. In particular, 'home' comes to mean the desire for connection and relation that is often realized through storytelling, which emerges in these texts as a mode of making kin, generating diaspora, and queerly reproducing culture.

Diaspora cultures are forms of utopianism that rework traditions in pursuit of 'their particular utopia', according to Gilroy.[17] These novels suggest that it is precisely through an imagining of a queer—that is, non-genealogical and non-national—diaspora that the possibility of a global diaspora space might

---

13 Fabian, *Time and the Other*.
14 Weheliye, *Habeas Viscus*, p. 3.
15 Sylvia Wynter, 'Beyond the Word of Man: Glissant and the New Discourse of the Antilles', *World Literature Today* 63.4 (1989), pp. 637–48.
16 Braidotti, *Transpositions*, p. 1. Braidotti takes the term 'geno-centric' from Anne Fausto-Sterling, *Sexing the Body: Gender Politics and the Construction of Sexuality* (New York: Basic Books, 2000), p. 235.
17 Gilroy, *There Ain't No Black in the Union Jack*, p. 218.

be opened up, and thus the way to the global 'fraught co-existence' sought by Clifford. The experiences and practices of queered Black Atlantic kinship, which Jafari Allen suggests have 'always been about finding ways to connect some of what is disconnected, to embody and re-member', is a reminder not only of what should be remembered, of these histories and their ongoing impact.[18] Following Sandoval's argument that it is 'subordinated, marginalized, or colonized Western citizen-subjects' who have the most experience of both the 'aesthetics of "postmodern" globalization' and with 'what citizenship in this realm requires and makes possible',[19] these practices of decolonizing kinship—that is, of playing, drifting, dissolving, fighting, loving and working with others and into unknown otherwises—might also provide resources for coexisting and a life worth living in the worlds to come.

18 Allen, 'Black/Queer/Diaspora at the Current Conjuncture', p. 217.
19 Sandoval, *Methodology of the Oppressed*, p. 9.

Bibliography

Agamben, Giorgio. *Homo Sacer: Sovereign Power and Bare Life*, trans. Daniel Heller-Roazen (Stanford: Stanford University Press, 1998).
Agard-Jones, Vanessa. 'What the Sands Remember', *GLQ: A Journal of Lesbian and Gay Studies* 18.2–3 (2012), pp. 325–46.
Ahmed, Sara. 'Happy Futures, Perhaps', in E. L. McCallum and Mikko Tuhkanen (eds.), *Queer Times, Queer Becomings* (Albany: State University of New York Press, 2011), pp. 159–82.
Alexander, M. Jacqui. 'Erotic Autonomy as a Politics of Decolonization: An Anatomy of Feminist and State Practice in the Bahamas Tourist Economy', in M. Jacqui Alexander and Chandra Talpade Mohanty (eds.), *Feminist Genealogies, Colonial Legacies, Democratic Futures* (New York: Routledge, 1997), pp. 63–100.
Allen, Jafari S. 'Black/Queer/Diaspora at the Current Conjuncture', *GLQ: A Journal of Lesbian and Gay Studies* 18.2–3 (2012), pp. 211–48.
Anderson, Benedict. *Imagined Communities: Reflections on the Origin and Spread of Nationalism* (London: Verso, 1991).
Anderson, Linda. 'Autobiographical Travesties: the Nostalgic Self in Queer Writing', in David Alderson and Linda Anderson (eds.), *Territories of Desire in Queer Culture: Refiguring Contemporary Boundaries* (Manchester: Manchester University Press, 2000), pp. 68–81.
Appiah, Anthony. 'The Uncompleted Argument: Du Bois and the Illusion of Race', in Henry Louis Gates, Jr. (ed.), *"Race," Writing, and Difference* (Chicago: University of Chicago Press, 1986), pp. 21–37.
Apter, Emily S. and Maryse Condé, 'Crossover Texts/Creole Tongues: A Conversation with Maryse Condé', *Public Culture* 13.1 (2001), pp. 89–96.
Arnold, A. James. 'The Gendering of Créolité', in Marysé Condé and Madeleine Cottenet-Hage (eds.), *Penser la créolité* (Paris: Kartala, 1995), pp. 21–40.
Arrizón, Alicia. *Queering Mestizaje: Transculturation and Performance* (Ann Arbor: University of Michigan Press, 2006).
Arroyo, Jossianna. *Travestismos culturales: literatura y etnografía en Cuba y Brasil* (Pittsburgh: Instituto Internacional de Literatura Iberoamericana, 2003).

Asad, Talal. 'Anthropology and the Colonial Encounter', in Gerrit Huizer and Bruce Mannheim (eds.), *The Politics of Anthropology: From Colonialism and Sexism Toward a View from Below* (The Hague: Mouton, 1979), pp. 85–94.
Axel, Brian Keith. 'The Context of Diaspora', *Cultural Anthropology* 19.1 (2004), pp. 26–60.
——. 'The Diasporic Imaginary', *Public Culture* 14.2 (2002) pp. 411–28.
Barad, Karen. 'Nature's Queer Performativity', *Kvinder, køn og forskning [Women, Gender and Research]* 1–2 (2012), pp. 25–53.
Barnes, Julian. *Flaubert's Parrot* (London: Jonathan Cape, 1984).
Barrows, Adam. *The Cosmic Time of Empire: Modern Britain and World Literature* (Berkeley: University of California Press, 2011).
Bell, William. 'Not Altogether a Tomb: Julian Barnes's *Flaubert's Parrot*', in David Ellis (ed.), *Imitating Art: Essays in Biography* (London: Pluto, 1993), pp. 149–73.
Bennett, Herman L. 'The Subject in the Plot: National Boundaries and the "History" of the Black Atlantic', *African Studies Review* 43.1 (2000), pp. 101–24.
Berkhofer, Jr., Robert F. *The White Man's Indian: Images of the American Indian from Columbus to the Present* (New York: Alfred A. Knopf, 1978).
Berlatsky, Eric. '"Madame Bovary, c'est moi!": Julian Barnes's *Flaubert's Parrot* and Sexual "Perversion"', *Twentieth Century Literature* 55.2 (2009), pp. 175–208.
Berlet, Ira. 'Henry Bibb and the Detroit–Windsor Border as a Path to Manhood', Paper presented at the Mid-America Conference 'Transnationalism & Minority Cultures' (University of Oklahoma, 26–28 September 2013).
Bernabé, Jean, Patrick Chamoiseau, Raphaël Confiant. 'In Praise of Creoleness' [*Éloge de la créolité*], trans. Mohamed B. Taleb, *Callaloo* 13.4 (1990), pp. 886–909.
Blas, Zach. 'Opacities: An Introduction', *Camera Obscura* 31.2 (2016), pp. 149–53.
Boccardi, Mariadele. *The Contemporary British Historical Novel: Representation, Nation, Empire* (Basingstoke: Palgrave Macmillan, 2009).
Boucher, Philip P. *Cannibal Encounters: Europeans and Island Caribs, 1492–1763* (Baltimore: Johns Hopkins University Press, 1992).
Bradway, Tyler. '"Permeable We!": Affect and the Ethics of Intersubjectivity in Eve Sedgwick's *A Dialogue on Love*', *GLQ: A Journal of Lesbian and Gay Studies* 19.1 (2013), pp. 79–110.
Brah, Avtar. *Cartographies of Diaspora: Contesting Identities* (London: Routledge, 1996).
Braidotti, Rosi. 'Critical Posthuman Knowledges', *South Atlantic Quarterly* 116.1 (2017), pp. 83–96.
——. *Transpositions: On Nomadic Ethics* (Cambridge: Polity, 2006).
Brand, Dionne. *A Map to the Door of No Return: Notes to Belonging* (Toronto: Doubleday Canada, 2001).
——. *At the Full and Change of the Moon* (Toronto: Alfred A. Knopf Canada, 1999).
Braz, Albert. 'Mutilated Selves: Pauline Melville, Mario de Andrade, and the Troubling Hybrid', *Mosaic (Winnipeg)* 40.4 (2007), unpag.
Britton, Celia M. *Edouard Glissant and Postcolonial Theory: Strategies of Language and Resistance* (Charlottesville: University of Virginia Press, 1999).
——. *The Sense of Community in French Caribbean Fiction* (Liverpool: Liverpool University Press, 2008).
Brown, Jacqueline Nassy. 'Black Europe and the African Diaspora: A Discourse on Location', in Darlene Clark Hine, Tricia Danielle Keaton and Stephen Small (eds.) *Black Europe and the African Diaspora* (Urbana: University of Illinois Press, 2009), pp. 201–11.

Burnett, Paula. *Derek Walcott: Politics and Poetics* (Gainesville: University Press of Florida, 2000).

——. '"Where Else to Row, but Backwards?" Addressing Caribbean Futures through Re-visions of the Past', *ARIEL: A Review of International English Literature* 30.1 (1999), pp. 11–37.

Burton, Richard D. E. 'Comment Peut-on Etre Martiniquais?: The Recent Work of Edouard Glissant', *Modern Language Review* 79.2 (1984), pp. 301–12.

Butler, Judith. *Antigone's Claim. Kinship Between Life and Death* (New York: Columbia University Press, 2000).

——. 'Is Kinship Always Already Heterosexual?' *differences: A Journal of Feminist Cultural Studies* 13.1 (2002): pp. 14–44.

——. *Precarious Life: The Powers of Mourning and Violence* (London: Verso, 2004).

Carsten, Janet. *After Kinship* (Cambridge: Cambridge University Press, 2004).

Chamoiseau, Patrick. *Texaco* (Paris: Gallimard Folio, 1992).

——. *Texaco*, trans. Rose-Myrian Réjouis and Val Vinokurov (New York: Vintage International, 1998).

Chrisman, Laura. 'Whose Black World Is This Anyway?', in Bénédicte Ledent and Pilar Cuder-Domínguez (eds.), *New Perspectives on the Black Atlantic: Definitions, Readings, Practices, Dialogues* (Bern: Peter Lang, 2012), pp. 23–57.

Ciabattari, Jane. 'Giving Voice to Slaves' (Interview with Andrea Levy), *The Daily Beast*, 8 June 2010, http://www.thedailybeast.com/articles/2010/06/08/the-long-song-by-andrea-levy-interview.html (last accessed Mar. 2017).

Clandfield, Peter. '"What Is in My Blood?": Contemporary Black Scottishness and the Work of Jackie Kay', in Teresa Hubel and Neil Brooks (eds.), *Literature and Racial Ambiguity* (Amsterdam: Rodopi, 2002), pp. 1–25.

Clifford, James. *Routes: Travel and Translation in the Late Twentieth Century* (Cambridge, MA: Harvard University Press, 1997).

Cohen, Cathy J. 'Punks, Bulldaggers, and Welfare Queens: The Radical Potential of Queer Politics', *GLQ: A Journal of Lesbian and Gay Studies* 3 (1997), pp. 437–65.

Cohler, Deborah. 'Queer Kinship, Queer Eugenics: Edith Lees Ellis, Reproductive Futurity, and Sexual Citizenship', *Feminist Formations* 26.3 (2014), pp. 122–46.

Collett, Jessica L. and Ellen Childs. 'Meaningful Performances: Considering the Contributions of the Dramaturgical Approach to Studying Family', *Sociology Compass* 3–4 (2009), pp. 689–706.

Condé, Maryse and Madeleine Cottenet-Hage (eds.). *Penser la créolité* (Paris: Kartala, 1995).

Cott, Nancy F. *Public Vows: A History of Marriage and the Nation* (Cambridge, MA: Harvard University Press, 2000).

Dash, J. Michael. *Edouard Glissant* (Cambridge: Cambridge University Press, 1995).

Davies, Ceri. '"The Truth is a Thorny Issue": Lesbian Denial in Jackie Kay's *Trumpet*', *Journal of International Women's Studies* 7.3 (2006), pp. 5–16.

DeLoughrey, Elizabeth. 'Quantum Landscapes: A "Ventriloquism of Spirit"', *interventions* 9.1 (2007), pp. 62–82.

Derrida, Jacques. *Of Grammatology*, corrected edition, trans. Gayatri Chakravorty Spivak (Baltimore: Johns Hopkins University Press, 1997).

——. *Writing and Difference*, trans. Alan Bass (London: Routledge & Kegan Paul, 1978).

Dinshaw, Carolyn, et al. 'Theorizing Queer Temporalities', *GLQ: A Journal of Lesbian and Gay Studies* 13.2–3 (2007) pp. 177–95.

During, Simon. 'Rousseau's Patrimony: Primitivism, Romance and Becoming Other', in Francis Baker, Peter Hulme and Margaret Iversen (eds.), *Colonial Discourse / Postcolonial Theory* (Manchester: Manchester University Press, 1994), pp. 47–71.

Eckstein, Lars. 'Performing Jazz, Defying Essence: Music as Metaphor of Being in Jackie Kay's *Trumpet*', *Zeitschrift für Anglistik und Amerikanistik* 54.1 (2006), pp. 51–63.

Edelman, Lee. *No Future: Queer Theory and the Death Drive* (Durham, NC: Duke University Press, 2004).

Ellis, Nadia. *Territories of the Soul: Queered Belonging in the Black Diaspora* (Durham, NC: Duke University Press, 2015).

El-Tayeb, Fatima. *European Others: Queering Ethnicity in Postnational Europe* (Minneapolis: University of Minnesota Press, 2011).

Eng, David L. *The Feeling of Kinship: Queer Liberalism and the Racialization of Intimacy* (Durham, NC: Duke University Press, 2010).

——. 'Melancholia/Postcoloniality: Loss in *The Floating Life*', *Qui Parle* 11.2 (1999), pp. 137–50.

——. 'Queering the Black Atlantic, Queering the Brown Atlantic', *GLQ: A Journal of Lesbian and Gay Studies* 17.1 (2011), pp. 193–204.

——. 'Transnational Adoption and Queer Diasporas', *Social Text* 21.3 (2003), pp. 1–37.

Eng, David L. and Shinhee Han. 'A Dialogue on Racial Melancholia', *Psychoanalytic Dialogues* 10.4 (2000), pp. 667–700.

Eng, David L., Judith Halberstam and José Esteban Muñoz. 'What's Queer about Queer Studies Now?', *Social Text* 23.3–4 (2005), pp. 1–17.

Evans, Lucy. 'The Black Atlantic: Exploring Gilroy's Legacy', *Atlantic Studies* 6.2 (2009), pp. 255–68.

——. 'Tidal Poetics in Dionne Brand's *At the Full and Change of the Moon*', *Caribbean Quarterly* 55.3 (2009), pp. 1–19.

Fabian, Johannes. *Time and the Other* (New York: Columbia University Press, 2002).

Fausto-Sterling, Anne. *Sexing the Body: Gender Politics and the Construction of Sexuality* (New York: Basic Books, 2000).

Ferguson, Roderick. *Aberrations in Black: Toward a Queer of Color Critique* (Minneapolis: University of Minnesota Press, 2004).

Forte, Maximilian C. 'Extinction: Ideologies Against Indigeneity in the Caribbean', *Southern Quarterly* 43.4 (2006), pp. 46–70.

Foster, Christopher Ian. 'The Queer Politics of Crossing in Maryse Condé's *Crossing the Mangrove*', *Small Axe* 18.1 (2014), pp. 114–24.

Freeman, Elizabeth. 'Queer Belongings: Kinship Theory and Queer Theory', in George E. Haggerty and Molly McGarry (eds.), *A Companion to Lesbian, Gay, Bisexual, Transgender, and Queer Studies* (Oxford: Blackwell, 2007), pp. 295–314.

Froude, James Anthony. *The English in the West Indies, or the Bow of Ulysses* (London: Longmans, Green, and Co., 1888).

Genovese, Eugene D. *Roll, Jordan, Roll* (New York: Pantheon Books, 1974).

Gilroy, Paul. *Against Race: Imagining Political Culture Beyond the Color Line* (Cambridge, MA: Belknap Press of Harvard University Press, 2000).

——. *The Black Atlantic: Modernity and Double Consciousness* (Cambridge, MA: Harvard University Press, 1993).

——. *There Ain't No Black in the Union Jack: The Cultural Politics of Race and Nation* (London: Routledge, 1987).

Glissant, Édouard. *Caribbean Discourse: Selected Essays*, trans. J. Michael Dash (Charlottesville: University Press of Virginia, 1989).

——. *Poetics of Relation*, trans. Betsy Wing (Ann Arbor: University of Michigan Press, 1997).

Goffman, Erving. *The Presentation of Self in Everyday Life* (Edinburgh: University of Edinburgh Social Sciences Research Centre, 1956).

Goldberg, David Theo. *The Racial State* (Malden: Blackwell, 2002).

Goldberg, Jonathan. 'The History that Will Be', in Louise Fradenburg and Carla Freccero (eds.), *Premodern Sexualities* (New York: Routledge, 1996), pp. 3–21.

Gopinath, Gayatri. 'Bollywood Spectacles: Queer Diasporic Critique in the Aftermath of 9/11', *Social Text* 23.3–4 (2005), pp. 157–69.

——. 'Foreword: Queer Diasporic Interventions', *Textual Practice* 25.4 (2011), pp. 635–38.

——. *Impossible Desires: Queer Diasporas and South Asian Public Cultures* (Durham, NC: Duke University Press, 2005).

Goyal, Yogita. *Romance, Diaspora and Black Atlantic Literature* (Cambridge: Cambridge University Press, 2010).

Grandison, Julia. 'Bridging the Past and the Future: Rethinking the Temporal Assumptions of Trauma Theory in Dionne Brand's *At the Full and Change of the Moon*', *University of Toronto Quarterly* 79.2 (2010), pp. 764–82.

Greeson, Jennifer Rae. 'The Prehistory of Possessive Individualism', *PMLA* 127.4 (2012), pp. 918–24.

Gunew, Sneja. 'Resident Aliens: Diasporic Women's Writing', *Contemporary Women's Writing* 3.1 (2009), pp. 28–46.

Gyssels, Kathleen. 'The "barque ouverte" (Glissant) or *The Black Atlantic* (Gilroy): Erasure and Errantry', in Bénédicte Ledent and Pilar Cuder-Domínguez (eds.), *New Perspectives on the Black Atlantic: Definitions, Readings, Practices, Dialogues* (Bern: Peter Lang, 2012), pp. 59–82.

Halberstam, Judith [Jack]. *The Queer Art of Failure* (Durham, NC: Duke University Press, 2011).

Hall, Catherine. *Civilising Subjects: Metropole and Colony in the English Imagination, 1830–1867* (Cambridge: Polity, 2002).

Handley, George B. *Postslavery Literatures in the Americas: Family Portraits in Black and White* (Charlottesville: University Press of Virginia, 2000).

Hantel, Max. 'Toward a Sexual Difference Theory of Creolization', in John E. Drabinski and Marisa Parham (eds.), *Theorizing Glissant: Sites and Citations* (London: Rowman & Littlefield International, 2015), pp. 85–102.

Hargreaves, Tracy. 'The Power of the Ordinary Subversive in Jackie Kay's *Trumpet*', *Feminist Review* 74 (2003), pp. 2–16.

Harris, Wilson. *History, Fable and Myth in the Caribbean and Guianas* (Wellesley: Calaloux, 1995).

Hartman, Saidiya V. *Lose Your Mother: A Journey Along the Atlantic Slave Route* (New York: Farrar, Straus and Giroux, 2007).

——. *Scenes of Subjection: Terror, Slavery and Self-Making in Nineteenth-Century America* (New York: Oxford University Press, 1997).

——. 'The Time of Slavery', *The South Atlantic Quarterly* 101.4 (2002), pp. 757–77.

Hawking, S. W. 'Information Preservation and Weather Forecasting for Black Holes', Preprint, 22 January 2014, http://arxiv.org/abs/1401.5761

Hegel, G. W. F. *Hegel's Philosophy of Right*, trans. T. M. Knox (Oxford: Clarendon Press, 1942).
——. *Phenomenology of Spirit*, trans. A. V. Miller (Oxford: Oxford University Press, 1977).
Helmreich, Stefan. 'Kinship, Nation and Paul Gilroy's Concept of Diaspora', *Diaspora* 2.2 (1992), pp. 243–49.
Hird, Myra J. 'Chimerism, Mosaicism and the Cultural Construction of Kinship', *Sexualities* 7.2 (2004), pp. 217–32.
Hoad, Neville. *African Intimacies: Race, Homosexuality, and Globalization* (Minneapolis: University of Minnesota Press, 2007).
Homans, Margaret. *The Imprint of Another Life: Adoption Narratives and Human Possibility* (Ann Arbor: University of Michigan Press, 2013).
Hong, Grace Kyungwon. '"A Shared Queerness": Colonialism, Transnationalism, and Sexuality in Shani Mootoo's *Cereus Blooms at Night*', *Meridians: feminism, race, transnationalism* 7.1 (2006), pp. 73–103.
——. 'Existentially Surplus: Women of Color Feminism and the New Crises of Capitalism', *GLQ: A Journal of Lesbian and Gay Studies* 18.1 (2012), pp. 87–106.
——. 'The Future of our Worlds: Black Feminism and the Politics of Knowledge in the University under Globalization', *Meridians: feminism, race, transnationalism* 8.2 (2008), pp. 95–115.
——. *The Ruptures of American Capital: Women of Color Feminism and the Culture of Immigrant Labor* (Minneapolis: University of Minnesota Press, 2006).
Hong, Grace Kyungwon and Roderick A. Ferguson. 'Introduction', in Grace Kyungwon Hong and Roderick A. Ferguson (eds.), *Strange Affinities: The Gender and Sexual Politics of Comparative Racialization* (Durham, NC: Duke University Press, 2011), pp. 1–22.
Huggan, Graham. 'A Tale of Two Parrots: Walcott, Rhys, and the Uses of Colonial Mimicry', *Contemporary Literature* 35.4 (1994), pp. 643–60.
Hulme, Peter. *Remnants of Conquest: The Island Caribs and their Visitors, 1877–1998* (Oxford: Oxford University Press, 2000).
Hulme, Peter and Neil L. Whitehead (eds.). *Wild Majesty: Encounters with Caribs from Columbus to the Present Day: An Anthology* (Oxford: Clarendon Press, 1992).
Hutcheon, Linda. *The Politics of Postmodernism*, 2nd edition (London: Routledge, 2002).
Jackson, Shona N. *Creole Indigeneity: Between Myth and Nation in the Caribbean* (Minneapolis: University of Minnesota Press, 2012).
Jackson, Zakiyyah Iman. 'Animal: New Directions in the Theorization of Race and Posthumanism', *Feminist Studies* 39.3 (2013), pp. 669–85.
James, C. L. R. 'Black Studies and the Contemporary Student' [1969], in Anna Grimshaw (ed.), *The C. L. R. James Reader* (Cambridge: Blackwell, 1992), pp. 390–404.
Jerng, Mark C. *Claiming Others: Transracial Adoption and National Belonging* (Minneapolis: University of Minnesota Press, 2010).
Johnson, Erica L. 'Unforgetting Trauma: Dionne Brand's Haunted Histories', *Anthurium: A Caribbean Studies Journal* 2.1 (2004), unpag.
Johnson, Walter. *River of Dark Dreams: Slavery and Empire in the Cotton Kingdom* (Cambridge, MA: Belknap Press of Harvard University Press, 2013).
Jones, James F. Jr. *Rousseau's* Dialogues*: An Interpretive Essay* (Geneva: Librairie Droz, 1991).
Justice, Daniel Heath. '"Go Away, Water!": Kinship Criticism and the Decolonization Imperative', in Craig S. Womack, Daniel Heath Justice and Christopher B. Teuton (eds.), *Reasoning Together: The Native Critics Collective* (Norman: University of Oklahoma Press, 2008), pp. 147–68.

Kandiyoti, Deniz. 'Identity and its Discontents: Women and the Nation', in Patrick Williams and Laura Chrisman (eds.), *Colonial Discourse and Post-Colonial Theory* (New York: Columbia University Press, 1994), pp. 376–91.
Kay, Jackie. *Red Dust Road* (London: Picador, 2010).
———. *The Adoption Papers* (Tarset: Bloodaxe Books, 1991).
———. *Trumpet* (London: Picador, 1998).
Kincaid, Jamaica. *The Autobiography of My Mother* (London: Vintage, 1996).
King, Jeannette. '"A Woman's a Man, For a' That": Jackie Kay's *Trumpet*', *Scottish Studies Review* 2.1 (2001), pp. 101–08.
King, Tiffany Lethabo. 'Humans Involved: Lurking in the Lines of Posthumanist Flight', *Critical Ethnic Studies* 3.1 (2017), pp. 162–85.
Knepper, Wendy. *Patrick Chamoiseau: A Critical Introduction* (Jackson: University Press of Mississippi, 2012).
Koolen, Mandy. 'Masculine Trans-formations in Jackie Kay's *Trumpet*', *Atlantis* 35.1 (2010), pp. 71–80.
Lenik, Stephan. 'Carib as a Colonial Category: Comparing Ethnohistoric and Archaeological Evidence from Dominica, West Indies', *Ethnohistory* 59.1 (2012), pp. 79–107.
Lenon, Suzanne. '"Why Is Our Love an Issue?": Same-Sex Marriage and the Racial Politics of the Ordinary', *Social Identities* 17.3 (2011), pp. 351–72.
Lévi-Strauss, Claude. *A World on the Wane [Tristes Tropiques]*, trans. John Russell (New York: Criterion, 1961).
———. *Race and History* (Paris: UNESCO, 1958).
———. *The Elementary Structures of Kinship*, trans. James Harle Bell (Boston: Beacon, 1969).
———. 'The Structural Study of Myth', *The Journal of American Folklore* 68.270 (1955), pp. 428–44.
Levy, Andrea. *The Long Song* (London: Review, 2010).
———. 'The Writing of *The Long Song*', *AndreaLevy.co.uk*. http://www.andrealevy.co.uk//content/Writing%20Se%20Long%20Song.pdf (last accessed Oct. 2012).
Livingston, Julie and Jasbir K. Puar. 'Interspecies', *Social Text* 29.1 (2011), pp. 1–14.
Loichot, Valérie. *Orphan Narratives*. Charlottesville: University Press of Virginia, 2007.
———. '"We Are All Related": Edouard Glissant Meets Octavia Butler', *Small Axe* 13.3 (2009), pp. 37–50.
Lowe, Lisa. 'The Intimacies of Four Continents', in Ann Laura Stoler (ed.), *Haunted By Empire: Geographies of Intimacy in North American History* (Durham, NC: Duke University Press, 2006), pp. 191–212.
———. *The Intimacies of Four Continents* (Durham, NC: Duke University Press, 2015).
Luibhéid, Eithne. 'Queer/Migration: An Unruly Body of Scholarship', *GLQ: A Journal of Lesbian and Gay Studies* 14.2–3 (2008), pp. 169–90.
Luibhéid, Eithne and Lionel Cantú Jr. (eds.). *Queer Migrations: Sexuality, U.S. Citizenship, and Border Crossings* (Minneapolis: University of Minnesota Press, 2005).
Mackey, Nathaniel. *Bedouin Hornbook* (Charlottesville: University Press of Virginia, 1986).
———. 'Sound and Sentiment, Sound and Symbol', *Callaloo* 30 (1987), pp. 29–54.
McLeod, John. *Life Lines: Writing Transcultural Adoption* (London: Bloomsbury, 2015).
Macpherson, C. B. *The Political Theory of Possessive Individualism: Hobbes to Locke* (Ontario: Oxford University Press, 2011).

Maisier, Véronique. 'Patrick Chamoiseau's Novel *Texaco* and the Picaresque Genre', *Dalhousie French Studies* 57 (2001), pp. 128–36.
Martínez-San Miguel, Yolanda. *Coloniality of Diasporas: Rethinking Intra-Colonial Migrations in a Pan-Caribbean Context* (New York: Palgrave Macmillan, 2014).
——. 'Más allá de la homonormatividad: intimidades alternativas en el Caribe hispano', *Revista Iberoamericana* 74.225 (2008), pp. 1039–57.
Mauss, Marcel. *The Gift: Forms and Functions of Exchange in Archaic Societies* (New York: Norton, 1967).
Melville, Pauline. *The Ventriloquist's Tale* (London: Bloomsbury, 1998).
Merali, Zeeya. 'Stephen Hawking: "There Are No Black Holes"', *Nature,* 24 January 2014, http://www.nature.com/news/stephen-hawking-there-are-no-black-holes-1.14583 (last accessed Mar. 2017).
Mishra, Vijay. *The Literature of the Indian Diaspora: Theorizing the Diasporic Imaginary* (London: Routledge, 2007).
Morgensen, Scott Lauria. 'Settler Homonationalism: Theorizing Settler Colonialism within Queer Modernities', *GLQ: A Journal of Lesbian and Gay Studies* 16.1–2 (2010), pp. 105–31.
Morris, Kathryn E. 'Jamaica Kincaid's Voracious Bodies: Engendering a Carib(bean) Woman', *Callaloo* 25.3 (2002), pp. 954–68.
Moten, Fred. *In the Break: The Aesthetics of the Black Radical Tradition* (Minneapolis: University of Minnesota Press, 2003).
Moynagh, Maureen. 'The Melancholic Structure of Memory in Dionne Brand's *At the Full and Change of the Moon*', *The Journal of Commonwealth Literature* 43.1 (2008), pp. 57–75.
Muñoz, José Esteban. *Cruising Utopia: The Then and There of Queer Futurity* (New York: New York University Press, 2009).
——. *Disidentifications: Queers of Color and the Performance of Politics* (Minneapolis: University of Minnesota Press, 1999).
Murdoch, H. Adlai. 'Continental Creolization: French Exclusion through a Glissantian Prism', in Encarnación Gutiérrez Rodríguez and Shirley Anne Tate (eds.), *Creolizing Europe: Legacies and Transformations* (Liverpool: Liverpool University Press, 2015), pp. 57–79.
Naipaul, V. S. *The Middle Passage: Impressions of Five Societies—British, French and Dutch—in the West Indies and South America* (New York: Vintage Books, 1981).
Nash, Jennifer C. 'Practicing Love: Black Feminism, Love-Politics, and Post-Intersectionality', *Meridians: feminism, race, transnationalism* 11.2 (2013), pp. 1–24.
Nesbitt, Nick. *Caribbean Critique: Antillean Critical Theory from Toussaint to Glissant* (Liverpool: Liverpool University Press, 2013).
Ness, Robert. '"Not His Sort of Story": Evelyn Waugh and Pauline Melville in Guyana', *ARIEL: A Review of International English Literature* 38.4 (2007), pp. 51–96.
Neumann, Klaus. 'But Is It History?', *Cultural Studies Review* 14.1 (2008), pp. 19–32.
Nyong'o, Tavia. *The Amalgamation Waltz: Race, Performance and the Ruses of Memory* (Minneapolis: University of Minnesota Press, 2009).
Ortíz, Ricardo L. *Cultural Erotics in Cuban America* (Minneapolis: University of Minnesota Press, 2007).
Patterson, Orlando. *Rituals of Blood: Consequences of Slavery in Two American Centuries* (Washington: Civitas Counterpoint, 1998).
——. *Slavery and Social Death: A Comparative Study* (Cambridge, MA: Harvard University Press, 1982).

Bibliography

Patterson, Tiffany Ruby and Robin D. G. Kelley. 'Unfinished Migrations: Reflections on the African Diaspora and the Making of the Modern World', *African Studies Review* 43.1 (2000), pp. 11–45.
Patton, Cindy and Benigno Sánchez-Eppler (eds.), *Queer Diasporas* (Durham, NC: Duke University Press, 2000).
Pelt, April. '"Weary of Our Own Legacies": Rethinking Jane Eyre's Inheritance through Jamaica Kincaid's *The Autobiography of My Mother*', *ARIEL: A Review of International English Literature* 41.3–4 (2011), pp. 73–90.
Povinelli, Elizabeth A. 'Notes on Gridlock: Genealogy, Intimacy, Sexuality', *Public Culture* 14.1 (2002), pp. 215–38.
———. *The Empire of Love: Toward a Theory of Intimacy, Genealogy, and Carnality* (Durham, NC: Duke University Press, 2006).
Povinelli, Elizabeth A. and Kim Turcot DiFruscia. 'A Conversation with Elizabeth A. Povinelli', *Trans-Scripts* 2 (2012), pp. 76–90.
Puar, Jasbir K. *Terrorist Assemblages: Homonationalism in Queer Times* (Durham, NC: Duke University Press, 2007).
Puri, Shalini. *The Caribbean Postcolonial: Social Equality, Post/Nationalism, and Cultural Hybridity* (New York: Palgrave Macmillan, 2004).
Radcliffe-Brown, A. R. 'The Study of Kinship Systems', *The Journal of the Royal Anthropological Institute of Great Britain and Ireland* 71.1–2 (1941), pp. 1–18.
Reddy, Chandan. *Freedom with Violence: Race, Sexuality, and the US State* (Durham, NC: Duke University Press, 2011).
Reid-Pharr, Robert F. 'Engendering the Black Atlantic', *Found Object* 4 (1994), pp. 11–16.
Rhys, Jean. *Wide Sargasso Sea* (London: Penguin, 2001).
Rice, Alan. '"Heroes across the Sea": Black and White Fascination with African Americans in the Contemporary Black British Fiction of Caryl Phillips and Jackie Kay', in Heike Raphael-Hernandez (ed.), *Blackening Europe: The African American Presence* (New York: Routledge, 2004), pp. 217–31.
Richardson, Matt. '"My Father Didn't Have a Dick": Social Death and Jackie Kay's *Trumpet*', *GLQ: A Journal of Lesbian and Gay Studies* 18.2–3 (2012), pp. 361–79.
Rifkin, Mark. 'Remapping the Family of Nations: The Geopolitics of Kinship in Hendrick Aupaumut's "A Short Narration"', *Studies in American Indian Literatures* 22.4 (2010), pp. 1–31.
———. *When Did Indians Become Straight? Kinship, the History of Sexuality, and Native Sovereignty* (Oxford: Oxford University Press, 2011).
Riggs, Damien W. and Elizabeth Peel. *Critical Kinship Studies: An Introduction to the Field* (London: Palgrave Macmillan, 2016).
Rivera-Servera, Ramón H. *Performing Queer Latinidad: Dance, Sexuality, Politics* (Ann Arbor: University of Michigan Press, 2012).
Robbins, Bruce. 'Comparative Cosmopolitanisms', in Pheng Cheah and Bruce Robbins (eds.), *Cosmopolitics: Thinking and Feeling beyond the Nation* (Minneapolis: University of Minnesota Press, 1998), pp. 246–64.
Rody, Caroline. *The Daughter's Return: African-American and Caribbean Women's Fictions of History* (New York: Oxford University Press, 2001).
Rubin, Gayle S. 'The Traffic in Women: Notes on the "Political Economy" of Sex', *Deviations: A Gayle Rubin Reader* (Durham, NC: Duke University Press, 2011), pp. 33–65.
Rubin Gayle S. and Judith Butler, 'Sexual Traffic', *differences: A Journal of Feminist Cultural Studies* 6.2–3 (1994), pp. 62–99; rpt. in *Deviations: A Gayle Rubin Reader*, pp. 276–309.

Ruckel, Terri Smith. '"To Speak of My Own Situation": Touring the "Mother Periphery" in Jamaica Kincaid's *The Autobiography of My Mother*', *Anthurium: A Caribbean Studies Journal* 3.1 (2005), unpag.
Rupprecht, Anita. 'Excessive Memories: Slavery, Insurance and Resistance', *History Workshop Journal* 64.1 (2007), pp. 6–28.
Safran, William. 'Diasporas in Modern Societies: Myths of Homeland and Return', *Diaspora: A Journal of Transnational Studies* 1.1 (1991), pp. 83–99.
Sandoval, Chela. 'Dissident Globalizations, Emancipatory Methods, Social-Erotics', in Arnaldo Cruz-Malavé and Martin F. Manalansan IV (eds.), *Queer Globalizations: Citizenship and the Afterlife of Colonialism* (New York: New York University Press, 2002), pp. 20–32.
——. *Methodology of the Oppressed* (Minneapolis: University of Minnesota Press, 2000).
Sansavior, Eva. 'Playing the Field/Performing "the Personal" in Maryse Condé's Interviews', in Patrick Crowley and Jane Hiddleston (eds.), *Postcolonial Poetics: Genre and Form* (Liverpool: Liverpool University Press, 2011), pp. 71–88.
Schneider, David M. *A Critique of the Study of Kinship* (Ann Arbor: University of Michigan Press, 1984).
——. *American Kinship: A Cultural Account* (Chicago: University of Chicago Press, 1980).
Scott, David. 'Islands of *Créolité*?', *Small Axe* 13.3 (2009), pp. vii–x.
Scott, James B. 'Parrot as Paradigms: Infinite Deferral of Meaning in *Flaubert's Parrot*', *ARIEL: A Review of International English Literature* 21.3 (1990), pp. 57–68.
Secomb, Linnell. 'Empire and the Ambiguities of Love', *Cultural Studies Review* 19.2 (2013), pp. 193–215.
Sedgwick, Eve Kosofsky. *A Dialogue on Love* (Boston: Beacon Press, 1999).
——. 'Gender Criticism', in Stephen Greenblatt and Giles Gunn (eds.), *Redrawing the Boundaries: the Transformation of English and American Literary Studies* (New York: Modern Language Association of America, 1992) pp. 271–302.
Sexton, Jared. 'People-of-Color-Blindness: Notes on the Afterlife of Slavery', *Social Text* 28.3 (2010), pp. 31–56.
Sharpley-Whiting, T. Denean. 'Erasures and the Practice of Diaspora Feminism', *Small Axe* 17 (2005), pp. 129–33.
Shemak, April. 'Alter/natives: Myth, Translation and the Native Informant in Pauline Melville's *The Ventriloquist's Tale*', *Textual Practice* 19.3 (2005), pp. 353–72.
Siebers, Tobin. 'Ethics in the Age of Rousseau: From Lévi-Strauss to Derrida', *MLN* 100.4 (1985), pp. 758–79.
Silva, Denise Ferreira da. 'To Be Announced: Radical Praxis or Knowing (at) the Limits of Justice', *Social Text* 31.1 (2013), pp. 43–62.
Skeehan, Danielle C. 'Caribbean Women, Creole Fashioning, and the Fabric of Black Atlantic Writing', *The Eighteenth Century* 56.1 (2015), pp. 105–23.
Smith, Andrea. 'Queer Theory and Native Studies: The Heteronormativity of Settler Colonialism', *GLQ: A Journal of Lesbian and Gay Studies* 16.1–2 (2010), pp. 42–68.
Soto-Crespo, Ramón E. 'Death and the Diaspora Writer: Hybridity and Mourning in the Work of Jamaica Kincaid', *Contemporary Literature* 43.2 (2002), pp. 342–76.
Soyinka, Wole. *Myth, Literature and the African World* (Cambridge: Cambridge University Press, 1990).
Spillers, Hortense J. 'Mama's Baby, Papa's Maybe: An American Grammar Book', *Black, White and in Color: Essays on American Literature and Culture* (Chicago: University of Chicago Press, 2003), pp. 203–29.

Spivak, Gayatri Chakravorty. 'Bonding in Difference', in Alfred Arteaga (ed.), *An Other Tongue: Nation and Ethnicity in the Linguistic Borderlands* (Durham, NC: Duke University Press, 1994), pp. 273–85.
Stein, Mark. 'Life Border Writing', in Tobias Döring (ed.), *A History of Postcolonial Literature in 12½ Books* (Trier: WVT, 2007), pp. 169–80.
Steinwand, Jonathan. 'What the Whales Would Tell Us: Cetacean Communication in Novels by Witi Ihimaera, Linda Hogan, Zakes Mda, and Amitav Ghosh', in Elizabeth DeLoughrey and George B. Handley (eds.), *Postcolonial Ecologies: Literatures of the Environment* (Oxford: Oxford University Press, 2011), pp. 182–99.
Stephens, Thomas M. 'Creole, Créole, Criollo, Crioulo: The Shadings of a Term', *The SECOL Review* 7.3 (1983), pp. 28–39.
Stoler, Ann Laura. *Race and the Education of Desire: Foucault's* History of Sexuality *and the Colonial Order of Things* (Durham, NC: Duke University Press, 1995).
Strong, Thomas. 'Kinship Between Judith Butler and Anthropology? A Review Essay', *Ethnos: Journal of Anthropology* 67.3 (2002), pp. 401–18.
Terry, Jennifer. 'Theorizing Deviant Historiography', in Ann-Louise Shapiro (ed.), *Feminists Revision History* (New Brunswick: Rutgers University Press, 1994), pp. 276–303.
Thieme, John. 'Throwing One's Voice? Narrative Agency in Pauline Melville's *The Ventriloquist's Tale*', *The Literary Criterion* 35 (2000), pp. 170–92.
Thomas, J. J. *Froudacity: West Indian Fables by James Anthony Froude* (Philadelphia: Gebbie and Company, 1890).
Tinsley, Omise'eke Natasha. 'Black Atlantic, Queer Atlantic: Queer Imaginings of the Middle Passage', *GLQ: A Journal of Lesbian and Gay Studies* 14.2–3 (2008), pp. 191–215.
———. *Thiefing Sugar: Eroticism Between Women in Caribbean Literature* (Durham, NC: Duke University Press, 2010).
Todd, Zoe. 'An Indigenous Feminist's Take On The Ontological Turn: "Ontology" Is Just Another Word For Colonialism', *Journal of Historical Sociology* 29.1 (2016), pp. 4–22.
Trouillot, Michel-Rolph. *Silencing the Past: Power and the Production of History* (Boston: Beacon, 1995).
Tuhkanen, Mikko. 'Queer Hybridity', in Chrysanthi Nigianni and Merl Storr (eds.), *Deleuze and Queer Theory* (Edinburgh: Edinburgh University Press, 2009), pp. 92–114.
Vergès, Françoise. 'Creolization and Resistance', in Encarnación Gutiérrez Rodríguez and Shirley Anne Tate (eds.), *Creolizing Europe: Legacies and Transformations* (Liverpool: Liverpool University Press, 2015), pp. 38–56.
Walcott, Derek. *Collected Poems 1948–1984* (New York: Farrar, Straus and Giroux, 1986).
———. 'The Antilles, Fragments of Epic Memory: The 1992 Nobel Lecture', *World Literature Today* 67.2 (1993), pp. 261–67.
———. 'The Muse of History', in Alison Donnell and Sarah Lawson Welsh (eds.), *The Routledge Reader in Caribbean Literature* (London: Routledge, 1996), pp. 354–58.
Walcott, Rinaldo. 'Queer Returns: Human Rights, the Anglo-Caribbean and Diaspora Politics', *Caribbean Review of Gender Studies* 3 (2009), pp. 1–19.
Walker, Alice. 'As You Wear: Cross-dressing and Identity Politics in Jackie Kay's *Trumpet*', *Journal of International Women's Studies* 8.2 (2007), pp. 35–43.
Walters, Wendy W. *Archives of the Black Atlantic: Reading Between Literature and History* (New York: Routledge, 2013).

Waugh, Evelyn. *A Handful of Dust* and *Decline and Fall* (New York: Dell, 1934).
———. *Ninety-two Days: The Account of a Tropical Journey Through British Guiana and Part of Brazil* (New York: Farrar & Rinehart, 1934).
Weedon, Chris. 'Migration, Identity, and Belonging in British Black and South Asian Women's Writing', *Contemporary Women's Writing* 2.1 (2008), pp. 17–35.
Weheliye, Alexander G. *Habeas Viscus: Racializing Assemblages, Biopolitics, and Black Feminist Theories of the Human* (Durham, NC: Duke University Press, 2014).
Wekker, Gloria. *The Politics of Passion: Women's Sexual Culture in the Afro-Surinamese Diaspora* (New York: Columbia University Press, 2006).
———. *White Innocence: Paradoxes of Colonialism and Race* (Durham, NC: Duke University Press, 2016).
Wesling, Meg. 'Neocolonialism, Queer Kinship, and Diaspora: Contesting the Romance of the Family in Shani Mootoo's *Cereus Blooms at Night* and Edwidge Danticat's *Breath, Eyes, Memory*', *Textual Practice* 25.4 (2011), pp. 649–70.
Weston, Kath. *Families We Choose: Lesbians, Gays, Kinship* (New York: Columbia University Press, 1991).
———. "Forever Is a Long Time: Romancing the Real in Gay Kinship Ideologies', in Sylvia Yanagisako and Carol Delaney (eds.), *Naturalizing Power: Essays in Feminist Cultural Analysis* (New York: Routledge, 1995), pp. 87–110.
White, Deborah Gray. *Ar'n't I A Woman? Female Slaves in the Plantation South* (New York: Norton, 1985).
Whitworth, Michael H. *Einstein's Wake: Relativity, Metaphor and Modernist Literature* (Oxford: Oxford University Press, 2001).
Wright, Michelle M. *Becoming Black: Creating Identity in the African Diaspora* (Durham, NC: Duke University Press, 2004).
———. 'Can I Call You Black? The Limits of Authentic Heteronormativity in African Diasporic Discourse', *African and Black Diaspora: An International Journal* 6:1 (2013), pp. 3–16.
Wynter, Sylvia. 'Beyond the Word of Man: Glissant and the New Discourse of the Antilles', *World Literature Today* 63.4 (1989), pp. 637–48.
———. 'Sambos and Minstrels', *Social Text* 1 (1979), pp. 149–56.
Young, Robert J. C. *Colonial Desire: Hybridity in Theory, Culture and Race* (London: Routledge, 1995).
———. *Postcolonialism: An Historical Introduction* (Oxford: Blackwell, 2001).

Index

abortion 41, 108, 123, 139, 145
adoption 20n10, 23–24, 151, 163–64
Africa 25, 118, 141, 158, 168–69, 172
African diaspora *see* black Atlantic
    diaspora
afterlife of slavery *see* postslavery
Agamben, Giorgio 119
Agard-Jones, Vanessa 30
Ahmed, Sara 127
Alexander, M. Jacqui 112, 116
Allen, Jafari S. 1, 181
Amerindian *see* indigeneity
Anderson, Benedict 31, 54n43
Anderson, Linda 152n3
anthropology 26–28, 41
    kinship studies 12–14, 35–36, 59–62, 67, 69–70, 76
anticolonial sabotage 45–49, 56, 81
    see also defeatism
Appiah, Anthony 54n43
Apter, Emily 136n23
archive 28, 85–86, 96–97, 103, 105, 117, 168
Arnold, A. James 136n22, 148
Arrizón, Alicia 10–11
Arroyo, Jossiana 55
Asad, Talal 36
At the Full and Change of the Moon 26–30, 104, 105–28, 131, 139, 169, 179

The Autobiography of My Mother 26, 28, 30, 35–57, 59–60, 81, 178
Axel, Brian Keith 5, 116

Barad, Karen 178
Barnes, Julian 61–62, 77
barque ouvert 141
Barrows, Adam 71, 73, 77, 80
becoming 3, 31, 124, 128, 132, 148–49, 153, 155, 159–72, 176–77, 179
Bell, William 62
Bennett, Herman L. 28
Berkhofer, Jr., Robert F. 54n43, 56n50, 60
Berlatsky, Eric 62n9
Berlet, Ira 95
Bernabé, Jean 135–36, 141, 148
biopolitics 16, 24
black Atlantic diaspora 3, 10, 26, 29, 31, 107, 116, 133, 158, 176–77, 181
black Atlantic studies 2, 10–11, 95
Blas, Zach 135n18
blood 13, 19–21, 25, 45, 54, 80, 91, 100, 103, 108, 111, 113–16, 119, 123–25, 135, 139, 142, 163, 169–71, 177, 180
Boccardi, Mariadele 86
Boucher, Philip P. 52
Bradway, Tyler 161
Brah, Avtar 4–5

Braidotti, Rosi 175n1, 178n8, 179–80
Brand, Dionne 26–30, 104, 105–28, 131, 139, 169, 179
Brathwaite, Edward Kemau 127n52
Braz, Albert 61n5, 77–79
Britton, Celia M. 132n3, 136n23
Burnett, Paula 47–48, 61, 73
Burton, Richard D. E. 132n4
Butler, Judith 14–15, 17, 18, 20, 41, 109n12, 117–18, 123, 153–56, 159, 173, 178

camp 119
   see also plantation
capitalism 18, 23, 64, 87–88, 94, 95, 98, 108, 116, 156, 163–64, 175
Carsten, Janet 13
Catholicism 54, 69–70, 74–75
Chamoiseau, Patrick 26–27, 29–30, 131–49, 177, 179
citizenship 6, 94, 117–18, 123, 151, 158, 174, 179–81
civilization 2–3, 9, 14, 46, 49, 72–73, 95, 133, 140–41
Clandfield, Peter 157n14
Clifford, James 4, 5, 177n4, 181
coevalness *see* temporality
Cohen, Cathy J. 10, 116
Cohler, Deborah 22
colonial–anthropological discourse 2, 35–38, 46–57, 59–62, 65–68, 76, 79, 177–80
colonialism
   and knowledge production 60–62, 65–66, 78, 81, 147, 177–78
   and language 35, 37, 43, 49, 53
   and time *see* temporality
   see also colonial–anthropological discourse; historiography; kinship and colonialism
Condé, Maryse 136
Confiant, Raphaël 135–36, 141, 148
consanguinity *see* blood
cosmopolitanism 4, 8, 11, 31, 122, 125, 177
Cott, Nancy F. 92
créolité (creoleness) 135–36, 141, 148
creolization 135
creolized community *see* diaspora community

creolized kinship *see* kinship, queer
critical kinship studies 1, 2, 11–24
cultural reproduction 10–11, 14, 38, 42, 63–64, 67, 80, 132

Darwin, Charles 68
Dash, J. Michael 132
Davies, Ceri 152–53n3
defeatism 47–56
Deleuze, Gilles 7
DeLoughrey, Elizabeth 61n5, 68n18
Derrida, Jacques 37, 48, 50, 59, 63, 65, 72, 76, 78
diaspora
   aesthetics 31, 151, 154, 159–62, 170–74
   community 29–30, 41, 79–80, 131–32, 135, 137, 144–45, 148, 174, 175–77
   and ethnic purity 5, 8–9, 30–31
   and gender 5–6, 148, 152–53
   and heteronormativity 3, 7–11, 95, 98, 102, 116
   longings 24, 105, 117–18, 120–23, 179
   memory 4, 5, 9, 30, 87–88, 96–97, 106–07, 111–12, 121, 139, 141, 154, 161–69, 172
   queer diaspora 1, 8–11, 22, 26, 29, 31, 106, 115–16, 119, 126, 132–33, 154–55, 170, 177, 179–81
   relationality 2, 10–11, 26, 31, 35, 112, 116, 121, 136–37, 140, 144–46, 155, 175–77, 179–81
   shame 87, 93–94, 96, 103, 105, 117
   see also black Atlantic diaspora; kinship, diasporic; patriarchy; subjectivity; temporality
diaspora space 4, 26–27, 31, 169, 172, 176, 180
diaspora studies 1, 2, 3–11, 151–52, 173–74, 180
Dickens, Charles 77
Dombey and Son 77
drift 121, 127–28, 146, 148, 179
During, Simon 36

Eckstein, Lars 161, 170–71
Edelman, Lee 22, 29
Einstein, Albert 71–73
Ellis, Nadia 10–11

Index

El-Tayeb, Fatima 6
Eng, David L. 2, 8–9, 11–12, 22–23, 115–16, 125
Enlightenment 9, 42
ethnocentrism 37, 44, 50, 63–64, 79
ethnographic gaze 38, 49–50, 55, 81, 178
Euclid 73, 81
Evans, Lucy 5n14, 114

Fabian, Johannes 36, 49, 55n46, 71, 73, 76, 133
family stories 19, 26, 28–29, 35, 60, 78, 87–89, 105, 118, 120, 122, 137–39, 158, 164, 168–70
family tree 7–8, 114–15, 139, 169
fatherhood 40, 43–45, 109–12, 114, 139, 142, 145, 163–64, 167–68
Fausto-Sterling, Anne 180n16
Ferguson, Roderick 10, 17, 101, 116
forgetting *see* diaspora memory
Forte, Maximilian C. 56, 60
Foster, Christopher Ian 136n23
Freeman, Elizabeth 21–23, 119, 122
friendship 22–23
Froude, James Anthony 35, 38, 47–53, 56
futures, futurity 8, 10, 22, 41, 48–49, 93, 98, 105–08, 111–13, 118–19, 123–27, 151–54, 164–65, 172–73, 175–81
  indigenous futurity 60, 63, 66, 79, 81

Genovese, Eugene 91
Gilroy, Paul 4–9, 25, 133n6, 176, 180
Glissant, Édouard 29–30, 105, 121, 127n52, 131–41, 149, 177, 179
Goffmann, Erving 15
Goldberg, David Theo 157n13
Goldberg, Jonathan 78
Gopinath, Gayatri 8–9, 11–12, 23, 115–16
Goyal, Yogita 25
Grandison, Julia 106, 114
Greeson, Jennifer Rae 94
Gunew, Sneja 5n15, 177
Gyssels, Kathleen 133n6

Halberstam, Jack [Judith] 38, 42, 44, 102, 105
Hall, Catherine 95

Hantel, Max 135n18
Haraway, Donna 122
Hargreaves, Tracy 153
Harris, Wilson 46–49, 80
Hartman, Saidiya 19, 30, 90, 94, 109, 154
Hawking, Stephen 65, 73, 76–77
Hegel, G. W. F. 14–15, 117–18
Helmreich, Stefan 7, 11
Hesse, Barnor 99
Hird, Myra J. 13–14
historical novel 86, 127
historicity 106–07, 115, 126–28, 176, 178–80
historiographic metafiction 86
historiography 2, 3, 12, 20, 26–31, 35–48, 51–59, 67, 72, 81, 116, 124, 127, 133, 168, 178–79
  anticolonial 107, 131
  colonial historiography 37, 87–89, 93, 96–103, 105, 108, 111, 133, 137
  and fiction 85–88, 96–98, 103
  and gender 97–98, 102–04
Hoad, Neville 125–26
Homans, Margaret 24n124
Hong, Grace 17–18, 94, 101, 103
Huggan, Graham 47n26
Hulme, Peter 52, 55–56, 60
human, norms and definitions of 2, 3, 9, 14, 26, 37, 48, 60, 63, 70, 72, 95, 123, 139–41, 143, 154–55, 158, 175–76, 180
Hutcheon, Linda 86
hybridity 53

incest 12, 14, 28, 36, 60–61, 70–71, 75
indigeneity 26–28, 38, 50–57, 59–81
  indigenous extinction 49–57, 60, 79
  indigenous knowledge 74
  and purity 50–54, 64, 70, 79
  survival politics 60, 63, 66, 73, 75, 78–81, 79–80, 177–78
  see also cultural reproduction; ethnocentrism
indigenous studies 16–18, 22–23
intersubjectivity *see* subjectivity
intimacy 18, 21, 30, 35–41, 76–77, 89–90, 117, 139, 145, 153, 155, 161, 177

197

Jackson, Shona N. 79
Jackson, Zakiyyah Iman 176n2
Jagose, Annamarie 106
James, C. L. R. 3
Jerng, Mark C. 23–24
Johnson, Erica L. 106, 112–13, 125n42, 126
Johnson, Walter 101n25
Jones, Jr., James F. 55
Justice, Daniel Heath 18

Kandiyoti, Deniz 5n16
Kay, Jackie 25–27, 30–31, 151–74, 179
Kelley, Robin D. G. 3
Kincaid, Jamaica 26, 28, 30, 35–57, 59–60, 81, 178
King, Jeanette 152n3
King, Tiffany Lethabo 176n2
kinship
　affiliation 9, 11, 17, 19, 22, 24, 109, 115, 139, 161
　as a practice of resistance 2, 21, 24, 31, 36, 42–43, 109–11, 124, 128, 134, 136, 139, 147, 176–80
　biological/biogenetic 13–14, 20–21, 25, 38–45, 50–57, 110, 114–15, 119, 131, 139, 142, 144
　and colonialism 2, 16–18, 21, 26, 35–36, 39–41, 100–03, 108, 132–34, 176–78
　diasporic kinship 2, 11–12, 23, 126, 128, 135–38, 151–52, 159–61, 168–74
　Euro-American norms of 3, 12–13, 25, 29, 87, 92, 103, 107, 109–12, 117, 119, 122, 128, 136, 160
　failed kinship 38–39, 89, 91, 109
　'fictive kinship' 19–20, 22
　filiation 9, 11, 30, 42, 115, 132–40, 143, 179
　genealogy 11, 14, 16, 19, 30, 38, 52, 61, 63, 77, 79, 102–03, 108–22, 132–33, 138, 142–44, 154, 164, 173, 176
　and indigeneity 16–18
　and naming 90, 93, 110
　national norms of 2, 6, 29–30, 42, 64, 102–04, 112

normative *see* kinship, Euro-American norms of; kinship, national norms of
　and possession/property/ownership 43, 89–94
　queer kinship 2, 21–23, 79–80, 102, 108–16, 119, 124, 127–28, 135–37, 142, 144–49, 155, 160–62, 167–74, 177, 179, 181
　and slavery 2, 18–21, 30, 43, 89–92, 100–03, 108–11
　and social status 90–95, 102
　and the state 14–16, 117–18, 139, 151–52, 154, 160, 163, 173–74
　'wounded kinship' 19, 133
kinship studies
　see anthropology; critical kinship studies
Knepper, Wendy 136n22
Koch-Grundberg, Teodor 68n18

Lacan, Jaques 14
language *see* colonialism and language; narration
Latino/a studies 10–11
Lenik, Stephan 54
Lenon, Suzanne 157
Lévi-Strauss, Claude 12–15, 27–28, 36, 40–41, 56, 59–72, 79–80
　Tristes Tropiques 28, 35, 37, 46–50
Levy, Andrea 26–30, 85–104, 127, 131, 143, 178
liberalism 9, 16–17, 21, 23, 26, 29, 64, 88, 94, 98, 117, 154, 156–57, 174, 175–79
literature *see* narration
Livingston, Julie 176n2
Loichot, Valerie 19–20, 133, 138
The Long Song 26–30, 85–104, 127, 131, 143, 178
Lord, Audre 25
love *see* intimacy
Lowe, Lisa 9, 28–29

Mackey, Nathaniel 19n94
Macpherson, C. B. 94
Maroon, Nanny 100, 102
Martínez-San Miguel, Yolanda 1n1, 27
Medicine, Bea 18
melancholia 125–26

Melville, Pauline 26–28, 57, 59–81, 177–78
memory *see* diaspora, memory
mestizaje 10–11
métissage 135
migration 8, 27, 120–23, 175–77
Mishra, Vijay 30–31
Morgensen, Scott Lauria 56, 60
Morris, Kathryn E. 55–56
Moten, Fred 19, 171
motherhood 25, 41, 108–16, 121–22
mourning 30–31, 125–26, 151–56, 159, 164–69, 172–74
Moynagh, Maureen 106, 113–14, 125–26
Muñoz, José Esteban 22n112, 125
Murdoch, H. Adlai 151n2
mythology 63–66, 71–74, 78–81

narration 24, 27–29, 35, 49, 56, 59, 62–63, 68, 72, 74, 77, 81, 111, 116, 127, 131–32, 142, 148–49, 155, 161, 169, 172–74, 177–81
   see also family stories; historiography; narrative authority
narrative authority 87–89, 95–98, 102–03
Nash, Jennifer C. 18n90
Nassy Brown, Jacqueline 6
nation
   and heteronormativity 6, 9, 29–30, 94–95, 98, 102, 105, 116, 131, 136, 152, 155–60, 163–64
   national consciousness, identity 112
   and women/femininity 5–6, 98, 102–04, 112–13, 138, 157, 159
   see also historiography; kinship, national norms and definitions of
Native American, *see* indigenous studies, indigeneity
necropolitics 56
Negritude 95, 141
neoslave narratives 28, 86
Nesbitt, Nick 132n3
Ness, Robert 65
Neumann, Klaus 105
Newtonian time 73
Nyong'o, Tavia 11

Ortíz, Ricardo L. 10

patriarchy 3, 7, 20, 25, 29, 37–44, 88, 95–102, 109, 121–23, 143, 158, 164
Patterson, Orlando 18–20, 109–10, 134, 158
Patterson, Tiffany Ruby 3
Peel, Elizabeth 11n53
Pelt, April 51
personhood 3, 17, 23–24, 40, 120, 134, 146, 175–76
plantation 124, 134, 140, 143–46
politics of love *see* intimacy
possessive individualism 94, 106, 118, 127
postcolonial studies 2, 16–17, 27, 65–67, 175–77
posthumanism *see* human, norms and definitions of
postslavery 18–19, 26, 29, 31, 85, 87, 93–98, 101–04, 107, 116–17, 128, 132, 154, 158, 168
Povinelli, Elizabeth 15–17, 20, 30, 36, 41, 69n19, 133
primitiveness 9, 46, 48, 51, 61, 67–68, 79
progress 10, 46, 49, 64–65, 67, 70–71, 87, 93–95, 98, 103, 117, 133, 140
Puar, Jasbir K. 157n13, 176n2
Puri, Shalini 27

quantum physics 65, 73, 76–78
queer diaspora *see* diaspora
queer latinidad 22
queer studies 2, 10, 21–24

Radcliffe-Brown, A. R. 12, 15
realism 59, 62–63, 77–78
recognition 3, 117–19, 122–23, 148, 154–57, 159, 164, 173, 179
Reddy, Chandan 22
Reid-Pharr, Robert F. 5n15
'Relation' (Glissant) 133–35, 138–40, 149
relativity, theory of 71–74
respectability politics 95, 98, 102
Rice, Alan 157–58n14
Richardson, Matt 157–59, 164
Rifkin, Mark 16–24, 36n8, 133–34
Riggs, Damien W. 11n53
Rivera-Severa, Ramón 22
Robbins, Bruce 122

Rousseau, Jean-Jacques 36–37, 42, 48, 55, 57, 59, 72
Rubin, Gayle 15, 40n13
Ruckel, Terri Smith 49–50
Rupprecht, Anita 86

sabotage *see* anticolonial sabotage
Safran, William 3–4
Sandoval, Chela 18, 31, 179, 181
Sansavior, Eva 136n23
savagery *see* primitiveness
Schneider, David 12–20, 27, 36, 135
Scott, David 136n22
Scott, James B. 62n10
Secomb, Linnell 24n126
Sedgwick, Eve Kosofsky 30, 105, 160–61, 171
Sexton, Jared 119
Sharpley-Whiting, T. Denean 5n17
Shemak, April 61n5, 67, 81n41
Silva, Denise Ferreira da 118
Skeehan, Danielle C. 124
slavery 26–27, 89–96, 99–103, 106–11, 136, 158, 180
  and the body 107–11, 124
  see also kinship and slavery; postslavery
Smith, Andrea 56, 60, 67n17
Soto-Crespo, Ramón E. 53
Soyinka, Wole 169
Spillers, Hortense 19–21, 95, 109–10, 134, 158
Spivak, Gayatri Chakravorty 173
Stein, Mark 152n3, 161
Steinwand, Jonathan 127
Stephens, Thomas M. 136
Stoler, Ann Laura 54n43
storytelling *see* narration
subjectivity
  diasporic 2, 4–6, 10–11, 22, 24–31, 40, 112–14, 120, 123, 131, 151, 153–55, 158, 169, 173–74, 175–81
  and history 106, 114
  intersubjectivity 6, 24, 42, 124, 126, 136, 159–63, 167, 170–73, 179
  and kinship 23–24, 40–42, 151, 176–77

temporality 22, 31, 60, 71–81, 105–06, 116, 124, 154, 160, 163, 171, 178–79
Terry, Jennifer 97, 127
Texaco 26–27, 29–30, 131–49, 177, 179
Thieme, John 77
Thomas, J. J. 46–49
Tinsley, Omise'eke Natasha 21, 29, 120
Todd, Zoe 176n2
trauma 106, 112–13, 118, 125–26
travel writing 28, 35, 46–52
Trouillot, Michel-Rolph 29, 106–07, 126
Trumpet 25–27, 30–31, 151–74, 179
Tuhkanen, Mikko 135n18

utopia 3, 8, 144–45, 180

The Ventriloquist's Tale 26–28, 57, 59–81, 177–78
Vergès, Françoise 147

Walcott, Derek 35, 47–49, 59, 168
Walcott, Rinaldo 135n18
Walker, Alice 152–53n3
Walters, Wendy W. 85–87
Waugh, Evelyn 65–68, 76–78
Weedon, Chris 19n97
Weheliye, Alexander 20, 180
Wekker, Gloria 26, 103n27
Wesling, Meg 10n44, 116
Weston, Kath 22
White, Deborah Gray 99n22
Whitehead, Neil L. 52
whiteness 8, 93, 99, 103n27, 143–44, 157, 159
Whitworth, Michael H. 73
World War I 117, 140
World War II 140
Wright, Michelle 5–6, 25, 95
writing *see* narration
Wynter, Sylvia 180

Young, Robert J. C. 42, 53, 65